CONTENTS

KT-525-386

List of Figures

List of Profiles

List of Tables

PREFACE

Access to History Context

Structure

In some ways *Access to History: Context* volumes are similar to most textbooks. They are divided into chapters, each of which is focused on a specific topic. In turn, chapters are divided into sections which have self-explanatory headings. As is the case with most textbooks, *Context* authors have organised the chapters in a logical sequence so that, if you start at the beginning of the book and work your way through to the end, everything will make sense. However, because many readers 'dip' into textbooks rather than reading them from beginning to end, care has been taken to make sure that whichever chapter you start with you should not find yourself feeling lost.

Special Features in the Main Text

Points to Consider – at the start of each chapter this shaded box provides you with vital information about how the chapter is organised and how the various issues covered relate to each other.

Issues boxes are a standard feature of each chapter and, like Points to Consider boxes, are designed to help you extract the maximum benefit from the work you do. They appear in the margin immediately following most numbered section headings. The question(s) contained in each issues box will tell you which historical issue(s) the section is primarily going to cover. If the section you intend to start with has no issues box, turn back page by page until you find one. This will contain the questions the author is considering from that point onwards, including the section you are about to read.

Boxed sections appear in both the margin and the main column of text. In each of the boxes you will find a self-explanatory heading which will make it clear what the contents of the box are about. Very often, the contents of boxes are explanations of words or phrases, or descriptions of events or situations. When you are reading a chapter for the first time you might make a conscious decision to pay little attention to boxed entries so that you can concentrate your attention on the author's main message.

Q-boxes appear in the margin and contain one or more questions about the item they appear alongside. These questions are intended to stimulate you to think about some aspect of the material the box is linked to. The most useful answers to these questions will often emerge during discussions with other students.

Activities boxes – as a general rule, the contents of activities boxes are more complex than the questions in Q-boxes, and often require you to undertake a significant amount of work, either on your own or with others. One reason for completing the task(s) is to consolidate what you have already learned or to extend the range or depth of your understanding.

Profiles – most of these are about named individuals who are central to an understanding of the topic under consideration: some are about events of particular importance. Each Profile contains a similar range of material. The two aspects you are likely to find most useful are:

▼ the dated timeline down the side of the page; and
▼ the source extracts, which provide you with ideas on what made the subject of the Profile especially notable or highly controversial.

Profiles also provide useful points of focus during the revision process.

End-of-chapter Sections

The final pages of each chapter contain different sections. It is always worthwhile looking at the **Summary Chart** or **Summary Diagram** first. As their names suggest, these are designed to provide you with a brief and carefully structured overview of the topic covered by the chapter. The important thing for you to do is to check that you understand the way it is structured and how the topics covered inter-relate with one another.

The **Working on...** section should be studied in detail once you have finished your first reading of the main text of the chapter. Assuming that you read the Points to Consider section when you began work on the chapter, and that you followed any advice given in it when you read the chapter for the first time, the Working on... section is designed to suggest what form any further work you do on the chapter should take.

The **Answering extended writing and essay questions on...** sections, taken as a whole throughout the book, form a coherent body of guidance on how to tackle these types of examination questions successfully.

The same is true of the **Answering source-based questions on...** sections which have been carefully planned bearing in mind the ways you need to build on the skills you have already developed in this area. You may find these sections particularly helpful during the time you are preparing for an exam.

The last part of each chapter contains a **Further Reading** section. These are of vital importance to you in chapters covering topics you are expected to know about in some detail. To do well in any History course it is essential to read more than one book. However, it is possible to find individual books which can act as your guide and companion throughout your studies, and this is one of them. One of the major ways in which it fulfils this function is by providing you with detailed guidance on the way you can make the most effective use of your limited time in reading more widely.

This book is an integral part of the *Access to History* series. One of its functions is to act as a link between the various topic books in the series on the period it covers, by drawing explicit attention in the Further Reading sections to where, within the series, other material exists which can be used to broaden and deepen your knowledge and understanding. Attention is also drawn to the non-*Access to History* publications which you are likely to find most useful. By using material which has been written based on the same aims and objectives, you are likely to find yourself consistently building up the key skills and abilities needed for success on your course.

Revision

Context books have been planned to be directly helpful to you during the revision period. One of the first things many students do when starting to revise a topic for an examination is to make a list of the 'facts' they need to know about. A safer way of doing this (because it covers the possibility that you missed something important when you originally worked on the topic) is to compile your lists from a book you can rely on. *Context* volumes aim to be reliable in this sense. If you work through the chapter which covers the topic you are about to revise and list the events contained in marginal 'events lists' and in boxed lists of events, you can be confident that you have identified every fact of real significance that you need to know about on the topic. However, you also need to make a list of the historical issues you might be asked to write about. You can do this most conveniently by working through the relevant chapter and noting down the contents of the 'issues boxes'.

For almost everybody, important parts of the revision process are the planning of answers to all the main types of structured and essay questions, and the answering of typical questions (both those requiring extended writing and those based on source material) under exam conditions. The best way to make full use of what this book has to offer in these respects is to work through the two relevant sets of end-of-chapter sections (Answering extended writing and essay questions on… and Answering source-based questions on…) in a methodical manner.

Keith Randell

POLITICS AND PARTIES, 1900–14

CHAPTER 1

POINTS TO CONSIDER

In one sense there was enormous change in Britain between 1900 and 1999, and that is the subject of this book. Yet in another sense there was considerable continuity. The basic questions that confronted late Victorian Britain were still being asked at the beginning of the new millennium in 2000. How much power should the State have over ordinary people's lives? What were the best means of Britain's earning its living? How much should people pay in taxes? How could poverty be tackled? Should wealth be re-distributed by the government taking it from the wealthy to give to the poor? How far should the government be responsible for running the economy? How much attention should Britain spend on protecting itself against potential enemies? What was its international role? How closely should it tie itself to alliances and agreements with other countries? What should be its relations with Ulster? Such questions were as pressing in 1999 as they had been in 1900. Answers to these questions involve political decisions. That is where the parties come in. This chapter shows how the political parties responded to such questions in the period between the beginning of the century and the outbreak of the Great War in 1914.

1 The Conservatives and Liberals at the Beginning of the Twentieth Century

ISSUE:
What were the main issues that divided the parties?

In 1900 British politics was dominated by two main parties, the Conservatives (also known officially as Unionists because of their opposition to home rule for Ireland) and the Liberals. In addition there were two smaller but still influential parties – the Labour Party, which came into being in 1900 as the Labour Representation Committee (LRC), and the Irish Nationalists. In 1906, after having been in power for 11 years, the Conservatives suffered a crushing electoral defeat at the hands of the Liberals. If we examine the reasons for the Liberal landslide we will gain further understanding of the great issues in British politics in the late Victorian and **Edwardian** eras.

GOVERNMENTS OF THE LATE VICTORIAN AND EDWARDIAN ERAS

1895 –1902	Conservatives under Lord Salisbury;
1902 –05	Conservatives under Arthur Balfour;
1905 –08	Liberals under Henry Campbell-Bannerman;
1908 –14	Liberals under Herbert Asquith.

EDWARDIAN

Strictly speaking, the adjective Edwardian refers to the reign of Edward VII (1901–10). However, it is accepted practice among historians to extend the term to include the early years of the reign of George V between his accession in 1910 and the outbreak of the First World War in 1914.

Q Why did the Conservatives suffer such a heavy defeat in 1906?

'CHINESE SLAVERY'

Balfour's government was accused of having permitted large numbers of Chinese labourers, referred to as 'coolies' or slaves, to be brought from Asia to work in appalling conditions for pitiful wages in the gold and diamond mines of southern Africa.

THE TAFF VALE JUDGEMENT, 1901

The Conservatives did not come well out of the controversy surrounding this legal decision, which restricted the right of trade unions to strike. When Balfour's government declared that it would take no steps to reverse this ruling against the trade unions it reinforced the conviction among the workers that Conservatism was fundamentally opposed to their interests (see page 18).

Table 1 The election results for 1900 and 1906 (showing seats won).

The 1900 and 1906 Election Results		
	1900	**1906**
Conservatives	402	157
Liberals	184	400
LRC (Labour in 1906)	2	30
Irish Nationalists	82	83

There is an interesting political saying: oppositions do not win elections, governments lose them. This maxim can certainly be applied to the Liberal victory of 1906, which was largely due to the mistakes of the Conservatives. In 1902, Arthur Balfour had inherited a number of growing problems, which caused his government to become increasingly unpopular. Among these were: **'Chinese slavery'**, **the Taff Vale judgement**, the effects of the Anglo-Boer War, and the tariff reform question. It was the last two issues in this list that created the greatest difficulties for the Conservatives.

a) The Anglo-Boer War, 1899–1902

This war was part of an attempt to reimpose British control on southern Africa. In the London Convention of 1884 Britain had accepted the division of southern Africa between the British, in Cape Province and Natal, and the Dutch Boers (farmers), in the Transvaal and the Orange Free State. However, although Britain formally recognised Boer rights of self-government in the Transvaal, it continued to claim ambiguously that it exercised 'suzerainty' (authority) over the region. This became a crucial issue after gold was discovered in the Transvaal in 1886.

There is now little doubt that Britain deliberately provoked the war. Ever since the Boers had separated from the British and set up their own republics, the demanding question was who was to have the final authority. Was southern Africa to be a British-dominated federal dominion or a Boer republic? For Joseph Chamberlain, the Colonial Secretary, British supremacy in southern Africa was essential in order to maintain Britain's strength as an imperial power. Chamberlain, therefore, plotted successfully with the aggressive British High Commissioner in the Cape to make such unreasonable demands on the Boers that they would be put in such a position that they would have no choice but to fight. The war that was to last three years broke out in 1899.

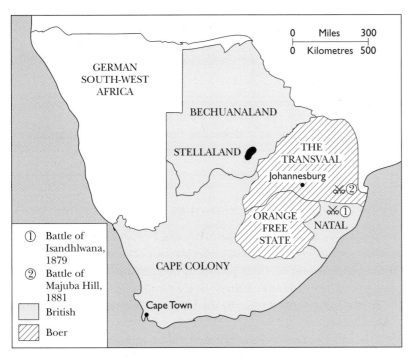

Figure 1 Map of southern Africa on the eve of the Anglo-Boer War.

From the beginning there was a significant group in Britain who were deeply unhappy with the war. Referred to as 'pro-Boers', they questioned the morality of Britain's stance. Initially, however, the war was widely popular in Britain, and Prime Minister Salisbury sought to gain from this by calling an election in 1900. The Conservatives deliberately played upon the patriotism of the electorate in what became known as the 'Khaki election'. Although the Conservative majority was slightly reduced, the government still had a comfortable majority over the Liberals.

However, from then on things went badly for the Conservatives. Although the war was eventually won, their handling of it proved dismal. The pro-Boers drew constant attention to the failure of British forces to win the war quickly. Still more discomfiting to the government were the reports of the extreme measures which the British forces employed in trying to break Boer resistance. The most notorious of these was the internment of civilians in 'concentration' camps, where the cramped and unhygienic conditions frequently led to the spread of fatal diseases. Henry Campbell-Bannerman, who had become Liberal leader in 1899, accused Salisbury's government of employing 'the methods of barbarism'. Lloyd George, a dynamic young Liberal, declared: 'we have now taken to killing babies'. Britain's inhumane strategy against Boer civilians, added to the fact that it took the might of the British imperial army three long years to overcome an outnumbered and outgunned group of farmers, caused embarrassment at home and aroused ridicule abroad.

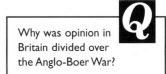

Why was opinion in Britain divided over the Anglo-Boer War?

Having read section 1a, write down a list of points in response to each of the following questions.

▼ Why did Britain become involved in a war with the Boer Republics? Were there any real British interests at stake?
▼ Why did the war as it developed became increasingly unpopular with certain sections of British opinion?

ISSUE:

Why were the early years of the century dominated by the tariff reform issue?

b) Tariff Reform (also known as Imperial Preference)

In the late Victorian and Edwardian years, British manufacturers and traders expressed deep anxiety over a number of developments that threatened to reduce their profits, if not put them out of business altogether. They identified the following causes of concern:

▼ Britain had been overtaken by the USA and Germany in iron and steel production.
▼ The machines and industrial processes which had earlier given Britain its lead had become outdated, particularly in the coal and textile industries.
▼ Too little capital was being put into new machinery and new methods.
▼ Many British manufactured goods were more expensive than foreign ones, which led to lower exports and higher imports.
▼ Falling profits led to lower investment and workers being laid off.

PROTECTION
is the belief that, in order to safeguard domestic manufacturing and agriculture from competition from abroad, the British government should use its powers to impose tariffs on foreign goods, thus making it unprofitable to import them.

The manufacturers demanded that Britain return to a policy of **protection**. This renewed a battle that had run throughout the nineteenth century between the advocates of **free trade** and the supporters of protection. The issue in the form of tariff reform became the major economic question of the pre-1914 years. Tariff reform was a policy, most closely associated with Joseph Chamberlain, of protecting home produced food and manufactured goods by placing restrictive duties on imports unless they came from the British dominions and colonies. Goods from these countries would receive preferential treatment. The idea behind this was to develop the British Empire as a worldwide protectionist trading union. The modern parallel is the European Union which seeks to create a free-trade system between its own members, but which follows a firmly protectionist policy towards non-member nations.

In a misjudged attempt to out-manoeuvre the Liberals on economic matters, Arthur Balfour's Conservative government (1902–05) adopted tariff reform as its official programme in 1903. But few Conservatives were genuinely happy with it. They accepted it because it seemed to offer a means of raising revenue without resorting to taxation. The lack of conviction among the Conservatives was eagerly exploited by the Liberals, who were able to project them-selves as the defenders of cheap food for the people against the dear-food tariff reformers. In the fierce 'free trade versus protection' debate that followed, the electorate judged that the protectionists had lost the argument. The result was a sweeping victory for the Liberals in the 1906 election. Henry Campbell-Bannerman, who had already become Prime Minister of a minority Liberal government two months earlier, following Balfour's resignation, now headed a Liberal ministry with a majority of 243 over the Conservatives.

ACTIVITY

Having studied the material in section 1b, prove to yourself that you have grasped the main ideas by explaining in a few sentences what the essential differences were between free trade and tariff reform as economic policies.

FREE TRADE

was associated with the ideas of the outstanding Scottish economist, Adam Smith, one of the great influences on economic thinking in the nineteenth century. He had argued in *The Wealth of Nations* (1776) that trade flourished best and brought the largest returns when it was left entirely free of government interference. His basic contention was that the attempt to protect home products by placing tariffs on imported goods had the reverse effect; it impeded the flow of trade and so reduced the export of British manufactures.

Figure 2 Two conflicting views of the effects of free trade. Liberal Party and Conservative Party election posters in 1906.

ACTIVITY

Study the posters in the light of what you have read in this section. In what ways do they present the tariff reform and free trade arguments?

ISSUE:
Why had a third main political party developed by the beginning of the twentieth century?

2 The Labour Party

Parliamentary reforms in 1867 and 1884 had given the vote to an increasing number of working men. It had been the hope of many Liberals that the workers would regard the Liberal Party as able to speak for them. However, there was a strong feeling among the working class organisations, such as the trade unions, that the Liberal party was too broadly based to be able to focus effectively on the concerns of the workers. What the workers needed was an entirely separate political party that would directly represent them. The outcome was the amalgamation in 1900 of a variety of reforming and radical groups into the Labour Representation Committee, which became the Labour Party in 1906.

SOCIALISM

Socialism has shades of meaning. It can refer to Communism, the Marxist movement that advocated revolutionary class conflict. But socialism, usually spelt with a small 's', can also refer to the radical but non-revolutionary movement which held that the power of the State should be used to correct the economic injustices and inequalities existing in society. This form of socialism was a strong influence in the early Labour Party.

Main Groups that Formed the Labour Party

▼ Trade unions, which wanted a distinct political party to represent them.
▼ The Social Democratic Federation (SDF), a Marxist group led by H.M. Hyndman, which wanted class war against the ruling establishment.
▼ Fabians (intellectuals such as George Bernard Shaw), who wanted to spread **socialism** not by revolution but by propaganda and education.
▼ Co-operative societies, which wanted the poorer consumers to be protected by a political party that could speak for them.

In its early days the Labour Party judged that it could best exert political influence by co-operating with the Liberals. This resulted in the Lib-Lab pact, an agreement made in 1903 between Ramsay MacDonald and Herbert Gladstone, the respective chief whips of the Labour and Liberal parties, that their candidates would not compete against each other in parliamentary elections. Some Labour supporters were not very impressed with this and felt that the party before 1914 was little more than an ineffectual pressure group. Beatrice Webb, a leading Fabian, reflected in 1914: 'if we are honest, we have to admit that the party has failed'. What she had in mind was Labour's failure to take over from the Liberals.

Nevertheless, gains had been made. The Liberals now had a radical rival. As Table 3 on page 14 shows, Labour increased its seats from 30 in 1906 to 42 in 1910. Although this was reduced by by-election losses to 37 by 1914, it was still a considerable achievement. An addi-

How effective was the young Labour Party?

tional boost came from the fact that in the period before 1914 a growing number of trade unions, including the powerful Miners' Federation, affiliated (became members as a block) to the Labour Party. This added numbers to the party and increased its financial income. There was also the happy circumstance for Labour that, after the 1910 elections had destroyed the Liberals' majority, Asquith's government needed to be on good terms with the minority parties in order to maintain its control of the House of Commons (see page 15).

3 The Liberal Reforms, 1906–14

ISSUE:
Why was social reform such a major concern in Edwardian Britain?

Living in the affluent world of the early 2000s, it is often difficult for us to appreciate how widespread poverty was in Britain at the beginning of the last century. Malnutrition, ill-health and squalid living conditions were the lot of the majority of the population. Poverty was as old as society but what had intensified it in Britain in the nineteenth century had been the rapid growth of population and its concentration in urban areas. As Table 2 shows, in the 40 years after 1871 the number of people living in the major industrial areas virtually doubled. The **Poor Law** and the other welfare schemes that existed were simply incapable of dealing with the widespread destitution that followed the unplanned and, therefore, uncontrolled urban growth. Overcrowding, poor sanitation, and disease were the result. It is true that central and local government in the Victorian age had begun to take measures to alleviate the worst of the cond-itions but their efforts fell far short of the needs. It was also the case that wage rates had risen but not to a level where the majority of workers had genuine control over their lives.

The Poor Law

This dated from the early-seventeenth century and was a system for providing relief for those in poverty. As amended in 1834, the Poor Law dealt with pauperism by ending outdoor relief for the able-bodied. In its place parish workhouses for the destitute were set up to be run by Boards of Poor Law Guardians. To deter the idle poor from entering them, it was laid down that conditions in the workhouses were to be deliberately 'less eligible' (harsher) than that of the lowest paid labourer. Although the regime had been softened by the early-twentieth century, the workhouse was still officially the main plank in public welfare provision.

Table 2 The Growth of the Conurbations in late Victorian and Edwardian Britain.

	Greater London	S.E. Lancs	W. Midlands	W. Yorks	Merseyside
1871	3,890,000	1,386,000	969,000	1,064,000	690,000
1901	6,856,000	2,117,000	1,483,000	1,524,000	1,030,000
1911	7,256,000	2,328,000	1,634,000	1,590,000	1,157,000

What highlighted these problems and forced politicians to react to them was the publication around the turn of the century of a number of studies which provided hard evidence of the squalor and deprivation that shaped the lives of the mass of people living in Britain. Prominent among the reports which moved them were the pioneering studies produced by Charles Booth and Seebohm Rowntree.

Source A From *Poverty: A Study of Town Life* by Seebohm Rowntree, 1901.

Life in Class A. Income under 18s. [90p] weekly for a moderate family. Three examples of cases considered within this group.
1. No occupation. Married. Aged 64. Two rooms. The man has 'not had his boot on' for 12 months. He is suffering from dropsy. His wife cleans schools. This house shares one closet [WC] with eight other houses, and one water tap with four others. Rent 2s.6d.
2. Out of work. Married. Four rooms. Five children. Drinks. 'Chucked his work over a row'. Very poor; has to pawn furniture to keep his children. Rent 4s.
3. Widow. Four rooms. One baby. Semi-lunatic family. Receives Poor Relief. Son, who is wage earner, is weak bodily and mentally. Ditto the daughter. Nice house, but dirty. 4s. per week is received for an illegitimate child being brought up here. This house shares one closet with another house, and one water tap with three other houses.

We are faced by the startling probability that from 25 to 30 per cent of the town population of the United Kingdom are living in poverty. In this land of abounding wealth, during a time of perhaps unexampled prosperity, probably more than one fourth of the population are living in povery.

It was such evidence as this that quickened the desire of all three parties to tackle poverty. The Labour Party came into being at this time specifically to defend the working class. 'New Liberalism' was the response of the radical-Liberals who wanted their Party to commit itself fully to social reform. Nor should it be forgotten that the Conservatives, although dismissed by their political opponents as reactionaries who did not want social change, had taken significant steps towards reform. Because of the reputation that the Liberals were to gain as a reforming government after 1905, sight has sometimes been lost of how much ground had been prepared by the preceding Conservative administrations.

Major Social Reforms of the Conservative Governments, 1886–1905

▼ provision made to improve working-class housing.
▼ steps taken to prevent cruelty against children.
▼ landlords rather than tenants to be responsible for paying tithes.
▼ Factory Act of 1891 improved safety conditions in the mines.
▼ Education Act of 1891 established free elementary education.
▼ measures to improve the conditions of shop assistants and mill hands.
▼ factory acts tightening safety regulations.
▼ Workmen's Compensation Act of 1897 provided payments for injuries sustained at the work place.

Yet, while it is important to acknowledge the record of the Conservatives, it was the Liberals who formed the first great reforming ministry of the new century. Asquith's pre-war Liberal government undertook a range of reforms that created the basis on which Britain's social policy was built during the rest of the century.

a) Social and Economic Reforms, 1906–11

The term New Liberalism refers to the ideas of the radicals and more progressive thinkers among the Liberals who wanted their party to embrace social reform policies that would both deal with the economic problems and appeal to the working class, which, with the widening of the franchise in the late-nineteenth century, was a growing electoral force. The New Liberals argued that the state must play the leading role in the improvement of social conditions, and that if it failed to do so the result would be the growth of socialism and class conflict. An important voice in the formulation of New Liberal thinking was J.A. Hobson. He urged the Liberal party to recognise 'the sovereignty of social welfare' and make social reform a priority.

New Liberalism seemed to have come into its own with the crushing Liberal election victory in 1906. It was Henry Campbell-Bannerman, Prime Minister from 1905 to 1908, who set the Liberals on the path to reform by claiming that the 1906 election had given the party a mandate to pursue radical policies. The pace of reform quickened still more in 1908 when Campbell-Bannerman retired and was replaced by Herbert Asquith, who was to remain Prime Minister for the next eight years. What proved to be one of the new leader's

ISSUE:
Were the reforms the implementation of New Liberalism?

THE MAIN REFORMS

1906 Trade Disputes Act protected union funds from claims for damages arising from strikes; education measures, introduced school meals and medical examinations;

1907 –12 prison reforms introduced the probation service, ended imprisonment for debt, and created special provisions for young offenders;

1908 old age pensions introduced;

1909 Trade Boards Act laid down minimum wages in the notorious 'sweated' industries, such as the clothing trade;

labour exchanges set up;

Development Commission set up to organise the funding of State welfare;

1911 National Insurance Act; Shops Act established the legal right of shop workers to a weekly half-day holiday.

OLD AGE PENSIONS, 1908

The first pensions granted 5s (25p) a week to people over 70 years of age who had incomes of less than £31.10s (£31.50) a year and who had not previously received help from the Poor Law. The pension was non-contributory, i.e., it was funded entirely from government revenues.

Why did the 1909 Budget cause bitter controversy?

shrewdest moves was the appointment of the radical David Lloyd George as Chancellor of the Exchequer. Lloyd George brought a dynamic thrust to the government's programme. He and Winston Churchill, who took over from him at the Board of Trade, were largely responsible for the reputation that the pre-1914 Liberal government gained as a great reforming ministry. Three particular measures illustrate the character of the Liberals' approach to social welfare – **old age pensions**, **the 'People's Budget'**, and **National Insurance**.

Pensions for the elderly was not a new idea. Other countries, Germany for example, had already adopted them, and they had been considered by all the parties during the previous 20 years. But what made them so contentious in 1908 was not the principle behind them but the method of paying for them. To meet the cost of the old age pensions Lloyd George planned to raise revenue by increased taxation of the propertied classes. This was the purpose of his 1909 budget, which became known as 'the People's Budget'.

Main Terms of the 'People's Budget', 1909

▽ Standard rate of income tax to be raised to 1s 3d (approx 6p) in the pound on incomes up to £3,000 p.a.

▽ A new 'super tax' of 5d (approx 2p) in the pound on incomes over £3,000 p.a.

▽ Death duties to be paid on estates valued at over £5,000.

▽ A levy of 20 per cent on the unearned increase in property values when land changed hands.

It was the proposal to impose death duties and to tax increases in land values that aroused the fiercest opposition of the landed interests. The Conservatives attacked the budget by asserting that the unprecedentedly heavy taxation of landowners was a deliberate act of class war by Lloyd George. He retaliated by claiming that it was indeed a war budget but not of the kind described by the Conservatives:

> This is a War Budget. It is for raising money to wage implacable warfare against poverty and squalidness. I cannot help hoping and believing that before this generation has passed away we shall have advanced a great step towards that good time when poverty and wretchedness and human degradation which always follow in its camp will be as remote to the people of this country as the wolves which once infested the forests.

Source B From a speech by Lloyd George in the House of Commons, 1909.

Yet what incensed his opponents was that, for all his grand language, only a portion of the proposed revenue from the budget was earmarked for pensions. The greater part of the £16 million that Lloyd George was hoping to raise was to go towards the costs of the new warships that were being built for the navy.

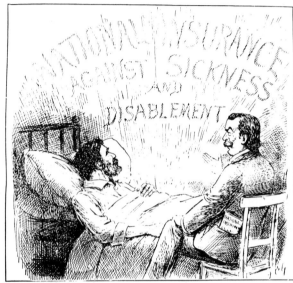

THE DAWN OF HOPE.

Mr. LLOYD GEORGE'S National Health Insurance Bill provides for the insurance of the Worker in case of Sickness.

Support the Liberal Government
in their policy of
SOCIAL REFORM.

Figure 3 National Insurance – The Dawn of Hope – Liberal Party poster, 1911. Lloyd George in his best bedside manner shows the sick patient that National Insurance will protect him.

Main Terms of the National Insurance Act, 1911

▽ Cover was provided for workers aged between 16 and 70 against sickness and unemployment.

▽ It did not apply to all industries, but was targeted at those where unemployment was consistently high.

▽ The scheme was to be funded by compulsory weekly contributions: 4d from the employer, 3d from the employee, and 2d from the state.

▽ Contributions were to be paid by buying adhesive stamps which were then affixed to a card.

ACTIVITY

Having studied section 3a, write down a set of paragraphs in answer to the following question:

▼ In what sense may the Liberal reforms be said to be a fulfilment of 'New Liberalism'?

Interestingly, the National Insurance Act met strong resistance from the very people it was intended to benefit. Its compulsory character was particularly disturbing to the five and half million people, many of them working class, who already paid privately into schemes run by insurance companies and trade unions. The workers doubted that they were going to gain more from an imposed State plan than from their own private insurance. The popular press attacked the compulsory contributions as theft from the workers' pay packets. Lloyd George responded by claiming that the workers were 'getting 9d for 4d'. As the originator of the scheme Lloyd George showed remarkable skill in meeting the objections to it. He quietened the protests from the insurance companies, which feared losing out to the State scheme, by making them an integral part of the operation of the new plans. He was also able to overcome the complaints of the Labour Party, which had wanted national insurance to be paid for by higher taxes on the wealthy. Lloyd George pacified Labour by promising to introduce payment for MPs, a commitment which he honoured in 1911.

The resistance of the workers and the Labour Party to measures, which were supposedly in their interest, is at first sight surprising. What it shows is that attitudes to welfare reform in the Edwardian period were often complex. It is notable that Churchill's Trade Boards Act of 1909, which aimed at providing minimum wages in the 'sweated' industries where unscrupulous employers exploited cheap labour, was also initially opposed by the unions. The reason was that they feared that the effect of a minimum wage would be job cuts by the employers. The minimum wage was also seen as undermining the customary right of unions to negotiate differentials, that is, separate rates of pay for different levels of skill. It was also dislike of the State's interfering between employer and worker that led the unions to look suspiciously at the labour exchanges introduced by Churchill in 1909.

The fact was that many working-class people had a well-founded distrust of State intervention, which they saw as patronising and disruptive. Their practical experience of officialdom in such developments as the workhouse, compulsory education, slum clearance and vaccination had seldom been a happy one. Too often they felt they were being pushed around by State-employed snoopers. Workers sus-

Q Why did the working classes initially oppose the Liberal welfare reforms?

pected that State welfare was primarily intended to keep them in their place and make them conform. R.H. Tawney, one of the outstanding social historians of his day and a strong Labour Party supporter, explained the workers' reasoning.

> The middle and upper class view in social reform is that it should regulate the workers' *life* in order that he may *work* better. The working-class view of economic reform is that it should regulate his *work*, in order that he may have a change of living. Hence to working people licensing reform, insurance acts, etc. seems beginning at the wrong end.

Q
Did the Liberal social reforms mark the beginning of the welfare state in Britain?

Source C R.H. Tawney writing in 1912.

The Liberal social-reform programme has come to be seen as a key stage on the path to the modern **welfare state**. It is worth restating the main Liberal social reforms: old age pensions, labour exchanges, National Insurance, and the Development Commission. These did not create a full welfare state; the resources simply did not exist for that. But what can be said is that the Liberals had taken significant steps towards what has been termed 'the social service state', a centrally organised administration capable of improving the living and working conditions of large portions of the British population.

THE WELFARE STATE
is the notion of the State operating a fully funded programme to provide all the essential social, health and educational needs of all its people, regardless of their income or social status. A neat way of putting it is to say that the welfare state protects everyone 'from the cradle to the grave'.

ACTIVITIES

▼ Having read the chapter so far, explain briefly why the working classes were initially suspicious of state welfare.

▼ Write down in your own words the ways in which the Liberal social reforms prepared the way for the welfare state. For more details on this, you may care to look ahead to pages 132–36.

4 The Pre-War Crises, 1911–14

ISSUE:
Why did Liberal Britain experience a series of major social and political crises in this period?

Chief Political and Constitutional Reforms, 1911–14

▼ payment of MPs (£400 p.a.) introduced, 1911. This allowed those without a private income to consider standing for Parliament.
▼ Parliament Act, 1911, removed the power of the House of Lords to veto Bills passed by the House of Commons.
▼ Home Rule Act for Ireland, 1912.
▼ Trade Union Act, 1913 legalised union funds being used for political purposes.
▼ Welsh Church disestablished, 1914.

The period from 1911 to 1914 was a particularly troubled time in Britain. Four major crises occurred: a) conflict between the Lords and Commons, b) suffragette agitation, c) industrial strife, d) the Ulster crisis. These proved so disruptive that they seemed to threaten the social and political order. The seriousness of the crises has been interpreted by some observers as evidence of the failure of the Liberals to deal with the problems of their time. Before examining that view, let us examine the major features of the crises.

a) The Conflict Between the Lords and Commons, 1909–11

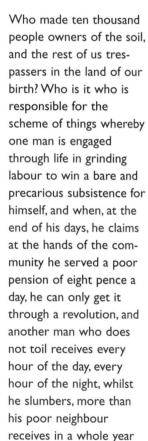

Why did the Unionists attack the People's Budget?

A major struggle between the House of Commons and the House of Lords had become increasingly likely after the Liberals won their landslide victory in 1906. Unable to outvote the government in the Commons, the Conservative opposition resorted to using its in-built majority in the Lords to block measures to which it objected. These included major licensing and education bills. Matters came to a head in the controversy over the People's Budget of 1909, in which Lloyd George had proposed special taxes on rich landowners to pay for old age pensions (see page 10).

Who made ten thousand people owners of the soil, and the rest of us trespassers in the land of our birth? Who is it who is responsible for the scheme of things whereby one man is engaged through life in grinding labour to win a bare and precarious subsistence for himself, and when, at the end of his days, he claims at the hands of the community he served a poor pension of eight pence a day, he can only get it through a revolution, and another man who does not toil receives every hour of the day, every hour of the night, whilst he slumbers, more than his poor neighbour receives in a whole year of toil?

Source D From a speech by Lloyd George in the House of Commons, 1910.

The Unionists decided to resist the budget on the grounds that it was an unprecedented attack upon the rights of property. They argued that this entitled them to ignore the long-standing convention that the Lords did not interfere with finance bills. Lloyd George, the Chancellor of the Exchequer and a strong opponent of aristocratic privilege, thought the whole affair could be turned to the Liberals' advantage. He led the Liberals in denouncing the peers' attempt to maintain their privileges at the expense of the old and the poor of the nation. In a memorable turn of phrase he mocked the Lords for being not, as the peers claimed, 'the watchdog of the constitution' but 'Mr Balfour's poodle'. Lloyd George savaged the peers for opposing the will of the British people.

Table 3 Results of the two elections in 1910, showing the narrow gap between Liberals and Conservatives.

The 1910 Election Results			
Conservatives	Liberal	Labour	Irish Nationalists
Jan/Feb	273	275	40	82
December	272	272	42	84

The Lords lost the battle that followed. In 1910, after two general elections had produced a stalemate that left the Liberals still in office since they could rely on the support of the Irish Nationalist and Labour MPs, the peers finally allowed Lloyd George's budget through. They were promptly presented with a Parliament Bill, which set out to limit their powers. For well over a year the Lords resisted, arguing that the 1910 elections had failed to give Asquith's government a clear mandate for such radical change. Added tension was created by the awareness on both sides that were the Lords' veto to be removed there would be nothing to prevent the Liberals from forcing Irish Home Rule through Parliament. The Lords gave in eventually under the threat of being swamped by 500 new Liberal peers whom King George V agreed, at Asquith's request, to create if the Lords' resistance continued. Even then, the narrow majority of 17 was achieved only by the decision of 37 Conservative peers to vote for the Bill rather than suffer the 'pollution' of their House.

Main Terms of the Parliament Act, 1911

The Lords' absolute veto was abolished by two key clauses:
- ▽ the delaying power of the Lords was to be restricted to two years;
- ▽ a Bill sent up by the Commons in three consecutive sessions would become law despite rejection by the Lords.

ACTIVITIES

- ▼ Having read the details in this section, explain in your own words the point of Lloyd George's jibe that the Lords were not the watch-dog of the constitution but 'Mr Balfour's poodle'.
- ▼ The clash between the Lords and Commons is the type of topic that calls for a group discussion. You and your student colleagues could divide into two groups, one arguing the case for the government, the other for the opposition peers. An opening question might be: 'Was the resistance of the House of Lords to the People's Budget and the Parliament Bill anything more than blind reaction?' Interestingly, the reform of the House of Lords again became an important issue in the late 1990s (see page 195). You might well find some of the points that came up then relevant to a discussion of the 1911 crisis.

Why did the 'votes
for women' question
cause acute problems for
the Liberals?

SUFFRAGISTS AND SUFFRAGETTES

Both groups fully supported female suffrage (votes for women), but whereas the suffragists were opposed to violent methods, the suffragettes believed that it was only by being prepared to break the law that women would be able to force a male-dominated parliament to respond to their demands.

b) The Suffragette Crisis

The extension of the vote to women might be thought to have been a cause that the Liberals would eagerly support. John Stuart Mill (1806–73), the great Liberal philosopher, had regarded it as an essential freedom in a civilised society. However, the impossibility of knowing how women would vote made a number of the leading Liberals hesitate to commit themselves to it. The slowness of Parliament to attend to the matter had led to the development of a **suffragist** and a **suffragette** movement. The major suffragette organisation was the Women's Social and Political Union (WSPU), founded in 1903 and led by the dynamic Emmeline Pankhurst. The WSPU undertook a campaign of disruption, which became increasingly violent as the Liberals persisted in their refusal to find parliamentary time to debate the question. Between 1911 and 1914, a series of suffragette outrages, which included arson and physical assault, showed the degree of WSPU frustration. But the violence tended to alienate moderate supporters. It also provided an excuse for the government to impose heavy prison sentences on convicted suffragettes. The issue of votes for women was no nearer to being settled when the war intervened in 1914. Mrs Pankhurst immediately called off her campaign and dedicated herself and her followers to the war effort.

'Votes for women' is now viewed as part of the broader campaign for female emancipation that developed in the twentieth century. However, at the time most politicians approached the matter primarily from a party political angle. For them a female electorate was an unknown quantity. They feared that it would have a harmful effect on their parliamentary strength. This worry applied to all the parties, Conservative, Liberal and Labour. They simply did not know how women would vote. For Labour there was the added complication that if the franchise were to be introduced only for selected groups of women this would weaken the case for complete male suffrage which was the Party's first priority. (In 1914, 40 per cent of adult males were still without the vote.) It should also be pointed out that the suffragettes were not always clear in their objectives. In 1910 Emmeline Pankhurst was willing to abandon the idea of working-class women gaining the franchise in return for Parliament granting it to women who owned or occupied property. This was doubtless a tactical move on her part, but it did emphasise how ambiguous the votes for women issue could be.

However, no matter what the ambiguities may have been, the Liberals were damaged by the suffragette issue. Their apparent reluctance to treat it as a question of principle weakened their moral standing, and their failure to resolve the issue proved a political embarrassment.

Figure 4 'The Cat and Mouse Act' – a graphic poster of 1913, showing the bitterness with which the Act was regarded by the suffragettes. The Act provided the means by which the authorities, without having to resort to the previous grim practice of force-feeding, overcame the resistance of the imprisoned suffragettes who went on hunger strike. The women were released on licence for short periods when their health deteriorated; once they had recovered they were reimprisoned.

ACTIVITY

The Liberals claimed that the votes for women issue was 'a constitutional not a moral question'. Explain what you think they meant by that and give your opinion on whether they were right to make that distinction.

Why were the years
1911–14 a time of
industrial strife?

**THE TRADE
DISPUTES ACT,
1906**
reversed the notorious Taff
Vale decision of 1901, which
had made trade unions liable
for claims for damages arising from strikes. The 1906
Act also legalised picketing
and sympathetic strikes, i.e.,
a strike by one union in
support of another.

SYNDICALISM
was a revolutionary philosophy, notably influential among
French and Belgian miners,
which called on workers to
abandon moderate methods
of trying to improve their
conditions and turn instead
to all-out disruption, with
the aim of smashing the
industrial-capitalist system.

c) Industrial Unrest

Despite the **Trade Disputes Act** of 1906, the years preceding the First World War were a particularly troubled period for the unions. By 1912 the cost of living was 14 per cent higher than in 1906 and unemployment had risen sharply during the same period. Despite the Liberal welfare measures, the gap between rich and poor was widening. Furthermore, the presence of Labour Party MPs in the Commons did not appear to have brought any clear benefits to the workers. Faced with these failures, many trade unionists began to doubt whether the existing political and parliamentary system could ever be made to respond to working-class needs. The belief that the legal and parliamentary systems were fundamentally hostile to their interests encouraged a number of unions to consider direct action. The increase in trade union membership from 1.9 million in 1900 to 4.1 million in 1914 was a measure of the growing frustration of the industrial workers. Few British workers were drawn to **syndicalism** but in the excited atmosphere of pre-war Britain direct action became increasingly attractive to the more militant unions.

In 1911 the miners, who had a reputation as one of the most combative British unions, went on strike demanding a minimum wage. The strike was strongest in South Wales where syndicalism had made its greatest impact. The miners' call for sympathetic action from other industrial workers was answered in the summer of 1912 when three major unions – the dockers, the railwaymen and the seamen – came out on strike. The government regarded the situation as so serious that they became involved in the negotiations between employers and workers. Lloyd George persuaded the bosses to increase their wage offer. The strike was called off but matters were far from settled.

In 1914 another major disruption threatened when the miners linked with the dockers and railwaymen to form a 'triple alliance'. Although the alliance did not develop into a general strike, it did frighten the government into urging the employers to consider granting further concessions to the unions. As with the Ulster question, so with the industrial relations conflict, it was the coming of the war in 1914 that brought a temporary suspension of the troubles.

ACTIVITY

Having examined the material in this section on the unions, write a few sentences saying whether you think unions were correct in claiming that parliament and the legal system had an inbuilt bias against the rights of workers.

d) The Ulster Crisis

In the nineteenth century there had been a strong movement for home rule (an independent government in Dublin responsible for Irish affairs) among Irish nationalists. But what made home rule such a contentious issue was the position of **Ulster**. For reasons which dated back to the sixteenth century, the northern Irish province of Ulster was peopled predominantly by Protestants of English and Scottish origin. They rejected any suggestion that the whole of Ireland should be separated from Britain, since this would, in their eyes, lead to the subjection of their province to the rule of an oppressive Catholic majority. Gladstone, the Liberal leader, had introduced Home Rule Bills in 1886 and 1893 but both had failed to pass through parliament. His attempts had split his party and had hardened the resolve of the Unionists to reject home rule on the grounds that it undermined the unity of the United Kingdom and betrayed Ulster.

The period following the failure of Gladstone's Home Rule Bills had been one of relative calm in Ireland, but by 1910 the situation had become dangerous again. The Irish Nationalist MPs in the Commons gained a sudden increase in influence after the two general elections in 1910, which left the Liberal government dependent on them for its Parliamentary majority. Such were the growing tensions in Ireland that Asquith's Liberal Government turned again to home rule as the only solution. In 1912, in a Commons evenly split between Liberals and Unionists, the government relied on the 84 Irish Nationalists, led by John Redmond, to force through the Third Home Rule Bill. Since the Conservatives' customary ability to veto measures passed by the Commons had been ended by the reform of the House of Lords in 1911, there was now nothing to stop home rule from eventually becoming law.

Sinn Fein

In 1908 a number of nationalist groups in Ireland came together under the banner of Sinn Fein ('Ourselves Alone'), a political party which claimed that Ireland was a free nation temporarily enslaved by the British. It sought the creation of a *Dail* (Parliament) to rule in the name of the Irish people. According to its chief spokesman, Arthur Griffith, Sinn Fein's aim was to break both the political and the economic stranglehold Britain had over Ireland. It opposed the Third Reform Bill in 1912 on the grounds that it did not go far enough in advancing Ireland's independence.

ISSUES:
Why was Ulster so bitterly opposed to home rule?
Did the Liberals' Third Home Rule Bill create more problems than it solved?

ULSTER
was the most industrially advanced region in Ireland. This made nationalists determined that the area would remain part of the nation should Ireland ever be granted home rule or complete independence. Clearly Ulster Unionism and Irish nationalist separatism were incompatible. It was their defence of the right of Ulster to remain part of the United Kingdom that had turned the overwhelming majority of the Conservative Party and a number of Liberals into 'Unionists'.

MAJOR DEVELOPMENTS IN THE ANGLO-IRISH QUESTION, 1908–14

1908 Radical Nationalist groups amalgamated to form **Sinn Fein**;

1910 two elections left Irish MPs holding the balance in Commons;
Edward Carson elected Chairman of the Irish Unionist Party;

1911 the Parliament Act ended the Lords' absolute veto;

1912 Commons passed the Third Home Rule Bill;

1913 Lords rejected the Home
Rule Bill;
Ulster Volunteer Force
formed by the Unionists;
Irish Volunteers formed by
the Nationalists;
1914 the Curragh mutiny;
Britain went to war against
Germany;
home rule suspended until
the end of the war.

○   ○

Oglaigh na hEireann.

ENROL UNDER THE GREEN FLAG.

Safeguard your rights and liberties (the
few left you).

Secure more.

Help your Country to a place among
the nations.

Give her a National Army to keep her
there.

Get a gun and do your part.

JOIN THE

IRISH VOLUNTEERS

(President: EOIN MAC NEILL).

The local Company drills at_____

Ireland shall no longer remain disarmed and impotent.

Figure 5 Enrol under the Green
flag. A 1914 Nationalist poster,
calling on Irish patriots to enlist
in the Irish National Volunteers, a
counter army to the Ulster
Defence Volunteers.

Ulster's
Solemn League and Covenant.

Being convinced in our consciences that Home Rule
would be disastrous to the material well-being of Ulster
as well as of the whole of Ireland, subversive of our
civil and religious freedom, destructive of our citizenship and
perilous to the unity of the Empire, we, whose names are under-
written, men of Ulster, loyal subjects of His Gracious Majesty
King George V., humbly relying on the God whom our fathers in
days of stress and trial confidently trusted, do hereby pledge
ourselves in solemn Covenant throughout this our time of
threatened calamity to stand by one another in defending for
ourselves and our children our cherished position of equal citizenship in the United Kingdom and in using all means which may be
found necessary to defeat the present conspiracy to set up a
Home Rule Parliament in Ireland. ¶ And in the event of
such a Parliament being forced upon us we further solemnly and
mutually pledge ourselves to refuse to recognise its authority.
¶ In sure confidence that God will defend the right we hereto
subscribe our names. ¶ And further, we individually declare
that we have not already signed this Covenant.

The above was signed by me at_____
"Ulster Day," Saturday, 28th September, 1912.

_____

——— God Save the King. ———

Figure 6 Ulster-Unionist post-
card of the Solemn League and
Covenant. Claims vary, but it is
likely that over 250,000
Unionists signed this Covenant.

The Ulster Protestants reacted to the Third Home Rule Bill by swearing to the Covenant. This was a document pledging those who signed it to use 'all means which may be found necessary' to resist home rule for Ireland. The Covenanters claimed that the Liberal government had no electoral mandate for home rule. Led by Edward Carson, they prepared to fight to prevent what they regarded as the subjection of Protestant Ulster to the Catholic south. Andrew Bonar Law, the Conservative leader, added fuel to the flames when he declared, 'I can imagine no length of resistance to which Ulster will go, which I shall not be ready to support'. By the summer of 1914 Ireland had split into two armed camps, the nationalist Irish Volunteers confronting Carson's Ulster Volunteer Force. Civil war seemed imminent, a situation made worse by the **Curragh Mutiny**.

Asquith managed to defuse the situation by calling a constitutional conference in June 1914. Reluctantly both sides agreed to consider a form of compromise: Ireland would be partitioned between the Catholic south, which would be granted home rule, and the Protestant north, which would remain part of the United Kingdom. In July 1914, with war against Germany imminent, it was further agreed the Home Rule Bill would be suspended for the duration of the conflict. This produced a temporary easing of the situation, but it was clear that the issue was far from resolved. After 1914 Ireland was destined to undergo still greater turmoil before anything approaching a genuine settlement was reached.

Why was Ireland on the verge of civil war in 1914?

THE CURRAGH MUTINY, 1914

A number of British officers, stationed at the Curragh army base in southern Ireland, who were sympathetic to the Ulster Protestants, resigned their commissions to avoid being sent north against the Ulster Volunteers. Technically this was not a mutiny since their resignations meant they were no longer in the army, but in the tense atmosphere the word was seized on by the press to show how dangerous the Irish crisis was.

5 The Debate on the Crises of 1911–14

In 1934 George Dangerfield, a historian, wrote a provocative book entitled *The Strange Death of Liberal England* in which he argued that the great pre-war crises indicated that by 1914 the Liberals were incapable of dealing effectively with the social and economic pressures of the early-twentieth century. He concluded that the Liberal Party by 1914 was on the point of extinction. Other historians were keen to develop his thesis. They argued that the fierce confrontations between employers and workers, the violence of the suffragettes, Ireland on the verge of civil war, and the battle between Lords and Commons, were all signs that Britain had entered an era of 'class politics'. It was a new form of political warfare with which the Liberal Party was not equipped to cope.

Superficially, the extreme opposition to the Liberal governments does seem to indicate that their policies had failed to satisfy the major demands of the time. However, although Dangerfield's interpretation

ISSUE:
Did the crises mark 'The Strange Death of Liberal England'?

What challenges have there been to Dangerfield's thesis?

remains a provocative starting point, it has been largely superseded by another school of thought which stresses that, difficult though matters were for the liberals, they were still in office in 1914 after nine years of unbroken government. All challenges to their authority had been overcome. Contentious measures such as the People's Budget, National Insurance, the Parliament Act and Home Rule had been forced through Parliament. Asquith's Cabinets had remained united throughout the troubles; no minister resigned office before 1914. The Conservatives, despite recovering in the 1910 elections from their landslide defeat four years earlier, had not been able to oust Asquith's government. Although the Conservatives made electoral gains in the south of the country, the Liberals maintained their traditional support in the industrial and working-class regions. Paul Adelman remarks: 'The Liberal Party may have been losing ground to the right, but it was warding off the challenge from the left'.

It is the resurgence of the Liberal Party in this period rather than its decline that has been strongly emphasised by two modern scholars, Peter Clarke and Ross McKibbin. It is true that the Labour Party had grown in membership in the country at large, mainly through trade-union affiliation. Yet, on its own admission, it had been only a marginal political influence before 1914. Clarke suggests that the Labour party had begun to see its future role not so much as a separate radical force but as a part of a Liberal-Labour 'progressive' movement.

All this tends to indicate that the problems of pre-1914 Britain were not a proof of the failure of Liberal policies since 1905. The decline of the Liberals as a political party may well owe more to the impact of the Great War and the political realignment that it caused (see page 44).

ACTIVITY

Having read sections 4 and 5, write a page or so of comments and observations to show that you understand the essential argument behind the idea that the period 1911–14 marked 'the strange death of Liberal England'. Headings such as Industrial Troubles, Lords v. Commons, Ulster, Votes for Women, Dangerfield's Argument, Opposing Views, would help you arrange your thoughts.

▼ Working on Politics and Parties, 1900–14

Your aim should be to familiarise yourself with the main issues of the period and the ways in which the parties approached them. Ask yourself what the chief differences were between the Conservative, the Liberal and Labour parties in their attitude towards the political social and economic problems of the day. Use the Issues and Activity boxes as guides as you read back over the chapter. You will have gathered that the Liberals dominated the greater part of the period. It is logical, therefore, to pay them the greatest amount of attention. The following questions are central and will help you test how much you have grasped.

1 Why did the Liberals after 1905 give so much attention to social reform?
2 How well did the Liberals deal with the major crises that confronted them between 1911 and 1914?

Summary – Politics and Parties, 1900–14

Year	Conservatives	Liberals	Labour
1899–1902	took Britain into the Anglo-Boer War	Pro-Boers opposed the war	
1900	Khaki election victory		LRC formed
1902–05	Conservatives under Balfour		
1903			Lib-Lab pact
1905		Formed government under Campbell-Bannerman	
1906	Split by tariff reform issue – lost heavily in election	Won landslide victory	Labour Party formed – gained 30 MPs
1908–14		Churchill and Lloyd George introduced a major reform programme	
1909	Strong resistance to People's Budget taxation proposals	Lloyd George's People's Budget	Miners' Federation affiliated to the party
1911–14	Resistance to home rule	Major crises – Lords, Ulster, suffragettes, industrial strife	

Answering Extended Writing and Essay Questions on Politics and Parties, 1900–14

Before attempting any question always satisfy yourself that you under-stand exactly what you are being asked to do. Examination questions now invariably fall into one of the following three categories.

Types of question	Examples of typical questions
Structured (those that ask you to *describe* situations or developments)	1 In what ways were the Conservatives embarrassed by Britain's performance in the Anglo-Boer War? 2 Describe the difficulties faced by Balfour's government of 1902 to 1905. 3 Describe the main social reforms introduced by the Liberals between 1906 and 1914. 4 Trace the main steps that led to the formation of the Labour Party in 1906. 5 Describe the ways used by the Liberal government to overcome the Conservative opposition to the People's Budget of 1909. 6 Describe how the Liberal government attempted to deal with the major crises that confronted it between 1911 and 1914.
Causes (those that ask you to explain *why* things happened the way they did)	7 Account for the Conservatives' landslide defeat in the general election of 1906. 8 Explain why the Liberals introduced a range of social reforms in the period 1906–11. 9 Account for the determined resistance of the House of Lords to Lloyd George's Budget of 1909. 10 Why was Ulster on the verge of civil war in 1914?
Historical judgement (those that ask you to use your knowledge to make an assessment or judgement of historical events)	11 How far do you agree that 'the suffragettes used the wrong methods for the right reasons'? 12 How valid is the view that the period 1909–14 marked 'the strange death of Liberal England'?

Answering Source-Based Questions on Politics and Parties, 1900–14

Before tackling the questions, refresh your memory by re-reading pages 2–7 in this chapter. Read the following statement and then answer the questions which follow.

> The basic fact about British politics in [1906] … was the domination of the great Liberal Party. This meant, therefore, that far from expanding as an independent party … there was a distinct possibility that the Labour Party would be absorbed by the Liberals.

Source E From *The Rise of the Labour Party, 1880–1945* by Paul Adelman, 1986.

▼ QUESTIONS ON SOURCE

1. What was meant by there being 'a distinct possibility' of Labour being absorbed by the Liberal Party in 1906? **(3 marks)**
2. Explain why a distinct Labour Party was formed by 1906. **(7 marks)**
3. How successful was the Labour Party in increasing its support and achieving its aims between 1906 and 1914? **(15 marks)**

Points to note about the questions

The first thing you should note is the difference in the mark allocation as shown in the bracketed number after each question. Clearly this should determine the time and space you give to each answer. As a rough guide, question 2) should be twice as long as 1), and 3) twice as long as 2). Remember marks are not transferable. You cannot compensate for a poor answer by 'borrowing' marks from a good one.

Question 1 The clue to the answer is in the preceding lines of the source itself.

Question 2 Here you have to call on *your own knowledge* of why various groups wanted a separate party to represent the workers' interests.

Question 3 This requires a substantial answer. You need to introduce such points as Labour's increased number of MPs from 30 in 1906 to 42 in 1910, the growth in the number of trade union affiliations to the Labour Party, the social reforms and progressive labour relations measures passed by the Liberals, and the need of the government to be on good terms with the minority parties after the close results in the two 1910 elections. Remember to refer to the doubts expressed by Labour supporters about the party's ability to replace the Liberals.

Further Reading

Books in the Access to History series

Whigs, Radicals and Liberals, 1815–1914 by Duncan Watts has three informative chapters (5–7) on the Liberal problems and achievements in this period. The same author studies Conservative policies under Salisbury and Balfour in *Tories, Conservatives and Unionists 1815–1914* (chapter 6). Chapter 7 in *Government and Reform 1815–1918* by Robert Pearce and Roger Stearn is a very helpful study of the battle over the 1911 reform of the Lords. The relationship between the Liberals and the Labour Party is covered in *Labour and Reform: Working-Class Movements 1815–1914* by Clive Behagg, chapters 5 to 7, while the response of the parties to the social problems of late Victorian and Edwardian Britain is studied in chapters 5 and 6 in *Poverty and Welfare* by Peter Murray. The suffragette movement is the subject of *Votes for Women* by Paula Bartley who also has a helpful chapter on the same theme in her book, *The Changing Role of Women, 1815–1914*. Chapters 4 to 7 of *The Growth of Democracy in Britain* by Annette Mayer deal illuminatingly with parliamentary reform in this period. The Anglo-Irish question is illuminatingly covered in *Great Britain and the Irish Question 1800–1922* by Paul Adelman.

General

There are valuable up-to-date assessments of Balfour, Asquith, and Lloyd George in *Modern British Statesmen 1867–1945* edited by Richard Kelly and John Cantrell (Manchester UP, 1997). *The Rise of the Labour Party, 1880–1945* (1996), *The Decline of the Liberal Party* (1995), both by Paul Adelman, and *The Conservative Party and British Politics* by Stuart Ball (1995) (all published by Longman) are very helpful studies of the main parties. An illuminating treatment of the pre-1914 period is provided by *The Edwardian Age* by Vyvyen Brendon (Hodder & Stoughton, 1996). Two highly recommended analyses are *Edwardian England* by Donald Read (Harrap, 1972) and *The Edwardian Crisis, Britain 1901–1914* by David Powell (Macmillan, 1996). Useful short introductions to the Anglo-Irish question are *Home Rule and the Irish Question* by Grenfell Morton (Longman, 1980) and *Ireland and England 1798–1922* by Joe Finn and Michael Lynch (Hodder & Stoughton, 1995). The outstanding study of the question is *Modern Ireland 1600–1972* by R.F. Foster (Penguin, 1988). A work which will prove very helpful as a source of reference throughout this book is the *Complete A–Z 19th & 20th Century British History Handbook* by Eric Evans (Hodder & Stoughton, 1998).

BRITAIN AND THE FIRST WORLD WAR

CHAPTER 2

POINTS TO CONSIDER

Twice in the first half of the twentieth century Britain chose to enter European conflicts that subsequently developed into world wars. This involvement in war proved to be a major formative experience for Britain. Its political, economic, and social character was significantly altered. This chapter examines why Britain entered the 1914–18 war, outlines the main features of the military struggle, analyses the impact of the war on party politics, and surveys the economic and social changes the war brought about in Britain. You may not need to study all of these aspects but you are advised to gain as broad a picture as possible of Britain's part in a war which may truly be said to have changed the world.

1 Britain's Entry into the First World War

ISSUES:
Need Britain have gone to war in 1914? What British interests were at stake?

On the afternoon of 28 June 1914 in Sarajevo, the capital of Bosnia, a young man named Gavrilo Prinzip stepped onto the running board of a large open-top Daimler motorcar and shot dead its two main occupants. Prinzip was a member of a Serbian terrorist organisation dedicated to resisting what it regarded as Austria-Hungary's threat to the independence of Serbia. The two he assassinated were the royal couple, Archduke Franz Ferdinand, heir to the Austro-Hungarian throne, and his wife, who were on a goodwill tour of the Austro-Hungarian Empire. The terrorists had chosen the Bosnian capital as offering the best opportunity for a successful assassination attempt. Prinzip's shots changed the course of history. Within six weeks of the murder the whole of Europe was at war, a war that by its end four years later had come to include nations from every continent. Why this event in a distant Balkan country should have had such momentous repercussions is a question that demands explanation. In particular we need to understand why Britain became involved.

At first sight, the most obvious explanation of why Britain in 1914 joined France and Russia against Germany and Austria-Hungary is that Britain was a member of an alliance in conflict with an opposing alliance. But the notion that it was the alliance system that necessarily

THE GATHERING CRISIS

June 28 Assassination of Archduke Franz Ferdinand;
July 23 Austro-Hungarian issued ultimatum to Serbia;
24 Russia considered mobilising against Austria-Hungary; Grey proposed mediation;
25 Austria-Hungary mobilised on Russian frontier;
26 France began military preparations;
27 Germany rejected the idea of an international conference;
28 Austria-Hungary declared war on Serbia;
29 Germany warned Russia against mobilisation; Grey warned Germany that Britain would not remain neutral in the event of a general European war;
30 Russia mobilised against Austria-Hungary and Germany;
31 Austria-Hungary ordered general mobilisation;
Aug 1 Germany declared war on Russia;
2 Germany issued ultimatum to Belgium;
3 Germany declared war on France; Belgium rejected German ultimatum; British army mobilised;
4 German forces invaded Belgium; Britain issued ultimatum to Germany; Britain declared war on Germany.

Why was there such uncertainty over the British position?

involved Britain in war overlooks the key point that Britain did not consider itself to be in a binding alliance. It was not committed to fight on any other nation's behalf. Indeed, it had long been the central purpose of British foreign policy to evade such a commitment. The Liberals after 1905 were just as concerned to avoid formal European engagements as their Conservative predecessors had been. While it is true that early in the twentieth century Britain entered into agreements with the USA and **Japan**, it did not change its stance towards Europe. As we will see, Britain's **ententes** with France and Russia are best understood as attempts to avoid closer contacts with Europe.

The test of what the implications of the triple entente actually were came with the diplomatic crisis that followed the assassination at Sarajevo in June 1914. When, a month later, a war broke out between Austria and Germany on one side and Russia and France on the other, the great question facing Britain was whether it had any obligation to become involved. Oddly, neither the Prime Minister, the Cabinet, nor even the Foreign Secretary had a precise answer to that question.

A remarkable feature of British foreign policy before 1914 was that it had been regarded as the individual concern of the Foreign Secretary. Cabinet scrutiny was unsystematic and, except at times of crisis, seldom demanding. Edward Grey held the position of Foreign Secretary continuously from 1905. By nature a withdrawn man, he had chosen to act alone and in secret. Reluctant to be drawn into formal commitments, Grey tried to protect British interests by leaving the position deliberately vague. Foreign governments were known to complain that they could rarely be certain where Britain stood on international questions. The ententes with France and Russia were specifically not alliances. They were understandings rather than agreements. It is true that Britain held military talks with France and Russia after **the Agadir crisis** in 1911, but again no formal agreements were made. Since, therefore, Britain in 1914 was not formally committed to any of the European states involved in the crisis, no one could be sure what its obligations actually were.

The Triple Alliance (the Central Powers)	The Triple Entente (the Allied Powers)
Germany, Austria-Hungary, Turkey	France, Russia, Britain
joined by Bulgaria in 1915	joined by Serbia and Japan in 1914 Italy in 1915 Portugal and Romania in 1916 USA and Greece in 1917

Figure 7 The opposed sides.

The secrecy of Grey's diplomacy since 1905 and the uncertainty of Britain's diplomatic position resulted in considerable division within the Cabinet over the question of entering the war. The Liberal Party, which had strong non-interventionist traditions in foreign policy, did not immediately incline to war and the Labour Party under Ramsay MacDonald initially took a strong anti-war stance. Since Britain had made no formal pledges to either France or Russia, it would require a specific issue to tilt the balance in favour of war. That issue, Grey maintained, came in the form of Belgian neutrality. It was Germany's violation of that neutrality by sending its armies through Belgium in order to attack France that united the Cabinet and the nation after their initial wavering. Writing in retrospect, Grey argued:

> The real reason for going into the war was that, if we did not stand by France and stand up for Belgium against this aggression, we should be isolated, discredited, and hated; and there would be before us nothing but a miserable and ignoble future.

Source A From *Twenty-Five Years 1892–1916* by Edward Grey, 1926.

Grey wrote his post-war analysis in order to establish that it had been with the highest motives that the Liberal government had taken Britain into what proved to be a struggle of unimagined suffering. He presented the defence of Belgium as having been the great moral purpose which animated the nation in 1914. It is certainly true that it was the announcement of Germany's rejection of Britain's demand that Belgian independence be honoured that rallied the House of Commons in favour of Britain's declaration of war. Grey described the mood of the MPs:

> We felt to stand aside would mean the domination of Germany; the subordination of France and Russia; the isolation of Britain and ultimately that Germany would wield the whole power of the Continent.

Source B From *Twenty-Five Years 1892–1916* by Edward Grey, 1926.

This definition of what Grey called 'the true issue' is instructive. Britain, he said, could not stand aside and permit the German domination of Europe. Yet this, it should be noted, was a consideration that applied prior to, and regardless of, the German invasion of Belgium. Effective though the image of an idealistic Britain crusading to defend gallant little Belgium was in convincing waverers that this was why Britain was going to war, the true motivation was altogether more

Q

How critical was the issue of Belgian neutrality?

THE ANGLO-JAPANESE ALLIANCE, 1902

Britain and Japan recognised each other's interests in China. Each agreed to remain neutral in the event of the other going to war with a third power, or to assist if the other went to war with two or more powers. The treaty was to operate for five years with the option of renewal.

THE ANGLO-FRENCH ENTENTE, 1904

Britain promised to give France a free hand in Morocco while the French recognised British rights in Egypt. There were many expressions of mutual good will, but no formal alliance or military agreement was concluded.

THE ANGLO-RUSSIAN ENTENTE, 1907

Russia promised to refrain from interference in Afghanistan and Tibet. Both countries promised to respect each other's 'spheres of influence' in Persia. No military matters were discussed. The agreement in effect extended the Anglo-French Entente into a triple entente.

THE AGADIR CRISIS, 1911

Germany, in a show of strength aimed at forcing France to grant territory in compensation for German recognition of French control of Morocco, sent a gunboat to the Moroccan port of Agadir. Britain publicly declared its support for France and put the Royal Navy on full alert. However, the crisis ended when France proved conciliatory and Germany backed off.

Source C From a speech by Edward Grey in the House of Commons, 5 August 1914.

self-interested. Britain was not prepared to tolerate one nation upsetting the balance of power in Europe, thereby endangering its own security. It is difficult to see the issue of Belgian neutrality as anything other than a pretext for war. All the probabilities were that Britain would have gone to war alongside France against Germany in 1914 irrespective of the Belgian issue. The day after Britain had declared war, Grey justified the decision not in terms of the high-mindedness that he later expressed but by appealing to the need to defend British interests:

> I have acted not from any obligation of Treaty or honour, for neither existed. There were three overwhelming British interests which I could not abandon:
> **1.** That the German fleet should not occupy, under our neutrality, the North Sea and the English Channel.
> **2.** That they should not seize and occupy the North-Western part of France opposite our shores.
> **3.** That they should not violate the ultimate independence of Belgium and hereafter occupy Antwerp as a standing menace to us.

Figure 8 The New Diplomacy, a *Punch* cartoon of 1911, satirising Grey's secretive conduct of foreign policy and the irritation it caused among his radical and socialist critics.

THE NEW DIPLOMACY.

ADVANCED DEMOCRAT (*to Foreign Secretary*). "LOOK HERE, WE'VE DECIDED THAT THIS ISN'T TO BE A PRIVATE ROOM ANY MORE; AND YOU'RE TO PUT YOUR CARDS ON THE TABLE AND THEN WE CAN ALL TAKE A HAND."
FOREIGN SECRETARY. "WHAT. AND LET MY OPPONENTS SEE THEM TOO?"

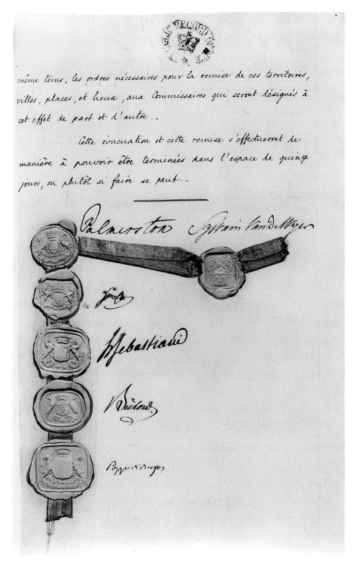

Figure 9 A British government poster showing the signatures on the treaty of 1839, which guaranteed Belgian neutrality. It was this treaty that the German Chancellor, Bethmann-Hollweg, referred to disparagingly to as 'the scrap of paper' when he learned that Britain was considering entering the war in accordance with its 1839 commitment.

A further factor was the pressure applied during the decade before 1914 by the chiefs of the armed services for increased resources. Under the Liberals, defence expenditure rose from £35 million to £91 million. The Admiralty was particularly insistent in demanding the building of more Dreadnoughts, the great battleships that represented British naval strength. The claim was that Germany's growing warship programme had to be countered by an equivalent expansion of the Royal Navy. There was a conviction among the service chiefs that Germany was bent on outstripping Britain militarily as a first step to waging an aggressive war. They believed there could be no other explanation for Germany's naval programme, which far exceeded any real defence needs it might have. Winston Churchill expressed the view of the military when he

Q How important was the arms race in pushing Britain towards war?

declared that, given their respective overseas commitments, Britain's navy was a necessity whereas Germany's was a luxury.

Table 4 A comparison of British and German military strength in 1914.

	Germany	Britain
Army		
divisions	50	8
reserve divisions	32	28
Navy		
cruisers	12	66
battleships	45	60
destroyers	144	300
submarines	28	78

Q

Were the British government and people eager for war in 1914?

In examining the factors that predisposed Britain to war in 1914, allowance has also to be made for the question of national prestige. Lloyd George, the Chancellor of the Exchequer, and one of the Liberals who had held strong anti-war sentiments at the time of the Boer War, was unambiguous in declaring that there were limits to the amount of German aggression Britain would tolerate. In 1911 he had warned the German government against taking a belligerent stance in foreign affairs and stated the case for possible British intervention:

> I believe it is essential in the highest interests, not merely of this country, but of the world, that Britain should at all hazards maintain her place and prestige amongst the Great Powers. If a situation were to be forced on us, in which peace could only be preserved by allowing Britain to be treated as if she were of no account in the Cabinet of nations, then I say emphatically that peace at that price would be a humiliation intolerable for a great country like ours to endure.

Source D From Lloyd George's speech at London's Mansion House, 1911.

However, Lloyd George's precise attitude at the time of the government's decision to declare war is not entirely clear. Official records of the Cabinet's discussions were not kept; we have to rely on the later comments of those involved. At one point, he appears to have been willing to resign from the Cabinet and oppose the war, should Germany draw back from violating Belgium. But there is reason to doubt his sincerity. Frances Stevenson, his mistress, wrote in her diary account of the time that Lloyd George's mind was already made up in favour of war and that the invasion of Belgium simply provided a 'heaven-sent excuse for supporting a declaration of war'. He himself later said that what helped persuade him to support the declaration was the urgent clamour for war that he witnessed among the ordinary people as he drove through the crowded streets of London. Whatever may have been the responsibility of Grey and Asquith's government for Britain's entering the war, it cannot be claimed that the British people were dragged into the struggle against their will.

There are a number of prominent British historians who argue that the Liberal government's decision to go to war was ultimately taken for domestic political reasons. Among the most provocative analysts are K.M. Wilson and Niall Ferguson, who suggest that Asquith's government declared war for fear that, if it did not, it would be pushed from office by the Conservatives, who from the beginning of the Serbian crisis had been wholly committed to war. Ferguson believes that, after the bitter political battles over such issues as the People's Budget, the House of Lords and Ulster (see pages 10, 14, 19), the Liberals were not prepared to allow the Conservatives to out-manoeuvre them by presenting themselves as the patriotic party that truly represented the mood of the nation. After surveying the various alternative explanations, Ferguson concludes:

How much did the domestic political situation in Britain influence the decision for war?

There was, however, another and arguably even more important reason why Britain went to war at 11p.m. on 4 August 1914. Throughout the days of 31 July–3 August one thing above all maintained Cabinet unity: the fear of letting in the Conservative and Unionist opposition … [On] 2 August Bonar Law [the Conservative leader] wrote to Asquith making clear that 'any hesitation in now supporting France and Russia would be fatal to the honour and future security of the United Kingdom'. The 'united support' offered by Bonar Law 'in all measures required by England's intervention in the war' was nothing less than a veiled threat that Conservatives would be willing to step into Liberal shoes if the government could not agree on such measures. After years of bellicose criticism from the Tory press, this was the one thing calculated to harden Asquith's resolve.

Source E From *The Pity of War* by Niall Ferguson, 1999.

ACTIVITY

Having read the section above, consider the following list of reasons for Britain's going to war in 1914. Use your own judgement to put these in order of importance. Ask yourself whether there was one dominating factor or whether Britain's decision was based on a combination of some or all of them.

▼ Edward Grey's secret diplomacy from 1905 onwards.
▼ British reluctance to contemplate a German-dominated Europe.
▼ Mutual rivalry as expressed in the Anglo-German arms race.
▼ Britain's fear that it was losing its naval supremacy.
▼ Britain's membership of the Triple Entente.
▼ The popular desire in Britain for war.
▼ Britain's treaty obligations to Belgium.
▼ Britain's sense of prestige and honour.
▼ Britain's need to protect its economic interests.
▼ The Liberal government's fears of a Conservative challenge.

2 Outline of the Military Struggle, 1914–18

It is possible to gain an understanding of the Great War in which Britain engaged by outlining the major campaigns and battles that took place. Always refer to the maps in this book or in a historical atlas so that you can locate the key places mentioned.

The Marne, September 1914

This was the first major battle of the war in the west. In an attempt to achieve the rapid defeat of France, German armies pushed through Belgium and northern France with the aim of capturing Paris in a broad sweep from the west. They were halted at the River Marne by the French army under Joffre and the British Expeditionary Force (BEF) under Sir John French. The German failure to break through led the two sides to dig in facing each other, establishing the system of trench warfare which characterised the Western Front for the next four years.

Source F Siegfried Sassoon, a soldier-poet, quoting from an army lecture on bayonet use, 25 April 1915.

'If you don't kill him, he'll kill you. Stick him between the eyes, in the throat, in the chest, or round the thighs. If he's on the run, there's only one place; get your bayonet into his kidneys; it'll go in as easy as butter.'

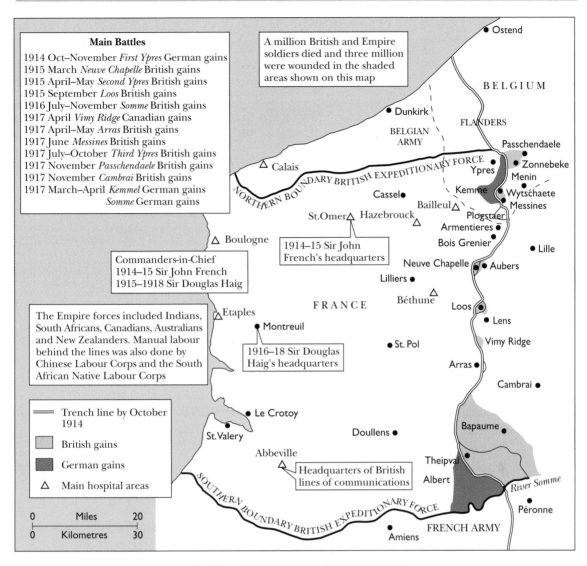

Main Battles

1914 Oct–November *First Ypres* German gains
1915 March *Neuve Chapelle* British gains
1915 April–May *Second Ypres* British gains
1915 September *Loos* British gains
1916 July–November *Somme* British gains
1917 April *Vimy Ridge* Canadian gains
1917 April–May *Arras* British gains
1917 June *Messines* British gains
1917 July–October *Third Ypres* British gains
1917 November *Passchendaele* British gains
1917 November *Cambrai* British gains
1917 March–April *Kemmel* German gains
Somme German gains

A million British and Empire soldiers died and three million were wounded in the shaded areas shown on this map

1914–15 Sir John French's headquarters

Commanders-in-Chief
1914–15 Sir John French
1915–1918 Sir Douglas Haig

The Empire forces included Indians, South Africans, Canadians, Australians and New Zealanders. Manual labour behind the lines was also done by Chinese Labour Corps and the South African Native Labour Corps

1916–18 Sir Douglas Haig's headquarters

Headquarters of British lines of communications

═══ Trench line by October 1914

▨ British gains

▨ German gains

△ Main hospital areas

0   Miles   20
0   Kilometres   30

Figure 10 Map of Europe showing the key features of the Western Front.

Gallipoli, April 1915–January 1916

In an attempt to break the stalemate on the Western Front, a major diversionary campaign was launched by the Allies against Germany's ally, Turkey. The aim was to capture Constantinople, so relieving pressure on Russia and increasing it on Germany. The campaign was a failure. After establishing a precarious hold on the Gallipoli peninsula at the entrance to the Dardanelles and holding it for ten months the Allies were finally forced to withdraw by the Turks. Of the 250,000 Allied casualties a significant minority were from the Australian and New Zealand contingents (ANZAC), which had distinguished themselves in the fighting.

Figure 11 A photo showing British troops preparing for a gas attack, Flanders 1915. Their gas masks are very rudimentary, made up of motoring goggles and pads of cotton wool soaked in chemicals and tied round the face with string. These gave little real protection.

Verdun, February–December 1916

Hoping to 'bleed France to death', the German high command began a major offensive against the French fortress of Verdun. The area was of little strategic importance but the Germans calculated, correctly as it proved, that the French would be prepared to fight to the death to preserve the historic site. It was the only major conflict on the Western Front where defence proved more costly than attack, the French losses of over 200,000 men slightly outnumbering those suffered by the Germans. It is estimated that some 20 million shells were fired in the course of the struggle at Verdun.

The Somme, July–November 1916

This proved to be the bloodiest engagement in British military history. With the intention of relieving the pressure on the French at Verdun, the British undertook a full-scale offensive against the Germans in the region of the River Somme. A massive preliminary bombardment failed to do serious damage to the German defences. When the British went 'over the top' on 1 July they walked into devastating machine-gun fire that cut them to pieces. On that first day of the battle the British suffered over 60,000 casualties. (To gain an idea of what that number means, consider that a full Old Trafford stadium, the home of Manchester United, today holds 61,000). By the time the battle was abandoned five months later, with a British gain of scarcely eight miles, the total casualties on all sides amounted to nearly a million. The Somme and Verdun became powerful symbols of the horror and sacrifice of the Western Front.

Jutland, 31 May–1 June 1916

This proved to be the only major engagement between the British and German navies in the 1914–18 war. As a battle it was indecisive since the opposing commanders were cautious and chose to break off the action rather than risk serious damage to their fleets. Nevertheless, Jutland had very important consequences. The German fleet went back to base and rarely ventured out after that. This effectively left Britain in control of the high seas, which enabled the Allied blockade of Germany to be cripplingly tightened. The Germans tried to compensate for their surface disadvantage by developing their submarine fleet. U-boat attacks on Allied merchant ships were so deadly that in the spring of 1917 Britain had nearly reached starvation point. However, Germany's declaration of unrestricted submarine warfare was a major factor in the United States' decision to enter the war on the side of the Allies in April 1917. Churchill showed his understanding of the significance of Jutland by suggesting that Admiral Jellicoe, the British commander, was 'the only man on either side who could have lost the war in a day'.

Passchendaele (also known as the Third Battle of Ypres), July–November 1917

This battle was in many respects a repeat of the Somme tragedy exactly a year earlier. Anxious to restore Allied morale which had been damaged by of a series of mutinies, the most serious being among the French troops, Douglas Haig, the Commander-in-Chief after 1915, ordered another massive British push to be launched at Ypres, the scene of bitter fighting since 1914. His aim was to break the German line at its northern end and recover the occupied Belgian ports. Haig had been encouraged by a recent British engagement at Arras (9–24 April) which, although it had achieved only limited gains (including the heroic capture of Vimy Ridge by Canadian troops), seemed to suggest that bombardment and infantry attack could be successfully combined. However, at Passchendaele continuous heavy rain reduced the ground to mud and slime and made effective infantry advances impossible. As at the Somme, German artillery and machine guns took a terrible toll of the British troops. When the battle finally petered out with no real gains made, Haig's army had suffered over 300,000 casualties.

A keen-edged sword,
a soldier's heart
Is greater than a
poet's art,
And greater hope than
a poet's fame
A little grave that has
no name.

Source G From a poem by Lance Corporal Francis Ledwidge, killed at Ypres, 31 July 1917.

Some of the German dead were young boys, too young to be killed for old men's crimes, and others might have been old or young. One could not tell because they had no faces, and were just masses of raw flesh in rags and uniforms. Legs and arms lay separate without any bodies thereabouts.

Source H From a report by Philip Gibbs, a British war correspondent, 4 July 1916.

Why did the war last so long?

Calm fell. From heaven distilled a clemency;
There was peace on earth, and silence in the sky;
Some could, some could not, shake off the misery;
The Sinister Spirit sneered: 'It had to be!'
And again the Spirit of Pity whispered, 'Why?'

Source I From the poem 'And there was a great calm', written by Thomas Hardy to mark the Armistice in November 1918.

Caporetto, 24 October–4 November 1917

Despite having been one of the members of the Triple Alliance, Italy chose in 1915 to enter the war on the Allied side. For two years it engaged in fighting on its north-eastern borders against Austria-Hungary. By October 1917 the Italian armies had lost nearly 600,000 men in battle. At Caporetto, Austrian forces supplemented by German contingents inflicted a crushing defeat on the Italians. British and French forces had to be rapidly sent to the Italian front to prevent the defeat becoming a total rout.

There was an expression frequently heard during the early days of the war that it would 'all be over by Christmas'. That expectation was to be cruelly shattered. The truth is Britain was not prepared for war in 1914. That is to say, it was not prepared for the war which actually took place. Nobody foresaw in 1914 what was to come – that the struggle would last for over four years and would be on such a scale and of such an intensity that it would change for ever people's understanding of the nature of war.

It was one of the tragic coincidences of history that the growth of technology gave both sides massive destructive power but did not allow either of them to establish overwhelming superiority over the other. In all major respects, the war was a very simple affair. Each side amassed huge numbers of troops and vast amounts of artillery. In the belief that sheer fire-power and weight of numbers would crush the enemy, large-scale infantry attacks were launched, preceded by a ferocious artillery bombardment, which was intended to wreck defences and break morale.

Yet, invariably what happened was that the bombardment, far from smashing the enemy defences, simply made the ground impassable. As the invading infantry, whose only armour was a tin helmet, tried to pick its way across the cratered surface of no man's land, the machine gunners would emerge from their deep trenches and with interlocking arcs of fire mow down the oncoming ranks. The lucky ones, those who were unscathed or only slightly injured, managed to crawl back to their lines. Too many, however, were either killed directly in the hail of machine-gun bullets or died from wounds and exposure in the shell holes into which they had scrambled for refuge. There were countless horrifying incidents of men, too weak to drag themselves out, drowning as water and liquid mud filled the shell holes. Attempts at rescue were seldom made. Early in the war it was soon realised that such efforts simply produced more deaths among the would-be saviours.

There were remarkable scientific advances during the war: the armoured tank and the bomber plane were among the spectacular

The German Offensive, 21 March–17 July 1918

By the beginning of 1918 the German high command knew that time was against them. Unless Germany soon won an overwhelming victory it would eventually be defeated. Despite Caporetto, the Austro-Hungarians needed constant German reinforcements to maintain themselves as a fighting force. Turkey, Germany's other main ally, was now more of a liability than a source of strength. No fewer than 27 states were now lined up against Germany and its allies. It was true that the collapse of the Russians following the October Revolution in 1917 had released 400,000 German troops for the Western Front, but this was more than offset by the USA's involvement in the war. From November 1917 a stream of fresh, well-equipped, American troops began to arrive in France. The Germans knew that unless they acted quickly the American forces would tip the balance irreversibly against them. Ludendorff, the German Chief-of-Staff, aimed to break the deadlock by reintroducing a war of movement. His basic plan was to attack the enemy line at the point where the French and British sectors merged, split the Allies and then seize the Channel ports.

The scheme came remarkably close to success. The initial thrust on a 40-mile front caused a large bulge in the British line as the Germans rapidly pushed forward. Ironically, it was the speed that proved the Germans' undoing. Such was their pace of movement that a gap opened between their forward troops and their supply lines. This gave the British time to recover. Under the overall command of France's Field Marshal Foch, the Allies then launched a series of counter attacks, which climaxed with the victory of the British army under Haig at Amiens. Ludendorff called this defeat on 8 August 'the black day of the German army'. It was the beginning of the end. Germany had little more to offer; the offensives had cost the lives of 300,000 German troops. The loss of morale was hastened by the collapse of the Turkish and Austrian armies on their respective fronts. Yet in the end it was the desperate domestic situation within Germany, where the population was starving and revolution had broken out, that led the German government to sign the Armistice in November 1918.

military developments. Yet none of these was enough to change the character of the war. The war on the Western Front was a war of attrition, a slogging match. The French and the British, and after 1917 the Americans, on one side and the Germans on the other, were

Why did the war cost so many lives?

'Good morning; good
morning!' the General said
When we met him last
week on our way to
the line.
Now the soldiers he
smiled at are most of
'em dead,
And we're cursing his staff
for incompetent swine.
'He's a cheery old card,'
grunted Harry to Jack
As they slogged up to
Arras with rifle and pack
But he did for them both
with his plan of attack.

Source J From a poem by
Siegfried Sassoon.

Were there any real
alternatives to British
strategy?

Why did the Allies
eventually prove
successful?

reduced to a form of warfare in which each tried to wear the other down. This is why the casualty figures were so high.

Ever since these terrible events occurred the question has been asked: Did it have to happen that way? Was there really no alternative? The short answer is no. The military technology of the time meant that the sides cancelled each other out. This remains a controversial issue. Many critics, then and since, have laid the greater part of the blame for the tragic human losses on the incompetence of the war staffs who planned the military strategies. The lack of imagination of the high command condemned millions to their deaths. 'Lions led by donkeys' is how one contemporary description put it, referring to the heroic volunteers and conscript troops who were sent to their deaths by generals who clung to the belief that the next great push would achieve the vital breakthrough long after the appalling casualty figures had made the futility of such warfare all too evident. Haig, the British Commander-in-Chief, has been the particular object for attack.

But he also has his defenders. He and his generals had to fight with the resources and with the knowledge at their disposal. There is also an argument for saying that the dogged methods did work in the end. It is also the case that the nearest there came to a military breakthrough occurred in the spring of 1918 when the German armies, applying the same basic strategy as had been used by the Allies at the Somme and at Passchendaele, launched a massive counter attack that broke the British and French line at many points and might well have won the war had they been able to maintain their supply lines.

It is always easier to fight wars in retrospect. The only way the slaughter could have been avoided was by not fighting at all, an option that was never open to the generals. Ending the war, like declaring it, was a political not a military decision. The first duty of the generals was to win the war with the means and the knowledge at their disposal. It was Lord Kitchener, the Secretary of State for War from 1914 until his death at sea in 1916, who remarked, 'We cannot make war as we ought, we can only make it as we can'.

In the end the Allies won because their greater economic resources enabled them to hold on longer. A leading modern military historian, John Terraine, has aptly described 1914–18 as 'the greatest war of the first industrial revolution'. It marked the point in historical development when the warring countries were enabled by their industrial strength to engage in total conflict. Speaking of the massive armies that every country put into the field, Terraine writes:

They all had to be clothed in the distinctive fashion of their calling, equipped with all its accoutrements, accommodated, moved over land and sea, medicated, fed – and buried. The Industrial Revolution took care of all these matters in a manner never before possible. The picture is awesome – the production figures of the war; the astronomical mileage of telephone wire and barbed wire; the quantities of sandbags; of pit-props; the diversity and numbers of trench warfare supplies; acreage of cloth for uniforms; horseshoes; tonnages of lint for bandages; the unimaginable totals of weapons; rifles, machine guns, small arms ammunition, artillery of all calibres, shells … shells … shells.

Source K From *The First World War* by John Terraine, 1983.

What these vast resources did was to sustain mass armies, made possible by the phenomenal growth of population in the century preceding 1914.

ACTIVITY

The rights and wrongs of the British strategy are a topic of endless debate. You can make your contribution to it by examining both sides of the argument. List the pros and cons of the strategy adopted. Can you suggest a realistic alternative?

SIZE OF THE BRITISH ARMY (to nearest hundred thousand)

1914 August – 734,000
1914 December – 1,186,400
1918 November – 5,900,000 (amounting to nearly 15 per cent of the UK population)

3 Wartime Politics in Britain, 1914–18

ISSUE:
Did the War fundamentally alter British party politics?

a) Asquith as War Leader, 1914–16

At the outbreak of war, the parties agreed to a political truce so as to leave Asquith's government free to conduct the war effort. However, by May 1915 serious criticism had begun to be made of Asquith's performance as wartime leader. A critical shell shortage and the failure of the Gallipoli campaign (see page 35) led to a Conservative demand for a government shake-up. Asquith gave way and accepted that the seriousness of the war situation required the setting up of a coalition government. Bonar Law and a number of other leading Conservatives entered the government.

As the war developed it was Lloyd George, not Asquith, who became the dominant figure in the government. Between 1914 and 1916 he held in turn the positions of Chancellor of the Exchequer, Minister of Munitions and War Secretary. To each post he brought intense energy and drive. This led him into conflict with the military commanders, whom he accused of incompetence. Lloyd

Q

Why did Lloyd George replace Asquith as Prime Minister in 1916?

KEY POLITICAL DEVELOPMENTS, 1914–18

1914 August: Outbreak of war; Political truce agreed.

1915 May: Formation of Coalition government under Asquith; leading Conservatives (Bonar Law, Balfour, Curzon) entered the Cabinet.

1916 December: Conservatives withdrew support from Asquith – Lloyd George became PM and formed new Coalition, containing Conservatives and Labour ministers; Liberal MPs split between the followers of Lloyd George, who received the government whip, and the Asquithians, who claimed to be the official Liberal Party.

1918 February: Representation of the People Act created universal male and partial female suffrage.
May: Lloyd George survived the Maurice Debate.
December: Lloyd George and the Coalition Liberals won the Coupon Election in alliance with the Coalition Conservatives.

ISSUE:
How far was Lloyd George responsible for Britain's winning the war?

George's exasperation with the way the war was being run expanded into the belief that what was needed was a much more dynamic political leadership. He proposed, therefore, the setting up of a three-man war council with himself as its chairman. The Conservatives let Lloyd George know that they were prepared to back him against Asquith.

A series of complicated manoeuvres followed in the autumn of 1916. The key question was whether Asquith would be willing to allow the proposed war council to function without him. In the end, judging that this would be too great an infringement of his authority as Prime Minister, he insisted that he must be the head of the council. Lloyd George offered his resignation, whereupon the Conservatives informed Asquith that they were not willing to serve in a Coalition government if Lloyd George was not a member. Asquith resigned leaving the way open for Lloyd George to become Prime Minister.

The leadership crisis in December 1916 revealed that once the Conservatives had turned against Asquith he had no other allies. The willingness of the Labour Party to support him earlier had reflected a commitment to the war effort generally rather than to him personally, while the Irish Nationalist MPs had largely lost interest in English domestic politics following the Easter Rising (see page 57). More significantly for the future of the Liberal Party, some 130 Liberal MPs declared their readiness to follow Lloyd George. This marked a split in the Liberal Party that was never fully healed.

ACTIVITY

Having read the section above, describe how the war effort had the effect of blurring the lines between the political parties, and explain why this worked to Asquith's disadvantage.

b) Lloyd George as War Leader, 1916–18

After 1918, Lloyd George was frequently referred to as 'the man who won the war'. No one person, of course, can win a modern war, but as a reference to the inspiration he brought to bear as war leader it is a fitting tribute. At the time he took over as Prime Minister in 1916 British morale was entering its lowest trough of the war. By early 1917, the success of the German U-boats in preventing vital supplies reaching Britain threatened to bring the country to its knees (see page 37). There was talk of a compromise peace and defeatism was in the air. Lloyd George's refusal even at this darkest hour to contemplate other than total victory inspired his colleagues, reassured the waverers, and put heart into the nation. It was characteristic of him that, having argued previously that the duties of the premiership were too heavy to allow the Prime Minister to run the war effort, Lloyd George continued to combine those two functions when he became Prime Minister himself.

Not everyone was happy with this. Lloyd George seldom attended parliament between 1916 and 1918. By relying increasingly on outside experts, rather than elected politicians, he appeared to some observers to be abandoning the traditional methods of parliamentary government. Critics suggested that Lloyd George was turning the British premiership into an American-style presidency. Some even accused him of becoming a dictator. This was what underlay his continuing battle with the military.

Lloyd George's Battle with the Military

The generals objected to what they regarded as a civilian politician attempting to decide questions of strategy. For his part, Lloyd George rejected the idea that the generals should make their demands for huge numbers of men and vast amounts of material without being directly answerable to the government for the use they made of them. It was a question of who was ultimately responsible for running the war. This dispute has been portrayed as a struggle to decide whether Britain in wartime was to be governed by politicians or generals. There are writers who see Lloyd George as having saved Britain from becoming a military dictatorship, but only at the price of its becoming a political one. Lloyd George's response was to claim that in wartime 'a perfectly democratic State has the right to commandeer every resource, every power, life, limb, wealth, and everything else for the interest of the State'.

---

c) The Impact of the War on the Parties

ISSUE:
Why did the war strengthen Labour and the Conservatives but damage the Liberals?

	Labour	Conservatives	Liberals
1914–15	Maintained political truce	Maintained political truce	Asquith led war effort
1915–16	Joined Asquith's Coalition	Joined Asquith's Coalition	Asquith formed Coalition
1916		Joined Lloyd George in opposing Asquith	Lloyd George replaced Asquith
1916–18	Entered wartime Coalition	Entered wartime Coalition	Lloyd George led the War Coalition Asquith led the Opposition

Table 5 How the parties behaved, 1914–18.

The war had a number of adverse effects on the Liberal Party, which left it gravely weakened. Although Asquith was replaced as Prime Minister in 1916, he continued as leader of the Liberal Party. He refused, however, to serve in Lloyd George's Cabinet. Instead, he led the parliamentary Opposition. This meant that from 1916 onwards the Liberals were divided between the Asquithians, who claimed to be the official Liberal Party, and the followers of Lloyd George. The Conservatives naturally gained from this split in the Liberal leadership. They also benefited from the forming of Coalition governments from 1915 onwards since they took key posts in the inner Cabinet. Thus, without an election victory, the Conservatives found themselves in positions of authority for the first time since 1905.

How did the war disadvantage the Liberals?

The main problem for the Liberal Party was that, although the majority of its members came to accept that the war had to be fought to the utmost, it was hard to accommodate it easily within the Liberal programme as developed since 1906. Having struggled to establish social issues as a priority, the Liberals now found themselves diverted from their welfare programme by the demands of war. Furthermore, having overcome the reactionary opposition of the Unionists on a whole range of issues before 1914, the Liberals now had to share government with them. All this tended to take the heart out of Liberal Party workers in the constituencies. In contrast, the Conservatives' traditional claim to be the 'patriotic' party served them well in wartime and led to a considerable recovery of popularity in the constituencies. An equally important factor accounting for Liberal Party decline was the **1918 Representation of the People Act**, introduced in the last year of the war. This trebled the electorate and had momentous political consequences.

THE REPRESENTATION OF THE PEOPLE ACT, 1918

▼ Gave the vote to all males over 21 and to all females over 30
▼ Tripled the electorate from 7 million to 21 million.

Labour's share of the vote in the 1918 election rose proportionally with the increase in the electorate from 7 per cent to 22 per cent. It increased its number of MPs from 42 to 60. The trend towards the replacement of the Liberal Party by Labour as the second largest single party had been established.

In a notable study written in 1966, Trevor Wilson suggested that the war was the essential reason for the decline in Liberal fortunes. Other historians have queried this and have argued that the war accelerated the decline rather than causing it. More recently, Martin Pugh has suggested that the key factor is not so much that the war undermined the Liberals as that they failed to seize the opportunity that the war offered them to unite as a party of government, lead the nation to military victory, and so consolidate the successes they had achieved between 1906 and 1914.

> ### ACTIVITIES
>
> George Dangerfield and Trevor Wilson both had interesting theories to explain the decline of the Liberal Party. Read back over section 3c and then write down the points where you think Dangerfield and Wilson differ and where they agree in their interpretations. It would help if you were to look ahead to the list of differences between the Liberal and Labour parties given on page 63. How important do you think were the parts played by the leading figures, Lloyd George and Asquith, in all this?

d) The Coupon Election, 1918

ISSUES:
Why did the Liberals perform so badly in this election?

In May 1918, General Maurice, the former Director of Military Operations, publicly accused Lloyd George of distorting troop numbers in order to suggest that the British army in France was stronger than it actually was. Asquith, taking the side of the generals, proposed a parliamentary vote of no confidence in the Coalition government. However, the Commons divided 293 to 106 in favour of Lloyd George. The result left Asquith and his supporters looking like a group of malcontents who had irresponsibly aimed to embarrass the government at a critical time in the war on the Western Front.

Politically, the importance of the Maurice debate was that it destroyed the chance of Liberal reunification. Asquith's attack on the government showed how considerable the differences were between himself and Lloyd George. This deepened the divide between the two factions in the Liberal Party and gave shape to politics for the following four years. Those who opposed Lloyd George in the debate were those who would stand as official Liberal Party candidates

The 1918 Election Result			
	Seats Won	**Total Votes**	**% Vote**
Coalition Conservative	335	3,504,198	32.6
Coalition Liberal	133	1,445,640	13.5
Coalition Labour	10	161,521	1.5
(Coalition totals)	(478)	(5,111,359)	(47.6)
Labour	63	2,385,472	22.2
Liberals (Asquithians)	28	1,298,808	12.1
Conservatives	23	370,375	3.4
Irish Nationalists	7	238,477	2.2
Sinn Fein	73	486,867	4.5
Others	17	810,980	8.0

Table 6 The 1918 election (the Coupon Election).

The result of 1918 broke the party not only in the House of Commons but also in the country. Local [Liberal] Associations perished or maintained a nominal existence. Masses of our best men passed away to Labour. Others gravitated to Conservatism or independence. Funds were depleted and we were short of workers all over the country. There was an utter lack of enthusiasm or even zeal.

Source L From a private letter of Herbert Gladstone's, written in 1919.

ISSUE:
Did the 1914–18 war create a new economic situation or simply accelerate existing trends?

What effect did the 1914–18 war have on government expenditure?

against him in the 1918 General Election. Bonar Law, the Conservative leader, and Lloyd George agreed to continue their Coalition into peacetime. A letter bearing their joint signatures was sent to all those candidates who were willing to support the Coalition. This written endorsement became known as 'the coupon', a wry reference to the ration cards introduced during the war, and led to the election being referred to as 'the Coupon Election'.

Although it brought immediate electoral success, Lloyd George's decision to polarise the Liberal split by carrying the Coalition into peacetime destroyed any chance the Liberal Party had of ever genuinely recovering. Kenneth Morgan, a biographer of Lloyd George, describes the coupon election as 'the greatest of disasters for the Liberal Party'. This modern judgement reinforces the view expressed nearer the time by Herbert Gladstone, the former Liberal Chief Whip (see source L).

ACTIVITY

Having read section 3d, use Table 6 to explain how and why Lloyd George's Coalition did so well in the Coupon Election of 1918.

4 The Economic and Social Impact of the First World War

Lenin, the Russian revolutionary, once observed that 'war is the locomotive of history'. He meant that modern war produces dynamic changes in the nations that fight them. The Great War certainly had profound economic and social effects in Britain. Four years of warfare could not have been sustained without an enormous physical effort. The ever-increasing demand for guns, ammunition and equipment became so great that it put tremendous strain on the heavy manufacturing industries. For long periods it seemed that the strain would prove too much, but by the end of the war industry had met the demands placed on it. A critical feature of all this was the increasing role played by the government in economic matters. Before 1914 much of the argument over free trade and protection had been about whether government should involve itself in economic planning. The demands of war ended the debate. It became accepted that if the nation was to survive there had to be a centrally directed war effort. The degree of government involvement is clear from the following details.

By 1917 spending by the government amounted to 60 per cent of **gross national product** (GNP). (The remarkable change this represented can be understood by noting that in 1813 at the height of the

Napoleonic wars British government spending amounted to only 7 per cent of GNP.) The government raised the capital needed by borrowing from banks at home and in North America. About two-thirds came from such loans. The remaining third was raised from increased taxation. This resulted in income tax being quadrupled between 1914 and 1918. Overall, government borrowing increased **the National Debt** from £650 million to £8,000 million.

The Defence of the Realm Act (DORA)

This act of August 1914 granted the State extensive powers. Among these were: government control of arms factories, censorship of the press, and restriction of freedom of information. Additional wartime measures included:

▽ Heavy duties on imports.
▽ Government control of the rail and coal industries.
▽ Ministry of Munitions set up to direct wartime industrial production.
▽ Trade unions were offered greater recognition and higher wages in return for their agreement to aid the war effort by not striking.
▽ Companies were required to accept restrictions on their profits and guarantee minimum wages to workers.
▽ To lessen social unrest, measures were introduced to improve living standards and control rents.
▽ Conscription was introduced, obliging males between 18 and 42 to serve in the armed forces.
▽ Food rationing was imposed.
▽ Restrictions were placed on the opening hours of public houses.
▽ Passports were required for travel abroad and limitations were placed on freedom of movement within Britain.

The war years were a growth period for British industry. Production expanded to meet the huge demand for goods and materials. But in many ways it was an unnatural growth that proved impossible to sustain in peacetime. Following a brief post-war boom between 1919 and 1921 a serious decline set in. Britain's **staple industries** returned to their long-term decline. It became evident that their output had been artificially stimulated by the demands of war. The truth was that British heavy industry had for many decades been seriously weakened by foreign competition, notably after the 1870s, from Germany and the USA. It had also been handicapped by its own inability to adapt to new trends. It had failed to re-invest or attract new investment. This meant that it lacked the capital to buy new machinery or develop modern production techniques. What the First World War did, therefore, was to hasten a decline that had already begun. Equally significant was the

GROSS NATIONAL PRODUCT (GNP)
This refers to the annual total value of goods produced and services provided by Britain at home and in trade with other countries. GNP should not be confused with Gross Domestic Product (GDP) which is a similar measurement but excludes foreign trade.

THE NATIONAL DEBT
This is the total amount owed by the government to its domestic and international creditors. At the end of the 1914–18 war Britain owed so much that a quarter of the revenue raised by the government had to be spent on paying the interest charges (£325 million) on the National Debt.

Q In what ways did the government extend its powers during the 1914–1918 war?

Q What changes did British industry experience during the war?

ACTIVITY

Basing your study of the statistics and information in section 4, draw up a list of the harmful effects of the war on the British economy.

ISSUES:

Was the war won on the home front? What social impact did the war have?

Source M From War and Our World: The Reith Lectures 1998 by John Keegan, 1999.

move away from free trade. The pressure of war led the government to impose restrictions and import duties on foreign imports.

One striking example of the war's impact was the behaviour of countries which before 1914 had been customers of Britain. Wartime blockades had obliged many of them to produce for themselves since they could no longer import supplies. A number developed their own manufacturing industries and simply stopped buying from Britain. Having been forced to become self-sufficient, these countries after 1918 protected their gains by tariffs and trade embargoes. Britain's dated basic industries were not able to adjust sufficiently to meet this change in the economic world order. Old-fashioned production methods left British manufacturers with high overheads. This made them reluctant to drop their prices since this would cut their profits. The consequence was a lack of competitiveness and a fall in demand for British-made goods. The rest of the world no longer wanted the products of Britain's traditional manufacturing industries at the prices British manufacturers were now forced to set.

a) The Home Front, 1914–18

So vital was the contribution of the civilian population to the war effort that it is arguable that the conflict was decided as much on the domestic front as on the military one. The efforts of the armies on the Western Front would have counted for little had they not been backed by a civilian population capable of sustaining the industrial output that the war demanded. This is part of the concept of total war. Everybody was a participant. There was another sense in which the civil population was directly involved in the struggle. The huge number of volunteers and conscripts who entered the armed forces meant there were hardly any families in Britain that were not personally affected by the war. Deaths and casualties at the Front brought bereavement and grief into all but a few British homes. As John Keegan movingly puts it:

The telegraph boy on his bicycle, pedalling the suburban street and symbol to the Victorians of a new and benevolent technological advance, became for parents and wives during both world wars literally an omen of terror – for it was by telegram that the awful flimsy form beginning 'We regret to inform you that' was brought to front doors, a trigger for the articulation of the constant unspoken prayer, 'Let him pass by, let him stop at another house, let it not be for us.'

In Britain during the First World War that prayer was not answered several million times; on seven hundred thousand occasions the telegraph boy brought the ultimate bad news of the death of a son, husband or brother.

When the results of the war are examined it is natural that death and casualty lists overshadow all other considerations. Yet there were aspects which historians now see as positive. When the war first broke out in 1914 there was fear that the disruption it would bring would cause severe distress to the mass of the working population. In the event, however, the war brought a number of advantages to the working class. This was largely because the war created a huge demand for extra industrial workers. The trade unions gained greatly from this since it increased their bargaining power; so essential were industrial workers to the war effort that their co-operation was vital. This was recognised in **the Treasury Agreement** of 1915. The war also had an important affect on the income and **status of women.**

Between 1914 and 1918 trade union membership rose from four million to six million. The stronger position of the unions resulted in higher wages and improved working conditions for workers. But this did not mean peace on the industrial front. Having declined during the first two years of the war, strike action increased during the last two. This was evidence of a powerful feeling among the workers that on both the home and war fronts the burden of winning the war was falling disproportionately on them. They were the class that was having to make the greatest sacrifice, and they doubted that the government, despite the many public tributes it paid them, fully understood this. This feeling was intensified when the returning troops observed how well many of those who had stayed behind in Britain had done out of the war.

How did the war affect the workers in Britain?

THE TREASURY AGREEMENT, 1915

This was negotiated by the Trades Union Congress (TUC) with Lloyd George, the Chancellor of the Exchequer. In return for accepting non-strike agreements and 'dilution' – the employment of unskilled men and women in jobs previously restricted to skilled workers – the unions were guaranteed improved wages and conditions. The real significance of the Treasury Agreement lay not in its details but in its recognition of the trade unions as essential partners in the war effort. They could no longer be regarded as outsiders. Lloyd George called the Treasury Agreement 'the great charter for labour'.

	Working Days Lost	No. of Strikes	No. of Strikers
1913	9,804,000	1,459	664,000
1914	9,878,000	972	447,000
1915	2,953,000	672	448,000
1916	2,446,000	532	276,000
1917	5,647,000	730	872,000
1918	5,875,000	1,165	1,116,000
1919	34,969,000	1,352	2,591,000

Table 7 Industrial strikes 1913–19.

Unhappily one of the most enduring legacies of the war was bitterness. Lloyd George remarked in 1919, 'Suspicion, resentment, misunderstanding and fear have poisoned the mind of mankind'. The destruction of a whole generation marked the end of innocence. Optimism died. Belief in the march of progress was now hard to sustain. John Maynard Keynes (see page 123) lamented: 'We have been moved beyond endurance. Never in the lifetime of men has the universal element in the soul burnt so dimly.' It is arguable that

How did the war influence cultural attitudes?

THE STATUS OF WOMEN

The response of women to the call to enter the factories to take the place of workers who had gone to the Front made them an indispensable part of British industry. Without them, the output of the munitions factories could not have been maintained. However, what makes historians cautious about seeing this as a permanent social advance is that once the war was over the great majority of them were replaced by male workers. In the inter-war years the number of women in the industrial workforce was not appreciably higher than it had been before the war. It was also the case that although women received the vote in 1918 (see page 44) it was restricted to those over the age of 30, hardly a reward to the younger female workers.

the fractured form of so much art, music and literature in the post-war period was evidence of the paranoia and alienation induced by the experience of war.

ACTIVITY

▼ How true is it to say that the war period was a time of advance for British workers?

▼ How does Source M support Lloyd George's assertion that the enduring legacy of the war was 'suspicion and fear'?

▼ Working on Britain at War, 1914–18

Your aim should be to gain as clear an idea as possible of the character of the war and its effects in Britain. Do not try to remember all the details of the military engagements, but do familiarise yourself with the broad strategies so that you are able to explain victory and defeat. An appreciation of the scale of the military struggle is essential to an order to understand its political, social and economic impact in Britain. A basic question that will help draw your ideas together and test just how well you have grasped the material is: Which played the more important part in securing Britain's victory in the war – the military front or the home front? You do not necessarily have to come down on one side or the other. However, in addressing the question you will cover all the important issues.

Answering Extended Writing and Essay Questions on Britain at War

Types of question	Examples of typical questions
Structured (those that ask you to *describe* situations or developments)	1 Trace the main steps that led to Britain's declaration of war on Germany in August 1914.
	2 Describe the changes in the status and conditions of the workers that occurred in Britain during the 1914–18 war.
	3 Describe the difficulties Lloyd George had with Britain's military leaders between 1916 and 1918.
	4 Describe how the power of the State grew during the war years, 1914–18.

Essay questions often present you with one of two kinds of challenge. Some ask for an analysis of the causes, or perhaps the causes and results, of an historical event or episode. Other questions require you to justify a historical judgement about a key event or individual.

Types of question	Examples of typical questions
Causes (those that ask you to explain *why* things happened the way they did)	5 Account for Britain's decision to go to war with Germany in 1914. 6 Explain why Lloyd George replaced Asquith as Prime Minister in December 1916. 7 Explain why the Liberal Party declined in the period 1914–18. 8 Account for Britain's ability to survive four years of warfare between 1914 and 1918.
Historical judgement (those that ask you to use your knowledge to make an assessment or judgement of historical events)	9 How far do you agree that British generals in the 1914–18 war had no alternative to the strategy they followed? 10 How important was sea power to Britain's survival during the First World War? 11 Examine the validity of the claim that Lloyd George was 'the man who won the war'. 12 'Britain's victory in 1918 owed more to German weakness than to British strength.' How far would you agree with this view?

Answering Source-Based Questions on Britain at War

Examiners specify that you should have the following skills when dealing with sources:

Types of question	
comprehension	a basic understanding of what the source says
cross-referencing	the ability to put a source in its historical setting
evaluation	the ability to judge the importance and reliability of a source
analysis	the ability to explain the significance of a source in relation to its wider historical background

Do not be frightened off by these terms. Try to understand them in relation to particular sources. Let us take a particular example. Re-read Source E on page 33 and then examine the following questions. You may feel the need to refresh your memory by reading section 1 again.

▼ QUESTIONS ON SOURCES

1. According to the writer of the source, what was the real reason that Britain went to war in 1914? **(4 marks)** (*Comprehension*)

2. Describe the circumstances that had placed the Cabinet in the position of having to make a decision on whether it should declare war. **(6 marks)** (*Cross-referencing*)

3. How reliable is this source as an explanation of the reason for the Cabinet's decision to declare war? **(8 marks)** (*Evaluation*)

4. What other factors would you need to consider if you were assessing the reasons for Britain's going to war with Germany in 1914? **(10 marks)** (*Analysis*)

Points to note about the questions

Question 1 You need to put into your own words what Ferguson says in Source E.

Question 2 Here you need to call on your own knowledge of the European crisis that that developed between late June 1914 and early August 1914.

Question 3 E is a secondary source. Does this make it reliable as a considered mature reflection of an important modern historian?

Question 4 Look at as many of the long- and short-term explanations for Britain's going to war as you can recall. Does Ferguson's argument fit in with or contradict all, some, or any of these?

Further Reading

Books in the Access to History *series*

The following both have substantial and informative sections on the origins of the war in Europe. *Rivalry and Accord: International Relations 1870–1914* by John Lowe, and *Britain and the European Powers 1865–1914* by Robert Pearce. An illuminating study of the war in all its aspects is *The First World War* by Vyvyen Brendon. The earlier chapters of *War and Peace: International Relations 1914–45* by David Williamson are relevant and helpful.

General

There are valuable and up-to-date assessments of foreign policy under Balfour and Asquith in *Modern British Statesmen 1867–1945* edited by Richard Kelly and John Cantrell (Manchester UP, 1997). There are helpful sections on the approach to the 1914–18 war in *The Edwardian Age* by Vyvyen Brendon (Hodder & Stoughton, 1996). Another informative study is *The Origins of the First World War* by G. Martel (Longman, 1988). *War & Society in Britain 1899–c.1948* by Rex Pope (Longman) is a short informed introduction that students would find helpful. An outstanding work to which over 50 leading social, political, military and medical historians contributed is *Facing Armageddon: The First World War Experienced* edited by Hugh Cecil and Peter Liddle (Leo Cooper, 1996). Of the many other readable books on the 1914–18 conflict the following are especially recommended: *First World War* by Martin Gilbert (HarperCollins, 1994), *The First World War* (Hutchinson, 1998) and *War and Our World: The Reith Lectures 1998* (BBC 1999), the last two both by John Keegan. *The Pity of War* by Niall Ferguson (Penguin, 1999) is long and detailed but more than repays any effort involved in reading it.

BRITAIN BETWEEN THE WARS, 1918–39

CHAPTER 3

POINTS TO CONSIDER

When the war ended in 1918 there were great hopes that Britain would reap the rewards of victory. But the post-war years proved troubled times. British industry continued to decline and the governments of the period seemed unable to find an answer to the growing economic problems. Matters became particularly difficult with the onset in the late 1920s of the Depression, a worldwide industrial down-turn. The 1930s became notorious as a decade of industrial stagnation and unemployment. Hunger marches and dole queues seemed to epitomise the period. Yet it was not an entirely dismal picture. In the parts of the country which the depression had not touched there were often hopeful signs of growth. Economic matters, therefore, take up a large part of the chapter. What we will be examining is the way the various governments of the inter-war years responded to the economic and financial crises that faced them. Space is also found for a survey of the main ways in which living standards developed during the period.

1 The Post-War Coalition

ISSUES:
Was Lloyd George 'the prisoner' of the Conservatives between 1918 and 1922?
Does the Coalition deserve its bad reputation?

Reconstruction, which had begun during the war, was continued under Lloyd George into the post-war period. A massive demobilisation programme was set in motion under Winston Churchill's direction. Ambitious proposals were drawn up for improved health facilities, unemployment pay and pensions. However, the grim economic circumstances in post-war Britain, caused by high inflation and declining orders for British goods, largely thwarted these schemes, although there was notable success in regard to housing. Over 200,000 council dwellings were built between 1919 and 1922. Throughout the Coalition years Lloyd George continued with his aim of creating greater co-operation in industrial relations. He maintained links with both employers and trade unions and encouraged them to think in terms of conciliation rather than confrontation.

It was Britain's inability to cope with the effects of the worldwide industrial slump that undermined Lloyd George's promise that the post-war nation would be 'a fit country for heroes to live in'. By 1922, unemployment had risen to over one million. Yet the government judged the economic situation to be so bad that it chose to restrict rather than expand social welfare provision. In a series of cuts,

GOVERNMENTS BETWEEN THE WARS

1918 –22	Liberal–Conservative Coalition under Lloyd George;
1922 –23	Conservatives under Andrew Bonar Law;
1923 –24	Conservatives under Stanley Baldwin;
1924	Labour under James Ramsay MacDonald;
1924 –29	Conservatives under Baldwin;
1929 –31	Labour under Ramsay MacDonald;
1931	National government (Lib-Con-Lab Coalition) under Ramsay MacDonald;
1935	National government under Baldwin;
1937 –40	National government under Neville Chamberlain.

GENERAL ELECTIONS BETWEEN THE WARS

1918	November – Coalition gained large overall majority;
1922	November – Conservatives gained majority;
1923	December – Conservatives lost overall majority;
1924	October – Conservatives regained overall majority;
1929	May – Labour became largest single party in Commons;
1931	October – National government gained majority;
1935	November – National government maintained its majority.

Why did the Coalition fall in 1922?

Chief Domestic Measures of the 1918–22 Coalition Government

▽ A major programme for the demobilisation of over one million servicemen.

▽ 1919 Addison's Housing Act for the first time provided local authorities with central government funds to provide council housing – 200,000 homes built by 1922.

▽ The 1920 Unemployment Insurance Act extended the 1911 Act to a wider range of industrial workers.

---

known as the 'Geddes Axe', after Sir Eric Geddes, Chairman of the special government-appointed committee which recommended them, revenue previously allocated to education, hospitals and housing was withdrawn. All governments tend to be judged primarily in relation to their economic record. The failure of the social and economic policies of the Coalition tended to dwarf its other activities.

After four years, the commonly held view of the Coalition was of a tired administration, led by an individual who was past his best and who was sustained in office only by a combination of his own love of power and a Conservative Party that lacked the courage to attempt to take on the full responsibility of government. Commentators spoke increasingly of the low tone of the Coalition, a reference to the unattractive mixture of economic incompetence, political expediency and financial corruption that had come to characterise it. The existence of the so-called 'Lloyd George Fund' provided an easy target for those wanting to blacken his name.

The 'Lloyd George Fund'

Lloyd George used his power of patronage as Prime Minister to employ agents to organise the sale of honours and titles on a commission basis. It was said that the asking rate during the Coalition years was between £10,000 and £12,000 for a knighthood, and between £35,000 and £40,000 for a baronetcy. During this period some 90 peerages and 20,000 OBEs were purchased by well-heeled, if not always well-born, social aspirants. Lloyd George argued unashamedly that it was a justifiable means of raising political funds, given that he did not have access to the donations that the Conservatives received from the business world or to the funds that came to the Labour Party from the trade unions.

The belief that Lloyd George was dishonest provided a powerful argument for those Conservatives who had begun to question their party's continued support for him. They pointed out that their support had always been conditional and suggested that the corruption of the Coalition, added to its failure in domestic, economic and foreign policy, was now beginning to taint the Conservative Party itself. Their chance to undermine him came shortly after when Lloyd George announced his intention of calling a general election. This was the moment for the Conservative Party to reconsider their relationship with Lloyd George. Should they, in the light of the obvious unpopularity of the Coalition, continue to support it? In a dramatic and decisive meeting of the Party, held at the Carlton Club in October 1922, the Conservative MPs voted by 187 to 87 to abandon Lloyd George and the Coalition by standing for election as a party in their own right.

The Carlton Club Meeting, 1922

The Carlton was the unofficial headquarters of the Conservative Party. At the meeting, Stanley Baldwin, soon to be the leader of the party, joined Bonar Law in persuading their colleagues to disassociate themselves from a Prime Minister no longer worthy of their trust. In an influential speech, Baldwin spoke of Lloyd George as 'a dynamic force which had already shattered the Liberal Party and which was well on its way to doing the same thing for the Conservative Party'. This meeting marked the critical moment when the Conservative Party guaranteed its survival as an independent political force.

The unpopularity of the Coalition and the wisdom of the Conservatives in abandoning it were shown in the results of the 1922 election. These were devastating for the Liberals, and revealed how badly damaged the party was by the division between the supporters of Lloyd George and the Asquithians. Lloyd George resigned following this overwhelming rejection. He was never to hold office again.

The 1922 Election Result			
	Seats Won	**Total Votes**	**% Vote**
Conservatives	345	5,500,382	38.2
Labour	142	4,241,383	29.5
National Liberal (Lloyd Georgians)	62	1,673,240	11.6
Liberals (Asquithians)	54	2,516,287	17.5

Table 8 The 1922 election result.

The Coalition of 1918–22 has not had a good press. Emphasis has traditionally been laid on its apparent failures. It has been seen as an

How poor was the record of the 1918–22 Coalition?

oddity in that it did not conform to the normal pattern of party politics. It is often suggested that by governing in peacetime without a genuine party majority, Lloyd George was doomed to eventual failure as 'the prisoner of the Tories'. His final defeat in 1922, following the withdrawal of Conservative support, is thus interpreted as in some way marking a return to normal two-party politics which had been disrupted by the war and Lloyd George's wish to perpetuate his own authority.

The objection to this line of argument is that it assumes that the two-party system is normal and necessary to British politics. What brought Lloyd George down was not his defiance of two-party politics, but the decision of the Conservatives to abandon him. Had it served their purpose to remain with him they would have done so. They were looking after their own interests, not defending some abstract political principle. It is in that sense that Lloyd George had been their 'prisoner' throughout the years of the Coalition. Since his own group of Liberal supporters was not enough to keep him in office he had always been dependent on the Conservatives. What blurred the historical picture, as Martin Pugh, a modern authority, has pointed out, was that the Conservatives after 1922 were at pains to portray Lloyd George as having been not their prisoner but a dictator over them. This was their way of absolving themselves from the mistakes of the Coalition years.

ACTIVITY

Read back over section 1, and then list the reasons why Lloyd George's post-war Coalition was less successful than the one he had led between 1916 and 1918.

ISSUE:
To what extent did the Treaty solve the Anglo-Irish question?

2 The Anglo-Irish Treaty, 1921 (often referred to as 'the Treaty')

The redeeming success of Lloyd George as Coalition leader was his negotiation of the Irish Treaty of 1921. To understand the importance of the Treaty and the scale of his success, it is necessary to examine the development of the Irish question after 1914. The suspension of the Home Rule Act at the start of the war had only shelved the Irish problem; it had not solved it. This became very apparent with the **'Easter Rising'** of April 1916, which the Cabinet feared might lead to further serious troubles in Ireland. Lloyd George was asked to find a solution. In taking up the task Lloyd George made it his main objective to prevent the Irish problem from undermining the British war effort. He immediately entered into discussions with Redmond, the Irish Nationalist leader, and Carson, leader of the Ulster Unionists.

Lloyd George proposed a compromise, referred to as the 'Heads of Agreement'. This granted immediate home rule for the 26 counties of southern Ireland with Ulster remaining part of the United Kingdom until after the war, when its permanent status would be settled. Lloyd George allowed Redmond to gain the impression that the separation of Ulster from the rest of Ireland was purely temporary. At the same time he reassured Carson that it would be permanent. However, for the moment, Lloyd George's manoeuvring came to nothing. When the Heads of Agreement were put to the Coalition Cabinet the Unionist members refused to ratify it. They claimed Lloyd George had gone too far to appease the Irish nationalists. When Redmond learned of this he broke off negotiations and the Agreement became a dead letter.

The failure to achieve a settlement undermined the position of those nationalists in Ireland who believed that a peaceful solution was possible and gave strength to those who argued that force was the only arbiter. The 80 Irish Nationalist MPs decided that they would no longer attend the Westminster Parliament. Notwithstanding this gesture of defiance, the Nationalist Party began to lose ground in Ireland to the more extreme Sinn Fein party whose leading members had played a prominent role in the Easter Rising. In 1917, the year in which Eamon de Valera became its leader, Sinn Fein won two by-elections.

The British government's attempt to extend conscription to Ireland in 1918 only made matters worse. Despite being outlawed, Sinn Fein won 73 seats in the 1918 Coupon Election, seats which it pointedly refused to take up at Westminster. Instead, in 1919 it defiantly set up its own *Dail Eireann* (Irish parliament) in Dublin. In the same year Sinn Fein's military wing, the Irish Volunteers, reformed itself as the Irish Republican Army (IRA), dedicated to guerrilla war against the British forces. IRA activists became so disruptive that Lloyd George sanctioned the recruitment of special irregular forces, such as the **Black and Tans**, to deal with the situation.

However, the terror and reprisals in which the Black and Tans engaged, while keeping the peace, led to their becoming the hated symbols of British authority in Ireland.

Although Lloyd George claimed 'to have murder by the throat', the ferocity of 'the troubles' between 1919 and 1921 finally convinced him that a constitutional settlement acceptable to both Nationalists and Unionists had somehow to be found. A Government of Ireland Act (1920) had already created separate parliaments for Southern and Northern Ireland. Neither parliament had recognised

THE 'EASTER RISING', 25–30 APRIL 1916

A breakaway group from the Irish Republican Brotherhood seized the General Post Office in Dublin and proclaimed the establishment of the Irish Republic. After four days of bitter fighting, the republicans were overwhelmed by a British force; their ringleaders were executed after a summary trial. The rising had been poorly supported but the executions turned the rebels into martyrs and intensified Irish bitterness. The Irish poet, W.B. Yeats, spoke of 'a terrible beauty' having been born, a reference to the terrible nature of violence and the uplifting beauty of sacrifice.

How did the failure to reach a settlement in 1916 affect the situation in Ireland?

THE BLACK AND TANS

Auxiliary forces known from the colour of their hastily designed uniform as the Black and Tans were recruited and sent to Ireland. The harsh methods they used soon led to their being hated by Irish Nationalists, who accused Lloyd George of employing them deliberately to terrorise the civilian population of Ireland.

> We find that the late Alderman MacCurtain, Lord Mayor of Cork, died from shock and haemorrhage caused by bullet wounds, and that he was wilfully murdered under circumstances of the most callous brutality, and that the murder was organised and carried out by the Royal Irish Constabulary, officially directed by the British government, and we return a verdict of wilful murder against David Lloyd George, Prime Minister of England; Lord French, Lord Lieutenant of Ireland; Ian MacPherson, later Chief Secretary of Ireland; Acting Inspector General Smith, of the Royal Irish Constabulary.

Source A From the statement of the jury at a Cork inquest, 1920.

How did Lloyd George manage to persuade the various parties to agree to a settlement?

---

the other, but their existence established a precedent for further negotiation. Accordingly, in 1921 Lloyd George gathered together a team of negotiators that included the new Conservative leader, Austen Chamberlain as well as Lord Birkenhead, previously one of the staunchest opponents of home rule. He then offered De Valera a truce and invited him and the other Irish leaders to London to discuss the drafting of a treaty of settlement.

When they arrived, Lloyd George shrewdly played upon the idea that he represented the last hope of a just settlement for Ireland. He suggested that if they could not reach an acceptable agreement under his sympathetic leadership it might well be that he would have to resign, to be replaced by Bonar Law whose objection to home rule would destroy any chance of settlement. His argument was persuasive enough to induce them to accept the appointment of a boundary commission charged with the task of detaching Ulster from the rest of Ireland. What this acceptance meant was that Irish Nationalists had given ground on the critical issue; they had dropped their previous insistence that Ulster must be part of an independent Ireland.

With this as a bargaining factor, Lloyd George was able to convince the Unionists that the rights and independence of Ulster had been safeguarded. In December 1921, after a long and complicated series of discussions in which all Lloyd George's arts of diplomacy, if not duplicity, were exercised, the parties finally signed the Irish Treaty, according southern Ireland Dominion status as the Irish Free State, with Ulster remaining part of the United Kingdom. This solved the major problem that had afflicted Anglo-Irish relations since the Union of 1800, but it left the Irish Nationalists deeply divided over the Treaty, which required the acceptance of partition and an oath of loyalty to the British Crown.

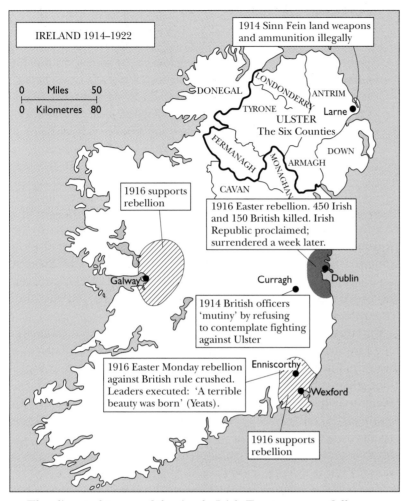

IRELAND 1914–1922

1914 Sinn Fein land weapons and ammunition illegally

DONEGAL
LONDONDERRY
ANTRIM
TYRONE
Larne
ULSTER
The Six Counties
FERMANAGH
DOWN
MONAGHAN
ARMAGH
CAVAN

1916 supports rebellion

1916 Easter rebellion. 450 Irish and 150 British killed. Irish Republic proclaimed; surrendered a week later.

Galway
Curragh
Dublin

1914 British officers 'mutiny' by refusing to contemplate fighting against Ulster

1916 Easter Monday rebellion against British rule crushed. Leaders executed: 'A terrible beauty was born' (Yeats).

Enniscorthy
Wexford

1916 supports rebellion

Figure 12 Map of the 1921 Treaty settlement showing the partition of the island of Ireland into the Irish Free State and Northern Ireland (comprising the six counties). Northern Ireland is sometimes loosely referred to as Ulster, although historically Ulster had been made up of nine counties – the six shown plus Donegal, Cavan, and Monaghan. The fact that Northern Ireland did not include these last three was of immense importance since it left the Protestants in a majority in the North.

The disputed terms of the Anglo-Irish Treaty were as follows:

I Ireland shall have the same constitutional status in the Community of Nations know as the British Empire as the Dominion of Canada, the Commonwealth of Australia, the Dominion of New Zealand, and the Union of South Africa, with a Parliament having powers to make laws for the peace, order and good government of Ireland and an Executive responsible to that Parliament, and shall be styled and known as the Irish Free State ...

4 The oath to be taken by Members of the Parliament of the Irish Free State shall be in the following form: I ... do solemnly swear true faith and allegiance to the Constitution of the Irish Free State as by law established and that I will be faithful to H.M. King George V, his heirs and successors by law in virtue of the common citizenship of Ireland with Great Britain.

Source B From the Treaty between Great Britain and Ireland, December 1921.

De Valera, leader of Sinn Fein and a survivor of the 1916 Rising, declared that dominion status under the Crown was unacceptable:

> The only banner under which our freedom can be won at the present time is the Republican banner. It is as an Irish Republic that we have a chance of getting international recognition ... Some might have faults to find with that and prefer other forms of government. But we are all united on this – that we want complete and absolute independence. This is the time to get freedom. Then we can settle by the most democratic means what particular form of government we may have.

Source C From a speech by Eamon De Valera, 1922.

As De Valera's speech indicated, the Treaty was unacceptable to a large number of nationalists. They regarded the oath of loyalty to the British Crown as a betrayal of Ireland. The result was a deep division within Ireland that marred the early years of the Irish Free State. A bitter civil war was fought in Ireland between 1922 and 1923 between the pro-Treaty Nationalists, led by Michael Collins, and the anti-Treaty Republicans led by De Valera.

In retrospect, the settlement of 1921 can be seen as both a remarkable historical achievement and a contemporary political failure. A British politician had had the vision to undertake successfully something which, since the 1801 Act of Union, had evaded all other statesmen who had approached it – a workable solution to the Anglo-Irish question. Of course, as subsequent events in Ireland were to show it was far from being a perfect solution. Nevertheless, judged against the scale of the problem originally confronting him, Lloyd George's achievement was highly impressive.

The political failure lay in the fact that the Treaty was necessarily a compromise. The Unionists were left feeling betrayed by Lloyd George's willingness to give in to what they regarded as Republican terrorism. The Nationalists could not forget his use of the Black and Tans; nor could they regard the Treaty as anything other than a concession reluctantly and belatedly extracted from a British government which granted it only when all other means of maintaining the union had failed. But above all it was the partition of Ireland that left the bitterest legacy. It would haunt future generations (see page 251).

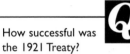

How successful was the 1921 Treaty?

ACTIVITIES

▼ Having read section 2, draw up a chronology of the main developments in Anglo-Irish relations between 1914 and 1921.

▼ How far is it an accurate or adequate statement to say that the Treaty of 1921 was both a historical achievement and contemporary failure?

DAVID LLOYD GEORGE (1863–1945)

Lloyd George was one of the most remarkable statesman of his or any age. The only PM not to have spoken English as his first language, he was characterised by his Welsh fire and oratory. During his 55 years in public life there was hardly a major issue in which he was not involved. He loved political battle, but he could also be disarmingly courteous and conciliatory. Although he remained a Liberal throughout his life, he was a keen advocate of coalition politics, believing that a pooling of the finest minds and talents from all the parties would serve Britain best. His humble Welsh background made him an upstart in the eyes of many and he was never fully trusted by his political contemporaries. His roguish private life did not help in this regard. As a young man he was notorious as a womaniser, was chased by jealous husbands, and was issued with more than one paternity order. His lifelong affair with his private secretary, Frances Stephenson, who bore him two children, was an open secret. Some critics regard his feud with Asquith as the major reason for the irreversible decline of the Liberal Party. Whatever the accuracy of that judgement, it remains the case that his burning hatred of social injustice, his arts as a diplomat and a negotiator, his populist belief that he truly understood the aspirations and needs of ordinary people, and the sheer range of activity in which he involved himself, combined to make him the most outstanding political figure of the first half of the twentieth century. In his House of Commons tribute in 1945, Winston Churchill emphasised that it was Lloyd George's work as a social reformer that ranked as his greatest achievement:

> There was no man so gifted, so eloquent, so forceful, who knew the life of the people so well. Much of his work abides, some of it will grow greatly in the future, and those who come after us will find the pillars of his life's toil upstanding, massive and indestructible.

Source D From a speech by Winston Churchill in the House of Commons, 28 March 1945.

1863	born in Manchester;
1864–77	brought up in Wales;
1884	qualified as a lawyer;
1888	married Margaret Owen;
1890	became Liberal MP for Caernarvon (remained MP for this constituency for the next 55 unbroken years);
1905	President of the Board of Trade;
1908	Chancellor of the Exchequer – introduced old age pensions;
1909	introduced 'People's Budget';
1911	introduced National Insurance Act;
1912	began a 33-year liaison with his mistress, Frances Stephenson;
1915	became Minister of Munitions in Asquith's Coalition;
1916	became Prime Minister;
1916–18	led Britain to victory;
1918	won the Coupon Election;
1918–22	PM of the peacetime Coalition;
1919	led British delegation at Paris peace talks;
1921	led negotiations that resulted in the Anglo-Irish Treaty;
1922	Coalition collapsed – he never held office again;
1926	became Liberal Party leader;
1936	visited Germany and met Hitler;
1937–39	attacked Neville Chamberlain's appeasement policy;
1940	declined invitation to join Churchill's Coalition;
1941	death of his wife, Margaret;
1943	married Frances Stephenson;
1945	created Earl Lloyd George of Dwyfor; died.

ISSUE:
Why were the
Conservatives in office
for such a short
period?

3 The Conservative Governments, 1922–24

After only eight months in office Bonar Law was forced to retire through ill health. His place as Prime Minister was taken by Stanley Baldwin, who judged that the best way to reverse the recession and tackle unemployment was to return to a policy of protection. He called a general election, hoping to gain a mandate for his plans. The results disappointed him. The Conservatives remained the largest single party in the Commons, but both the Liberals and the Labour Party improved considerably on their 1922 showing. Following a defeat on a confidence vote in the Commons, Baldwin resigned in January 1924. Since the Liberal and Conservative Parties had fought the election on opposite sides over protection, a coalition between them was unthinkable. Despite gaining 41 seats, the Liberals were now the third party and obviously could not form a government on their own. In a remarkable political development, the Labour Party, which had been in existence for barely 25 years, now found itself in government.

Table 9 The 1923 election result.

The 1923 Election Result		
	Seats Won	% Vote
Conservatives	258	38.1
Labour	191	30.5
Liberals	159	29.6

ISSUES:
How, by 1923, had
Labour come to
replace the Liberals as
the second largest
party?
Why, despite lacking a
majority, did Labour
take office in 1924?

4 The First Labour Government, 1924

The growth of Labour as a political force has as much to do with Liberal weakness as Labour strength. Despite dominating the political scene before 1914, the Liberals suffered serious internal divisions during the First World War and were never able to regain their position after 1918. Labour was able to take advantage of this. As the tables of election results indicate it continually bit into the Liberals' electoral support so that by 1923 it had pushed them into third place in British party politics.

Summary of Reasons for the Decline of the Liberals

▽ During the 1914–18 War the Liberal Party split between the supporters of Asquith and those of Lloyd George (see page 44).

▽ It never fully recovered from this and never again held office in its own right.

▽ Liberal values, such as the freedom of the individual, had been compromised by government measures during the war, e.g., military conscription.

▽ Before 1914 the party had always been able to rely on the parliamentary support of the Irish Nationalists. This was no longer available after Sinn Fein boycotted the House of Commons in 1918 and home rule for southern Ireland was implemented in 1922.

▽ the '**first past the post**' electoral system penalised the Liberal Party.

Summary of Reasons for the Rise of the Labour Party

▽ Working-class voters defected from the Liberal Party to the more radical, trade-union financed Labour Party.

▽ Its strong trade union links provided it with a sound financial base.

▽ The Labour Party had a good war record. After initial misgivings, it played a major role in the patriotic war effort.

▽ Its senior politicians gained experience as Cabinet ministers, thereby suggesting that the Party was capable of government.

▽ It improved its constituency organisation during the war and in 1918 adopted a formal constitution setting out its programme.

'FIRST PAST THE POST'

A succcessful candidate in a parliamentary constituency election is voted in on a simple majority. Since no account is taken of the proportion of votes, any majority larger than one is in a sense a wasted set of votes. The Liberals tended to have their votes piled up in particular constituencies rather than distributed evenly across all the constituencies.

Labour's taking office under MacDonald in 1924 was a truly remarkable turn of events yet in a sense it was on sufferance. Both the Liberals and the Conservatives calculated that as the young Labour Party was unlikely to be able to form a strong government they could use the position to their advantage. Asquith was willing to give conditional Liberal support to the Labour Party since it was a way of pushing the Conservatives from power. He also calculated that with Labour dependent on Liberal support he would be able to control the new government. For their part, the Conservatives believed that such was the inexperience of Labour that it would fail in office and discredit itself indefinitely as a party of government. That would leave the Conservatives free to continue their traditional rivalry with their real opponents – the Liberals.

At the time such calculations seemed sound enough. During its nine months of office in 1924 Labour introduced only three main

---

LABOUR GOVERN-MENT MEASURES IN 1924

▽ A Housing Act increased public funds to build new working-class homes.

▽ Restrictions on unemployment benefit were eased.

▽ More public funds were directed to educational provision.

THE ZINOVIEV LETTER

Shortly before the Election of October 1924, *The Daily Mail*, under the headline, SOVIET PLOT: RED PROPAGANDA IN BRITAIN: REVOLUTION URGED IN BRITAIN, reproduced a letter from Grigor Zinoviev, chief of the Comintern, the Soviet agency for spreading international revolution. It was addressed to the British Communist Party urging its members to infiltrate the Labour Party and use it to bring down the British State. The letter is believed by historians to have been a forgery, concocted either by Russian émigrés, MI5, or the Conservative Party, to suggest that the Labour Party was a front for Soviet subversion. To understand why this created such excitement it has to be remembered that Ramsay MacDonald's government had negotiated trade and diplomatic agreements with the Soviet Union.

measures and those were non-controversial. But the historical importance of the first Labour government was not what it did but the fact that it existed at all. Ramsay MacDonald's decision to take office was based on his conviction that the very act of forming a government would show that Labour had become a responsible part of the political system. It would prove that it could govern without red revolution breaking out. In this respect, MacDonald's was a notable achievement. He also judged that the Liberals were a spent force. His judgement was borne out by the election that followed in 1924. Although the Conservatives won well and took office, Labour lost only 40 seats and actually increased its share of the vote, this despite the problems caused by **the Zinoviev Letter**. The Liberals, however, suffered a disaster, losing 119 seats and 12 per cent of the share of the vote. The 1924 Election marks the point at which Labour superseded the Liberals as the second main party in Britain.

The 1924 Election Result		
	Seats won	**% Vote**
Conservatives	419	48.3
Labour	151	33.0
Liberals	40	17.6

Table 10 The 1924 election result.

Figure 13 'On the Loan Trail', a cartoon of October 1924 that ironically sums up the attitude of large sections of the press towards the affair of the Zinoviev Letter. The caption reads: 'In a document just disclosed by the British Foreign Office (apparently after considerable delay), M. ZINOVIEFF, a member of the Bolshevik dictatorship, urges the British Communist Party to use "the greatest possible urgency" in securing the ratification of Mr. MACDONALD's's Anglo-Russian Treaty, in order to facilitate a scheme for "an armed insurrection" of the British proletariat.'

ON THE LOAN TRAIL.

[In a document just disclosed by the British Foreign Office (apparently after considerable delay), M. ZINOVIEFF, a member of the Bolshevist Dictatorship, urges the British Communist Party to use "the greatest possible energy" in securing the ratification of Mr. MACDONALD's Anglo-Russian Treaty, in order to facilitate a scheme for "an armed insurrection" of the British proletariat.]

5 Baldwin's Government, 1924–29

Back in office in November 1924, after the short-lived Labour government had resigned, Stanley Baldwin formed a government that over the next five years introduced a number of important measures. His Chancellor of the Exchequer was Winston Churchill, who after 20 years as a Liberal had now returned to the Conservative Party. Baldwin accepted that tariff reform was no longer an acceptable policy and he quietly shelved it. Instead he adopted a broad policy aimed at improving British trade and finances; he also gave attention to a number of social reforms. However, one particular event has tended to overshadow his administration – the General Strike.

a) The General Strike, 1926

By 1925 the British coal industry was in a desperate state; orders were falling and overheads were increasing. The mine-owners sought to salvage something by reducing wages. Not surprisingly, the miners' union (the Miners Federation) resisted bitterly. When the TUC supported them a general strike seemed likely to occur in July 1925. However, Baldwin's government bought itself time by offering a temporary subsidy to maintain miners' wage levels and by setting up the Samuel Commission to examine the problems of the coal industry. In its Report in March 1926 the Commission recommended that the industry be totally restructured, but urged the miners in the meantime to accept a cut in wages. The Federation angrily rejected the Commission's proposals and called on the TUC again to support them by organising a general strike to begin on 30 April.

From the beginning, there was poor liaison between the TUC and the miners. Moreover, none of the TUC leaders genuinely wanted a strike on this scale; they hoped that, as had happened a year earlier, the government would back down rather than risk conflict. But, unlike 1925, the government was now prepared to call the TUC's bluff. Indeed, many in the Cabinet, most notably Churchill, wanted a show-down with the labour movement. However, talks in Downing

Street between government officials and TUC leaders seemed, by Saturday 1 May, to be on the verge of success. A compromise, by which the employers would withdraw their lock-out notices and the workers would lift their strike threats, was close to being agreed. But then there occurred an episode that destroyed the negotiations and made a strike unavoidable. On the evening of 2 May, news broke that the printers at the *Daily Mail* had refused to type-set a provocative editorial by the paper's editor. The key passage to which the printers objected read:

> The miners, after weeks of negotiation, have declined the proposals made to them, and the coal mines of Britain are idle.
>
> The Council of the Trades Union Congress, which represents all the other trades unions, has determined to support the miners by going to the extreme of ordering a General Strike.
>
> We do not wish to say anything hard about the miners themselves. As to their leaders, all we need say at this moment is that some of them are (and have openly declared themselves) under the influence of people who mean no good to this country.
>
> The General Strike is not an industrial dispute; it is a revolutionary movement, intended to inflict suffering upon the great mass of innocent persons in the community and thereby put forcible constraint upon the government.

Source E From *The Daily Mail*, 3 May 1926.

This was just what the government hawks, such as Winston Churchill, had been waiting for; Baldwin and his Cabinet were pressed into delivering an ultimatum to the TUC stating that no further talks could take place unless the 'overt action' of the printers was condemned by the TUC and all strike notices withdrawn. The TUC protested they had not known of the *Mail* printers' initiative and declared themselves still willing to negotiate. But by not waiting for the TUC's reply, the government closed the door to a settlement. The next day, 3 May, the government declared a state of emergency and the TUC began its long-threatened strike.

Despite its apparent militancy, the TUC's threats were largely bluff; it did not want a strike. As a consequence, the workers' side had made few preparations. It was only on the eve of the stoppage that the TUC hurriedly drafted its plans. In marked contrast, the government were fully ready. Indeed, the reason for the government's climb-down in 1925 had been to create time to prepare for a confrontation. The Emergency Powers Act of 1920 granted the Executive wide authority in the event of a major disruption of essential services. Under its terms, the government had set up the Organisation for the

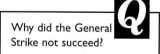

Why did the General Strike not succeed?

Maintenance of Supplies, which created a national network of voluntary workers to maintain vital services should a strike occur. Set against government preparations, the organisation of the strike by the TUC was rudimentary and ineffectual.

Given the government's readiness, the TUC's reluctance, and the general public's hostility, the strike stood no chance of success. There were violent clashes here and there between police and strikers but few unions were willing to support the miners in a fight to the finish. On 12 May, after ten days, the TUC called off the strike without winning any concessions from the employers or the government. The miners themselves carried on for another seven months before eventually they too gave in unconditionally. The government was quick to introduce a **Trade Disputes Act** in 1927 aimed at reducing union rights and so make another General Strike impossible.

> ### *TRADE DISPUTES ACT, 1927*
> ▼ Outlawed general and sympathetic strikes.
> ▼ Restricted strike action to specific disputes.
> ▼ Forbade trade union funds being used for political purposes unless the individual member chose to contribute by 'contracting in'.

Table 11 The path to the General Strike.

	Development	TUC Action	Government Action
July 1925	Mine owners reduced wages; Miners agreed to await Samuel Report	Backed miners' strike threat	Offered miners a wage subsidy; Set up Samuel Commission; Made preparations to meet a strike
March 1926	Samuel Commission urged miners to accept wage cuts; Federation called strike for 30 April	Gave Federation uncertain backing	
April–May 1926		Joined government in talks which seemed on verge of success	Hawks pressed for showdown
2 May	Printers at *Daily Mail* refused to set editorial	Denied knowledge of printers' action	Delivered ultimatum to TUC
3 May		TUC declared a General Strike	Declared a state of emergency

CHIEF MEASURES OF BALDWIN'S GOVERNMENT

1925 a Pensions Act enabled contributors to draw their pension at 65; Britain's currency was returned to the gold standard (see page 69);

1926 an Electricity Act set up the national grid to provide power throughout Britain;

1927 the BBC established a national radio broadcasting system; the Trade Disputes Act restricted trade union freedoms;

1928 the fifth Parliamentary Reform Act granted the vote to women on the same terms as men, i.e., all citizens over the age of 21;

1929 in an effort to stimulate production and commerce, a Local Government Act exempted all farms and 25 per cent of factories from local rates. The Act also effectively ended the old Poor Law, by abolishing the Boards of Guardians and phasing out the workhouses.

As the list of its measures shows, there was more to Baldwin's 1924–29 government than the General Strike. Nevertheless, the Conservative Party's 1929 election slogan 'safety first' was hardly an inspiring one after five years in office and its failure to control rising unemployment counted against it. In the election its share of the vote dropped by 10 per cent compared with 1924. The Liberal Party staged a recovery by nearly doubling its aggregate vote. But its share of the vote was too widely and thinly spread. The most impressive feature of the election was the increase in the Labour vote, sufficient to return it as the largest single party.

Table 12 The 1929 election result.

The 1929 Election Result			
	Seats Won	Total Votes	% Vote
Labour	288	8,389,512	37.1
Conservatives	260	8,656,473	38.2
Liberals	59	5,308,510	23.4

ACTIVITY

Having read section 5, write a set of headings giving the essential points in answer to the following questions. Was the strike avoidable? Which do you regard as the more convincing explanation of the failure of the General Strike – the government's foresight or the TUC's lack of preparation?

ISSUES:
How did Britain become caught in America's economic depression?
How accurate is it to say that the inter-war years were a period of depression in Britain?

1929 was a critical date in international history. It marked the beginning of a worldwide economic depression that was to last throughout the 1930s. Britain was one of the victims and we need to understand the pressures and difficulties that this created for the governments of the period. The following section describes the main features of the inter-war slump as it affected Britain.

6 The Depression

In 1929, the United States, the world's most powerful economic nation, experienced the 'great crash', the collapse of its stock market. This financial disaster was followed by a severe industrial depression between 1929 and 1932. In a desperate effort to limit the damage, the USA immediately introduced restrictive measures. It erected prohibitive trade barriers and recalled its foreign loans. Britain was one of the first countries to be harmed by these policies. Since the American market was now largely closed, the British manufacturing industries could not sell their goods. The staple industries, which were already in decline (see page 47), were particularly badly hit. There was the added problem for Britain that its trade with the USA had previously been the major means by which it had raised the capital to pay off its loans. Unable now to trade with America, Britain found itself in an impossible position. It was saddled with debts and could not raise the capital to meet them. It is true that Britain was itself owed large amounts by France, Russia, Italy and other allies

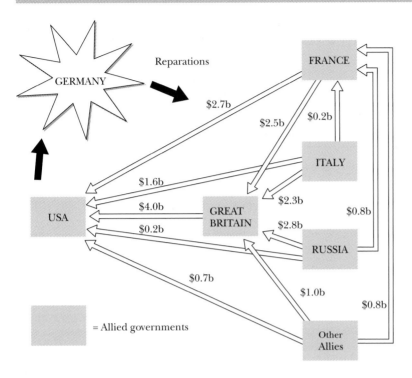

Figure 14 The links between the debtor and creditor nations that had been created by loans and borrowings among the Allies during the First World War. In theory, Germany was committed to paying large reparations to the Allies. But the relatively small amounts it did pay came from loans advanced by the USA. America stood at the centre of the whole interlocking system. This was why the health or otherwise of the United States' economy was of such vital concern to Europe. If things went wrong for the USA, Europe was bound to suffer also.

from the wartime. However, since these countries were also victims of the international depression there was little prospect of their paying their debts to Britain.

The problem was made worse by the effects of Britain's decision to return to the **gold standard** in 1925. The aim of Churchill, the Chancellor of the Exchequer, had been to strengthen the pound sterling by restoring it to its pre-war parity with the US dollar. This involved raising the pound's exchange rate from \$3.40 to \$4.86. While this bold step helped British financiers, it deepened the plight of British exporters who found it even harder to sell their goods abroad at the newly inflated prices. This was because the real gold value of Britain's pound sterling raised its exchange rate against all other currencies as well as the dollar. Foreign traders had to pay larger amounts of their own currency when purchasing British goods. This was an obvious disincentive to buying British. The return to the gold standard in 1925 thus added to the growing tendency for British goods to be priced out of the market.

Tables 13, 14 and 15 help to give us a picture of how the industrial depression, that was at its worst between 1930 and 1936, affected Britain. Tables 14 and 15 illustrate the blight affecting the staple industries in Britain. In 1936, a year in which a significant economic recovery began, the overall unemployment figure for all British trades

---

THE GOLD STANDARD

The term refers to the position in which a nation's coinage has a fixed gold content. In Britain, between 1821 and 1914, the sovereign coin was 92 per cent pure gold. This fixed gold value gave Britain's currency a strength that led foreign investors to buy sterling and use it as a common form of exchange. By 1914 nearly all trading nations had followed Britain in adopting their own gold standard, which gave great stability to international commerce. It was the economic disruption caused by the First World War that made it impossible for countries to maintain their gold standards.

What part did the gold standard play in Britain's difficulties?

Unemployment in Britain, 1921–40			
1921	1.58 million	1931	2.64 million
1922	1.50 million	1932	2.64 million
1923	1.28 million	1933	2.40 million
1924	1.12 million	1934	2.10 million
1925	1.22 million	1935	2.00 million
1926	1.28 million	1936	1.90 million
1927	1.12 million	1937	1.49 million
1928	1.20 million	1938	1.70 million
1929	1.28 million	1939	1.60 million
1930	1.98 million	1940	1.10 million

Table 13 Unemployment in Britain, 1921–40.

% Unemployed in Certain Trades in 1936	
All trades	12.5
Ship building	30.6
Coal mining	25.0
Shipping	22.3
All textile trades	13.2
Commerce & Finance	3.8
Printing & Paper	6.2
Skilled building crafts	6.3
Chemical trades	7.9
Engineering	8.3

Table 14 Percentage of unemployed in certain trades in 1936.

% Unemployed According to Region in 1936	
S E England	5.6
London	6.5
S W England	7.8
Midlands	9.4
NW England	16.2
N E England	16.6
Scotland	18.0
N Ireland	23.0
Wales	28.5

Table 15 Percentage of unemployed according to region in 1936.

Q

Which types of industry were worst affected?

THE SERVICE (OR CONSUMER) INDUSTRIES were those enterprises developed after the First World War to meet the growing demand for modern convenience and leisure goods, such as radios, refrigerators, vacuum cleaners, newspapers and magazines. The building, electrical engineering, printing and chemical trades rapidly expanded to provide these commodities which were directly aimed at stimulating consumer demand.

was 12.5 per cent. However, ship building, mining, shipping and textiles all showed much higher figures. In contrast, the **service industries** all had single figure rates of unemployment. The discrepancy is striking. Equally expressive are the statistics in Table 15, showing unemployment by region. Low in the relatively prosperous London and the South-East, unemployment was noticeably higher in the areas where the staple industries were concentrated: namely, manufacturing in Birmingham and the Black Country, coal and steel in Yorkshire and Wales, textiles in Lancashire, shipping and ship building on the

Tyne and in Scotland and Northern Ireland. The tables also indicate a parallel but opposite movement in British industry. At the same time as the north suffered a recession in the staple industries, the south enjoyed a boom in the new service industries.

Revisionist historians suggest it is inaccurate to speak of the inter-war 'Depression' or 'Slump' as if it had been a common experience in Britain. They regard it not as a single phenomenon but as several. What observers see depends on where they stand. Table 15 indicates that the depression was very much a regional affair. In those areas of Britain dependent on the old industries for their livelihood, the Depression was severe and enduring. If, however, the focus of attention is shifted to such regions as the Thames Valley or the Home Counties, the picture becomes one of remarkable growth. The increase in house-building and in the purchasing of cars and domestic commodities could be taken as both cause and effect of the good times prevailing in these areas.

Naturally enough, given the suffering it brought, unemployment is taken by analysts as the chief measure of the Depression. There is, however, a danger that such emphasis may lead to an exaggeration of how serious and long-lasting unemployment actually was. Economists often distinguish between two kinds of unemployment – **structural** and **cyclical**. Both types tend to be present in a time of industrial transition. There is the further consideration that productivity (i.e., the amount of production per worker) could grow at the same time as unemployment. An example of this can even be found within the same industry. In ship building, the process of shedding surplus labour, wretched though it was for the victims, considerably increased the output and efficiency of the individual workers who remained. If one measures productivity, as opposed to production, there are clear signs of growth, even in the staple industries.

Q

Was the Depression of the 1930s a national or a regional problem?

STRUCTURAL UNEMPLOYMENT

refers to the job losses that follow major and irreversible alterations in the economy. The staple industries in Britain experienced this type of unemployment. Coal is a good example. As British coal became more expensive to mine and therefore harder to sell in a competitive market, pits were forced to close or reduce their output, thus putting thousands out of work with no prospect of re-employment.

CYCLICAL UNEMPLOYMENT

is a temporary trend caused by fluctuations in supply and demand. An industry or enterprise with good long-term prospects might undergo a short-term fall in orders and lay off workers but with every intention of re-employing them when sales improved. Some retail or service industries were particularly subject to temporary or seasonal falls in demand.

ACTIVITY

After studying the statistics and details in section 6, jot down short responses to the following questions.

1 Why was unemployment such a persistent problem in Britain in the 1920s and 1930s?
2 Why did the incidence of unemployment show such regional variation?

ISSUE:
Did living standards rise or fall during the Depression?

a) Living Standards Between the Wars

The previous section suggested that the Depression was a patchy affair. It did not affect the whole of Britain equally. Unemployment and industrial decline were not universal. Indeed, in a number of areas there was spectacular growth. However, that was of little comfort to those in the depressed regions. They complained that a southern-dominated parliament and government did not fully appreciate the sufferings of their countrymen in the north. It was part of a north west-south east divide often described as the **'two nations'**. It was no consolation to the victims of the slump to be told that things were better elsewhere in the country. The grim reality for them is brought out in the accompanying passage written by a skilled engineer who lost his job.

Source F From *Memoirs of the Unemployed* edited by H.L. Beales and R.S. Lambert, 1934.

My wife had decided to try and earn a little money so that we might continue to retain our house. She obtained a job as house to house saleswoman, and was able to earn a few shillings to supplement our dole income. It was from this time that the feeling of strain which was beginning to appear in our home became more marked. I felt a burden on her. … Life became more and more strained. There were constant bickerings over money usually culminating in threats to leave from both of us. The final blow came when the Means Test [the intrusive official examination of the family's income] was put into operation. I realised that if I told the Exchange that my wife was earning a little they might reduce my benefit. If that happened home life would become impossible. When, therefore, I was sent a form on which to give details of our total income I neglected to fill it up. For this I was suspended benefit for six weeks. This was the last straw. Quarrels broke out anew … Eventually, after the most heartbreaking period of my life, both my wife and my son, who had just commenced to earn a few shillings, told me to get out, as I was living on them and taking the food they needed.

'THE TWO NATIONS'
was first used by Benjamin Disraeli, the Victorian statesman and novelist, as a subtitle to his novel, *Sybil* (1844), to define the division of Britain between the rich and the poor. The term came back into common usage in the 1980s and 1990s to describe the difference between the areas of Britain which were flourishing economically and those which were in relative decline.

Yet, after acknowledging the poverty that so many in the regions experienced, the fact remains that for other parts of the population the interwar years were a time of genuine economic advance. Figure 15 is instructive here. It shows that at no time did retail prices move ahead of wages; the lines of the graph remain parallel throughout the 1920s and 1930s, indicating that purchasing power was maintained even when wages appeared to fall. This meant that **real wages** increased. For those in work, times were better not worse during the Depression.

Between 1924 and 1935 real wages rose as a national average by 17 per cent. This gave the majority of people in Britain greater

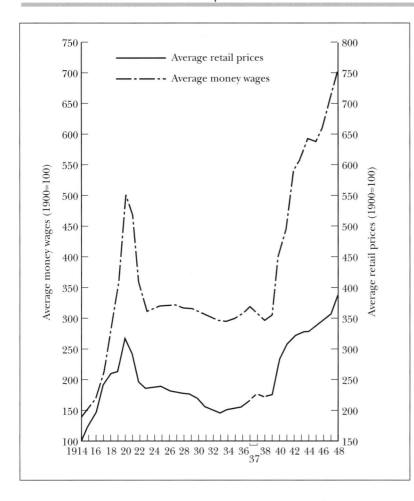

Figure 15 A graph comparing prices and wages in Britain, 1914–48.

purchasing power, a fact proved by the expanding sales of consumer goods, known popularly as **'mod cons'**. The women's cosmetics industry also experienced a very rapid growth as working-class women began to use the lipsticks, powders and perfumes that previously had been exclusive to the rich. Access to popular entertainment became widespread. Reading tabloid newspapers and magazines, listening to the radio, going to the cinema and watching professional sport became the main leisure activities of the British people. One measure of this is that between 1924 and 1935 cinema audiences grew from 36,000 a year to eight million.

In this same period over one million houses, many having indoor lavatories and hot running water, were provided at low rent by the local authorities. In addition to these 'council houses' two and a half million homes were provided by the building industry for private sale. This began a revolution in housing provision which was to be a notable aspect of social advance in the twentieth century. In 1914

REAL WAGES

The term refers to the purchasing power of earnings when set against prices. If prices are high money will buy less; if prices are low the same amount of money will buy more. For example, weekly earnings of £2 in one year might buy more than £3 would in a time of higher prices in another year. Therefore, although the £2 is obviously lower nominally than the £3, in *real* terms it has a higher purchasing value. If, as in the interwar period, wages go up at a faster pace than prices, there will be a rise in real wages.

MOD CONS

was short for modern conveniences. It referred to such items as motor cars, vacuum cleaners, refrigerators and radios.

only 10 per cent of the population had owned their own homes. By 1965 this proportion had grown to 60 per cent. A key feature of these houses was their use of electricity as the chief source of power. It was the spread of the national grid, which by 1940 was providing electricity to nearly all of urban Britain, that made possible the rise in living standards across the nation. This was of particular significance for women. By tradition they were the workers in the home. The drudgery that so many of them experienced was not ended by electricity but their burdens were lessened.

ACTIVITIES

Use the facts and figures presented in section 6 to answer the following questions. Express your answers in note form as a set of key points.

▼ How does the term the 'the two nations' help us to understand the effects of the interwar depression in Britain?
▼ Distinguish between wages and 'real wages'.
▼ What evidence is there to show that there was a general rise in living standards in Britain during the interwar years.

ISSUE:
Why did MacDonald's second government have such little success?

7 The Second Labour Government, 1929–31

Tragically for Labour, its second period of office coincided with the onset of the international depression. Whatever its reforming intentions may have been, the second Labour government was eventually overwhelmed by the economic crisis it inherited. In Britain unemployment had risen to nearly three million by 1931. To meet the hardship this brought to the victims, the government increased its expenditure on unemployment benefit. However, since the Depression caused a sharp fall in revenue from taxation, the government simply began to run out of money. The May Committee, set up to consider ways out of the crisis, recommended a wide range of cuts in public expenditure, including the reduction of pay for teachers, civil servants and those in the armed services. But the proposal that aroused the most dissension within the government was the suggestion that unemployment pay be cut by 10 per cent (the initial proposal had been 20 per cent).

Many in the Cabinet believed that if this were to be done it would destroy the very principle for which the Labour Party had been created – the protection of the working class. But MacDonald was also under pressure from the international bankers who were unwilling to

Did Ramsay MacDonald 'betray' his party in 1931?

advance further loans to Britain unless it reduced its welfare expenditure. He told his colleagues that there was no alternative but to make the cuts. When this proposal was put to a Cabinet vote, 10 of the 21 members rejected it.

This was the prelude to what became known in Labour Party history as 'the great betrayal'. Having failed to gain the necessary support from his colleagues, MacDonald declared his intention of resigning on his and their behalf. Instead, after consultations with both opposition leaders, Herbert Samuel of the Liberals and Stanley Baldwin of the Conservatives, he went to see the King, George V. MacDonald came back from the audience to tell his bemused colleagues in the last Labour Cabinet meeting, that he had agreed to stay on as Prime Minister in a new Coalition or 'National' government. MacDonald claimed that he was putting 'country before party', but many in the Labour ranks protested bitterly that it had all been a plot on his part to retain personal power and that the National government was already decided on long before he told the Cabinet. He was immediately expelled from his party and his name became reviled among succeeding generations of Labour supporters.

ACTIVITY

Ramsay MacDonald's decision to become leader of the National government still excites controversy. Your own views would be of value. How convincing do you find the claim that he was putting country before party? Were there any principles at stake in what he did? You are entitled to speculate what would have happened had he refused to make the cuts and resigned.

8 The National Government, 1931–40

Despite the extraordinary way it came into being, the National government proved highly popular at the polls. In the 1931 election it gained over two-thirds of the aggregate vote. The electorate broadly accepted that the exceptional crisis justified the creation of a new form of government whose first concern was, as MacDonald put it, not party politics but national recovery.

ISSUE:
Was the National government simply Conservative rule by another name?

The 1931 Election Result			
	Votes	**Seats**	**% vote**
Conservative	11,978,745	473	55.2
Liberal National	809,302	35	3.7
National Labour	341,370	13	1.6
Liberals	1,403,102	33	6.5
National Government (total)	(14,532,519)	(554)	(67.0)
Labour	6,649,630	52	30.6
Independent Liberal	106,106	4	0.5
Communist	74,824	0	0.3
New Party	36,377	0	0.2

Table 16 The 1931 election result.

> ### The New Party
>
> was founded by Oswald Mosley in 1931 following his resignation from Ramsay MacDonald's government over what he judged to be its failure to find an answer to unemployment. During his career Moseley had been variously a Conservative, an independent, and a Labour MP but he found none of the parties could accommodate his particular notion of progressive politics. The New Party fielded 24 candidates in the 1931 election, on a programme of curing joblessness. Its failure to arouse electoral support led Mosley to reject parliamentary politics. In 1932 he founded the British Union of Fascists (BUF), based broadly on Mussolini's Italian Fascist Party. However, although Mosley himself was an interesting character, his fascist movement never had the support to become more than a lunatic fringe, capable of causing disorder but never able to influence mainstream British politics.

Q What was the political character of the National government?

Despite its title 'National', the government first formed in 1931 was not a genuine coalition. From the beginning it was dominated by the Conservatives, who took the majority of the Cabinet posts. Only three of MacDonald's previous Labour Cabinet members stayed with him in 1931. The longer the government lasted the more apparent it became that it was a Conservative administration. This was especially evident in its economic policy which saw a return to protective tariffs in an attempt to stimulate industrial recovery. It is unlikely that these in themselves would have ended the Depression.

What helped the National government was the recovery in world trade that occurred towards the mid-1930s and was sustained by large-scale re-armament in the late 1930s. Although unemployment remained high for peacetime and was the outstanding domestic issue of the day, it did fall markedly from its peak of 2.6 million in 1932 to 1.7 million in 1938. A major benefit to the National government was the lack of an effective opposition in the Commons. The rapidly declining Liberal Party, and a Labour Party damaged by the 1931 split, were not a serious challenge. The 1935 election result showed that the National government had largely maintained its support. It was the last time in the century that a government would win more than 50 per cent of the total vote.

Apart from a set of largely ineffectual deflationary gestures, the National government did not really have a policy for dealing with unemployment. It shied away from the intervention advocated by Keynes (see page 123) and Oswald Mosley. The strongest criticism of the government tended to come from outside parliament. Although

The 1935 Election Result	Seats Won	Total Votes	% Vote
Conservatives (including National Labour and National Liberal)	432	11,810,158	53.7
Labour	154	8,325,491	37.9
Liberals	20	1,422,116	6.4

Table 17 The 1935 election result.

tiny in their membership the BUF and the Communist Party were very vocal in their condemnation of the economic policies of the day and tried to exploit the high levels of unemployment for political ends. But although tensions did occasionally take the form of **hunger marches** and political protests they were never a sustained threat to public order. The 1930s were certainly troubled times but Britain remained largely untouched by political extremism.

After MacDonald's retirement in 1935, he was followed as Prime Minister by the Conservative leader, Stanley Baldwin, who formed his third government. Much to the annoyance of his political opponents, Baldwin's policy of 'masterly inactivity' appeared to suit the situation. He continued to present the image he had developed as Prime Minister in the 1920s of the pipe-smoking Englishman who loved his country and its people and who could be relied upon in a crisis. This was evident in his tactful handling of the **Abdication crisis** in 1936. Baldwin was a great parliamentarian and was admired for his lack of pettiness and his generosity of spirit towards his political opponents. Indeed, it has been said of him that his calm leadership and lack of vindictiveness played no small part in Britain's avoiding the political extremism that marred so many European countries between the wars. When Baldwin retired in 1937 he was succeeded by Neville Chamberlain who was pre-occupied during the last three years of the National government with an increasingly threatening international situation (see page 93).

Historians have tended to find the period of the National government a dispiriting one. Inspired leadership was lacking and the politicians of the day had no answer to the economic difficulties that confronted them. Domestic policies seemed to be a matter of drift rather than direction. However, in the end it was not the National government's domestic record but its apparent failure in foreign affairs that has come in for the strongest criticism. The heaviest charge levelled against it is that it failed to prevent war with Germany in 1939. Whether that accusation is justified one of the main themes covered in Chapter 4.

HUNGER MARCHES were organised peaceful protests by the unemployed who felt they had no other way of drawing attention to their desperate condition than by taking to the streets. The most famous of these was the Jarrow March of 1936 which involved 200 unemployed Tyneside shipyard workers walking from Jarrow to London.

Q What strengths did Stanley Baldwin's personal qualities bring to the National government?

THE ABDICATION CRISIS, 1936 was precipitated by the wish of Edward VIII to marry Mrs Wallis Simpson, an American divorcée. Baldwin advised the King that to do so would not be compatible with his position as head of the Church of England, which did not recognise divorce. In December 1936, after just 325 days as uncrowned King, Edward put his personal desires before his sense of duty and announced his abdication. Six months later he married the woman whom, he told the nation in his abdication broadcast, he could not live without.

ACTIVITY

'Noisy but ineffectual' – this description was applied to both the Communist Party and the BUF. Why was it that neither of the two extremist parties in Britain gained any substantial following the 1930s? In organising your ideas on this, you need to consider the economic conditions as described in section 6, as well as the political developments covered in section 7.

Summary – Britain Between the Wars, 1918–39

Year	Conservatives	Liberals	Labour
1918–22	Continued to serve in Lloyd George's Coalition	Lloyd George won Coupon Election and formed peacetime Coalition	Party divided over support of Lloyd George
1922	The Party voted to abandon Lloyd George – Bonar Law becomes PM	Heavy defeat for Party in General Election	Made major gains in election
1923	Stanley Baldwin became PM – Party performed poorly in election	Party formally reunited under Asquith	
1924			Ramsay MacDonald formed first Labour government
1924–29	Baldwin headed Conservative government		
1926		Asquith retired – Lloyd George became Party leader	
1929–31			Second Labour government overtaken by financial crisis
1931	Party joined MacDonald in National government	Party divided over support for National government	Ramsay MacDonald 'betrayed' his Party to form National government – Arthur Henderson elected Party leader
1931–35			Ramsay MacDonald led National government
1935–37	Baldwin leader of National government		
1937–40	Neville Chamberlain leader of National government		

▼ Working on Britain Between the Wars, 1918–39

The Summary provides the basis for structuring your study. It was suggested in the 'Points to consider' section that a logical way to examine the period is to take the central theme of how the parties reacted to the important social and economic issues of the time. Using that as your base, you can construct your notes around the key issues and activities as they appear in the chapter. The following questions will help you:

1 Why, having dominated the pre-war period, was the Liberal Party never again in office after 1916?
2 Why did Conservatives hold office for so long between 1922 and 1939?
3 Why did the Labour Party replace the Liberals as the second largest political party between the wars?
4 Why did Britain experience serious economic difficulties between the wars and what effect did these difficulties have?

Answering Extended Writing and Essay Question on Britain Between the Wars, 1918–39

Types of question	Examples of typical questions
Structured questions (these usually have such openings as 'Describe...', 'Describe how...', 'Show how...', 'In what ways did?...' 'Describe the ways in which...'	1 Describe the difficulties faced by Lloyd George as leader of the peacetime Coalition, 1918–22. 2 Describe how Lloyd George attempted to deal with the problems in Ireland between 1916 and 1922. 3 Describe the ways in which Stanley Baldwin's government prepared for the General Strike of 1926 and dealt with it when it came. 4 In what ways did the economic depression affect Britain between the wars?
Questions on *causes* usually begin with leads such as: 'Why did ... ?', 'Explain why ... ', 'Account for ... '.	5 Why did the Conservatives abandon Lloyd George's Coalition in 1922? 6 Explain why the industrial depression that began in the USA in the late 1920s had a major influence on Britain's economy. 7 Explain why Ramsay MacDonald was so unpopular with the Labour Party after 1931. 8 Account for the decline of the Liberal Party between the wars. 9 Explain why the National government was in office for so long in the 1930s.

Types of question	Examples of typical questions
Questions calling for *historical judgement* usually take such forms as 'How far do you agree that ... ?', 'Examine the validity of the statement that ... ', 'How valid do you find the view that ... ?'	**10** How far do you agree that Lloyd George was the prisoner of the Conservatives during the period of the Coalition government, 1918–22? **11** Examine the validity of the statement that the General Strike of 1926 was 'an avoidable folly'. **12** How valid do you find the view that 'Ramsay MacDonald handled the financial and political crisis of 1931 as best he could he in the circumstances'?

Answering Source-Based Questions on Britain Between the Wars, 1918–39

In tackling questions on sources you need to understand what the examiners are expecting of you. The following exercise illustrates the type of questions that are set. It is on the theme of Lloyd George's attempt to resolve Anglo-Irish difficulties over Ulster. Re-read section 2 of this chapter and then study:

Source A, the statement of the Cork jury, on page 58,

Source B, the extract from the Treaty on page 59,

Source C, De Valera's statement, on page 60.

▼ QUESTIONS ON SOURCES

1. What can you learn from Source A about the attitude of the Cork jury towards British policy in Ireland in 1920? **(5 marks)**

2. Using your own knowledge, explain why Nationalists in Ireland objected to the oath of loyalty, as given in Source B. **(8 marks)**

3. What aspects of the Treaty, as quoted in Source B, are rejected by De Valera in Source C? **(10 marks)**

4. How valuable are these sources to the historian who is studying the importance of the Anglo-Irish Treaty of 1921? **(12 marks)**

5. Explain how these sources help to you to understand the Anglo-Irish question in the period 1914–22. **(15 marks)**

Points to note about the questions

Question 1 This tests your *comprehension*. It asks you to show that you have understood what is in the source. There is no need to bring your own knowledge into your answer.

Question 2 This is a *'stimulus'* question. It asks you to use your own knowledge to explain an aspect of the Anglo-Irish issue that you already know about.

Question 3 This is a *'cross referencing'* question. It requires you to compare the content of two sources and reach a conclusion based on the comparison.

Question 4 This is an *evaluation* question. It asks you to judge the usefulness of the sources.

Question 5 This is a *'lead-out'* question. It asks you to use the sources and your own knowledge to construct a historical explanation.

Source-based questions nearly always fall into one of these five categories. Get used to grasping exactly what the different types of question are asking you to do. Do check the mark allocation. This will tell you how important the question is and how long you need to spend on it.

Further Reading

Books in the Access to History series

Britain: Domestic Politics, 1918–1939 by Robert Pearce covers the political struggles of the interwar years while the same author's *Industrial Relations and the Economy: 1900–39* decribes the economic problems of the time. The Anglo-Irish question is treated in detail in *Great Britain and the Irish Question 1800–1922* by Paul Adelman.

General

There are valuable up-to-date assessments of Lloyd George, Ramsay MacDonald, Baldwin and Neville Chamberlain in *Modern British Statesmen 1867–1945* edited by Richard Kelly and John Cantrell (Manchester UP, 1997). *The Rise of the Labour Party, 1880–1945* (1996), *The Decline of the Liberal Party* (1995) both by Paul Adelman, and *The Conservative Party and British Politics* by Stuart Ball (1995), (all three published by Longman) are very helpful studies of the main parties. *Lloyd George and the Liberal Dilemma* by Michael Lynch (Hodder & Stoughton, 1993) examines Lloyd George's part in the decline of the Liberals. Authoritative works on the whole period are *The Conservative Party From Peel to Major* by Robert Blake (Arrow Books, 1997) and *The Conservative Century, The Conservative Party Since 1900* by Anthony Seldon and Stuart Ball (OUP, 1994). Two important books on the Liberal decline are *The Downfall of the Liberal Party 1914—35* by Trevor Wilson (Collins, 1966) and *The Liberal Party: Triumph and Disintegration, 1886–1929* by G.R. Searle (Macmillan, 1992). Still the best book for students on the General Strike is *The General Strike* by Margaret Morris (Penguin, 1976) but there is also a committed and entertaining pro-union account in *The General Strike of 1926* by R.A. Florey (Calder, 1980). Useful short introductions to the Anglo-Irish question are *Home Rule and the Irish Question* by Grenfell Morton (Longman, 1980) and

Ireland and England 1798–1922 by Joe Finn and Michael Lynch (Hodder & Stoughton, 1995). The outstanding study of the question is *Modern Ireland 1600–1972* by R.F. Foster (Penguin, 1988). A work which will prove very helpful as a source of reference throughout this book is *The Complete A–Z 19th & 20th Century British History Handbook* by Eric Evans (Hodder & Stoughton, 1998). An outstanding work by an outstanding British social historian, which covers many of the themes in this chapter, is *A History of the Modern British Isles 1914–1999* by Arthur Marwivk (Blackwell, 2000).

BRITAIN'S FOREIGN POLICY, 1918–39

CHAPTER 4

POINTS TO CONSIDER

In 1939, only 21 years after the 1914–18 conflict, which had been called the 'war to end wars', Europe was again at war. This gives the intervening years a tragic quality as if they were heading inevitably for disaster. But that is a view that comes with hindsight. Until 1939 arrived few people in Britain expected another war so soon. That, indeed, is the key to British foreign affairs in this period. So appalling was the memory of the Great War that politicians devoted themselves to pursuing policies that they believed would prevent war. The reasons why they failed are the themes of this chapter. We will be studying the contribution Britain made to the peace settlement of 1919, its commitment to peace through a policy of international collective security, and its efforts, when this policy appeared to have failed, to preserve peace through appeasement. The attempt to appease Germany was highly controversial at the time and continues to arouse debate among historians. Aspects of this controversy are studied in the final section of the chapter.

1 Britain and the Peacemaking

In the election campaign that followed the armistice in 1918 (see page 45), Lloyd George, sensing the strength of anti-German feelings in Britain, promised to punish the defeated enemy with great severity. He did this in order to maintain the popularity of his Coalition government.

However, such talk flew in the face of Lloyd George's own better judgement. He reasoned that the best hope for a lasting peace in Europe was to avoid leaving Germany with a permanent sense of grievance. At the Versailles Peace Conference, in the meetings of the **'Big Four'**, he tried to hold the balance between President Woodrow Wilson's American idealism and Clemenceau's French desire for revenge. Lloyd George believed that it made no sense to impose a humiliating peace settlement on Germany. He was opposed to the French demand for heavy war reparations and he argued against too much German territory being seized. He also prophesied, accurately as it turned out, that the victor nations would be unwilling in the future to risk war in defence of an unjust treaty.

> **ISSUE:**
> **What were Britain's real objectives at the Paris Peace Conference in 1919?**

> **THE BIG FOUR**
> All the Allies who had fought against Germany were represented at the Versailles peace talks, but the dominant bloc responsible for the final Treaty in June 1919 were the USA (led by Woodrow Wilson), France (led by Clemenceau), Italy (led by Orlando) and Britain (led by Lloyd George). In fact, since Italy's influence can be largely discounted, it would be more accurate to refer to the 'Big Three'.

The attitude of the British delegation at Versailles was summarised in the draft document drawn up by its secretary.

Source A From a memorandum written by Sir Maurice Hankey, Secretary to the British Delegation at Versailles, 19 March 1919.

Principles for a German Treaty

First: The enormity of their crimes must be brought home to the German people.

Second: Means ought to be found for providing them with the physical force for resisting Bolshevism.

Third: We ought to try and build up the self respect of the German people so that they may resist the approach of Bolshevism and believe in their own civilisation rather than in that which comes from Russia.

BOLSHEVISM
In 1917, the Bolsheviks (Marxist revolutionaries) had take power in Russia in the October Revolution. The new government under Lenin had torn up Russia's existing treaties, and had committed the unforgivable sin, in Allied eyes, of making a separate peace with Germany at Brest-Litovsk in March 1918. At the very time of the peacemaking at Versailles, a bitter civil war was being fought in Russia with Allied forces assisting the Whites (anti-Bolsheviks) against the Reds (pro-Bolsheviks).

Q Why did Lloyd George have only limited success at Versailles?

Q What was the main legacy of the Versailles settlement?

The British delegation used Hankey's memorandum as their guide in approaching the peace talks. The first point anticipated the most disputed clause in the final Treaty, that relating to Germany's 'war-guilt'. But beyond that, the British attitude as expressed in the principles was not a harsh one. Indeed, the striking feature of the second and third points is the desire to preserve the strength of Germany so that it could resist **Bolshevism**. In a real sense, Bolshevik Russia had replaced Germany as the great enemy, hence Britain's struggle with France at Versailles to prevent her being too severe on Germany.

Despite his status as a world statesman and his skilful diplomacy at Versailles, Lloyd George was only partially successful in the negotiations. He was unable to prevent heavy reparations being imposed on Germany or to stop the forcible incorporation of a number of German peoples into neighbouring foreign states. The Peace Settlement of 1919 did not so much mark an agreement between the victors as a compromise between the French desire for revenge and the American concept of a just peace, with Britain somewhere in the middle urging moderation. The French concern was to obtain a settlement that would leave Germany so reduced that it would never again be able to threaten France. But Britain had no wish to see Germany permanently disadvantaged. Quite the contrary; for Lloyd George the overriding consideration was that Germany be allowed to recover so as to provide a balance to French dominance in Europe.

Events were to show that the Versailles settlement created as many problems as it solved. The key issue was what was often called 'the German Question'. The 1919 settlement imposed on Germany left it embittered. It was not simply a matter of the loss of its colonies or the dismantling of its armed forces. What caused the greatest resentment among Germans was their being forced to accept the notorious 'war

The Main Terms of the Treaty of Versailles, 1919

▼ Germany returned Alsace-Lorraine to France.

▼ The Rhineland was demilitarised and placed under Allied occupation for 15 years.

▼ The Saar coalfields were placed under international control.

▼ Germany lost West Prussia and Posen to Poland; this had the effect of dividing East Prussia from the rest of Germany by the Polish 'corridor'.

▼ Danzig, formerly German, was declared an international city.

▼ These territorial changes deprived Germany of four million people.

▼ Germany had to surrender all its overseas colonies.

▼ Germany was deprived of its warships and aircraft and had its army limited to 100,000.

▼ Financial reparations, eventually amounting to £6.6 billion, were imposed on Germany.

▼ Germany had to accept the 'war guilt' clause, which asserted that the war had been deliberately brought about by Germany and its Allies.

▼ A League of Nations was set up as a permanent body for resolving international disputes.

Figure 16 Map of Europe showing the main territorial changes resulting from the Versailles settlement, 1919.

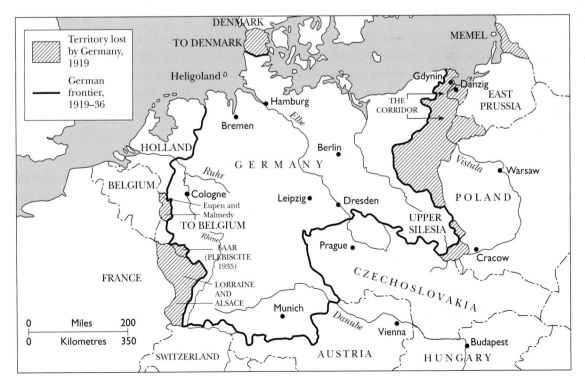

SELF-DETERMINATION

The right of a people to choose its own government and determine its own boundaries. The achievement of this principle had been one of the Allies' war aims and was a guiding aim in the redrawing of the map of Europe at Versailles. The anomaly was that the principle was not extended to the peoples of the defeated nations.

ISSUES:

How did Britain come to be involved in the Palestine question? Why did it cause Britain such problems?

ZIONISM

Confronted by growing anti-Semitism in the late-nineteenth century, world Jewry began to demand a Jewish national homeland in Palestine, a return to the biblical land of Zion. Theodor Herzl, a Hungarian Jew, convened the first Zionist Congress in 1897. In Britain the outstanding Zionist was Chaim Weizmann, destined to become the first President of Israel in 1948.

Source B From a letter by Arthur Balfour, the British Foreign Secretary to Lord Rothschild, of the British Zionist Federation, 2 November 1917.

guilt' clause and to agree to make huge reparations to the Allies for war damage. The loss of German territory in Europe was not extensive geographically but it did result in large numbers of German people being under alien rule after 1919. This, as Germany was quick to point out, contradicted the Versailles Treaty, which had aimed to shape post-war Europe on the principle of **self-determination**. At Versailles Lloyd George described the maintenance of future peace in Europe as being 'dependent upon there being no causes of exasperation to the vanquished which will leave them violently seeking redress'. He also warned the other Allies that nothing was more calculated to bring about a new war in Europe 'than that the German people should be surrounded by a number of smaller states each of them containing large numbers of Germans all clamouring for reunion'.

a) Britain and the League of Nations' Mandates

An important result of the acceptance of the principle of self-determination at Versailles was that the League of Nations became eager to encourage independence in the regions once controlled by the defeated German and Turkish empires. However, the League judged that many of the areas claiming independence in the post-war world were too vulnerable to become states immediately. Its solution was the mandate system. The League invited those nations among the victors with obvious geographical or historical ties to the areas claiming independence to take on a mandate to act as protectors until self-determination became possible. Under this scheme, Palestine and Mesopotamia (later Iraq) became British mandates. These were sensitive areas of the Middle East; the Palestine mandate, in particular, was to cause Britain major problems.

Palestine was inhabited by both and Arabs and Jews. They looked upon Britain's mandate as an obstacle in the path of their nationalist ambitions. In the twentieth century, Palestine, the Holy Land of biblical times, became a battle ground between **Zionism** and **Arab nationalism**. Britain had already been caught up in this struggle when it issued the Balfour Declaration in 1917.

His Majesty's Government view with favour the establishment in Palestine of a national home for the Jewish people, and will use their best endeavours to facilitate the achievement of this object, it being clearly understood that nothing shall be done which may prejudice the civil and religious rights of existing non-Jewish communities in Palestine, or the rights and political status enjoyed by Jews in any other country.

Britain's aim in issuing the Declaration had been to retain the support of world Jewry for the Allies in the First World War by accepting the Zionist demand for a homeland. At the same time it tried to calm Arab fears by suggesting that any settlement would leave untouched the rights of non-Jews in Palestine. In its eagerness to gain both Jewish and Arab assistance in the war against Germany, Britain had given contradictory promises to the two peoples. The consequence of this soon became evident. Violence followed as the Arabs resisted the inflow of Jews into the area. Under its League of Nations' mandate Britain had the responsibility for overseeing Jewish immigration into Palestine. British forces tried to keep the peace between the two sides but found themselves caught in the middle and resented by both Jews and Arabs. As Table 18 shows, Jewish immigration grew remarkably quickly in the 1920s and 1930s, but not fast enough for Zionists.

> ### ARAB NATIONALISM
> The First World War hastened the collapse of the tottering Turkish Empire. This encouraged large numbers of Arabs in North Africa and the Near East to assert their national and regional independence, a movement not dissimilar in character from Zionism, though bitterly opposed to it.

Figure 17 Map showing the sensitive areas of the Middle East.

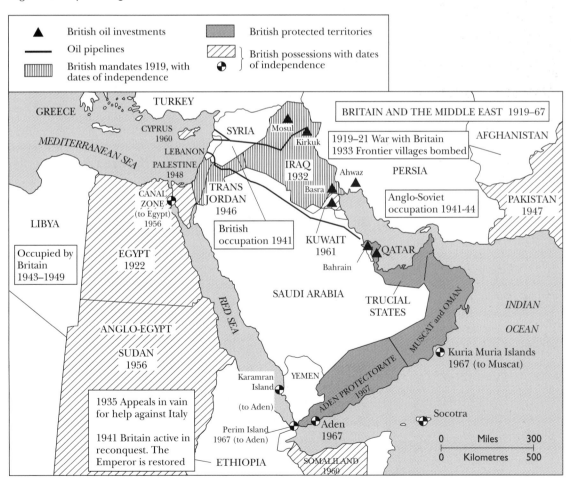

Table 18 Arab and Jewish populations in Palestine.

	1922	1932	1937	1940	1949
Arabs	590,000	770,000	850,000	950,000	250,000
Jews	84,000	180,000	400,000	460,000	720,000

A British proposal in 1937 to partition Palestine between Arabs and Jews was rejected by both sides. In the hope of achieving a compromise, the British government announced in 1939 that Jewish immigration would end after a final quota of 75,000 had been permitted to enter. But what complicated British efforts to balance the Arab-Jewish population were events in Europe. In the 1930s Adolf Hitler's Nazi regime began a fierce persecution of the Jews in Germany. Palestine was now not merely a home but a refuge. This explains the bitterness of the condemnations of British policy by Zionists, such as Golda Meir, a young Russian-American Jewess, who was to become Prime Minister of Israel in 1967.

Source C From a public protest by Golda Meir of the Zionist Federation, 1939.

> Our chief accusation against the government and its policy is that it forced us to sit here helplessly at a time when we were convinced that we could have rescued not millions but probably hundreds of thousands of Jews. We are convinced that due to this government policy, Jews went to their deaths because they were not allowed to enter the one country where they could have been saved.

When Britain went to war in Europe in September 1939, the Palestine question was still unresolved.

b) Britain and Bolshevik Russia

Britain had more success in regard to another demanding post-war question – its relations with Russia. Having earlier been an opponent of the Bolshevik regime, Lloyd George showed considerable skill in arranging a trade agreement between Britain and Soviet Russia in 1921 and preparing the ground for the international recognition of the new state. Unlike Churchill, who was an ardent anti-Bolshevik on principle, Lloyd George had opposed the Russian revolutionaries solely because they had withdrawn from the war against Germany. Once Germany had been defeated, Lloyd George was prepared to be more understanding of Lenin's government. It is true that he was responsible for sending British troops to Russia at the time of the Civil War between the Reds and the Whites (1918–20), but he claimed that it had never been his intention to interfere in the internal affairs of Russia; his only purpose was to

KEY EPISODES IN ANGLO-SOVIET RELATIONS

1918 –20 British forces fought in Russia against the Bolsheviks;

1921 Anglo-Soviet trade agreement signed;.

1924 Labour government gave diplomatic recognition to USSR; Conservative government withdrew recognition following the Zinoviev letter incident;

1926 British government accused the Soviet Union of promoting the General Strike;

1929 Labour government restored recognition of USSR.; new trade agreement signed;

1938 Stalin regarded the Munich agreement as an anti-Soviet move;

1939 British government did not respond to Soviet proposals for an Anglo-Russian alliance.

recover the valuable war materials Britain had previously shipped to imperial Russia.

2 Collective Security

After 1918 there was a natural reluctance among the British to become too closely involved in European affairs. Memories of the war and its horrors induced a general feeling that foreign policy was best when it was least active. Should problems arise it was hoped that Britain would be able to rely on the principle of collective security – the idea that nations would not have to act individually but would be able to protect themselves by joint action. A key aspect of this was the belief in the ability of the new international peacekeeping body, the League of Nations, to resolve international problems. Until well into the 1930s faith in collective security and in the League was a power-ful influence on the conduct of British foreign affairs. In the 1920s this faith did not seem entirely misplaced. Although there were occa-sional crises such as **the Chanak affair**, Britain was able to remain relatively detached from European problems.

The League of Nations

was the brainchild of President Woodrow Wilson and was the most idealistic feature of the post-war settlement. Article X, the key clause in the Covenant of the League, committed member states to act collectively to maintain the independence of each individual member. In the event of aggression against a member state, the Council of the League could impose various diplomat-ic and economic sanctions against the aggressor. Optimists believed that this would mean the end of international conflict. However, since the League had no military forces at its disposal it could not take armed action. A further crippling weakness was that, despite Woodrow Wilson's efforts, the USA, the world's most powerful nation, did not ratify the Covenant and never became a member of the League.

THE CHANAK AFFAIR, 1922
arose from the resentment of the defeated Turks at the dismemberment of their country under the terms of the Peace Treaty of Sèvres (1920). Under their new leader, Mustapha Kemal (Kemal Ataturk), the Turks threatened to take back by force the territories they had lost to their old enemy Greece. Lloyd George sided with the Greeks against their former oppressors. In September 1922 he ordered British reinforcements to be sent to Chanak on the Dardanelles, a likely area of confrontation. War threat-ened, but diplomacy eventu-ally prevailed and the Turks withdrew. At home, Lloyd George's action was con-demned by many Conservatives as an irres-ponsible piece of sabre rattling that might well have led to a major conflict.

Why did unrest persist in Europe after 1919?

THE WEIMAR REPUBLIC

replaced the second German empire in 1918. It took its name from the town of Weimar where the government relocated itself. The Weimar Republic had considerable success in the 1920s in re-establishing Germany as a responsible nation.

THE LOCARNO TREATY, 1925

An agreement, signed by France, Germany, Britain, Italy and Belgium, which confirmed Germany's western borders and accepted that the Rhineland should remain demilitarised. The agreement was widely regarded at the time as a final settlement of the war and as marking a new age of European peace.

Source D From *From Sarajevo to Potsdam* by A.J.P. Taylor, 1966.

Resentment with the peace settlement was not restricted to the defeated nations. Italy, as an enticement to her to enter the war, had been promised large additions of territory at the expense of the German, Austrian and Turkish Empires when the post-war settlement came to be made. The Allies did not keep these promises; Italian anger over this betrayal was exploited by Benito Mussolini and the Fascists, who came to power in 1922. Under Mussolini, the Italians began to plan the take-over of Abyssinia as compensation for what they had been denied at Versailles.

So it was that German and Italian bitterness became a major factor of interwar politics. Yet it is arguable that the crises that were to arise from German and Italian expansionism might not have occurred had not Europe undergone the economic depression that began in the late 1920s. Ten years after the Versailles Treaty, Europe appeared to have recovered from the worst effects of the war. Germany had stabilised itself under **the Weimar Republic** and **the Locarno Treaty** seemed to have pointed the way to international harmony.

These promising developments were undermined by the severity of the economic depression which begin in 1929 (see page 68) and allowed all the old hostilities and fears to resurface. In Germany it brought the Nazis from the fringe to the centre of politics and intensified the clash between Right and Left in all the European states. Renewed feelings of insecurity increased international suspicions. The problems that had dogged the peacemakers in 1919 re-emerged. Here it is important to stress that the decision of the USA not to join the League of Nations and its determination to avoid involvement in European affairs left a large gap in the international scene. The absence of the world's strongest nation meant that what in all probability would have been its moderating influence was not exercised on European developments.

The United States was in a frenzy of isolationism, reinforced by the Great Depression.

ACTIVITY

Having re-read section 2, write brief comments to show that you understand the meaning or the importance of the following: the principle of collective security, the Chanak Affair, the Locarno Treaty, the USA's non-membership of the League of Nations.

3 The Failure of Collective Security

ISSUE:
Was Britain's pursuit of collective security ever a realistic policy?

The outstanding feature of British policy towards Europe between the wars was the reluctance to take military action. It was not until 1939 that Britain was prepared to intervene forcibly. The reasons for Britain's hesitancy, which have long been a matter of historical argument, are the subject matter of the next two sections. One way of understanding Britain's approach is to see it as **appeasement**. This term is usually applied specifically to the period after 1936 when Britain had to deal with the problem of German expansion under Hitler, but as the following section indicates appeasement as a policy had begun earlier.

From 1932 onwards Italy's aggressive designs in north Africa became increasingly apparent. France and Britain were disturbed by this development but their response was complicated by their attitude to the German question. Hitler, the German Chancellor, who had led his Nazi party to power in 1933, began to re-arm Germany. This made the French and British reluctant to take too firm a line in opposing Mussolini over Abyssinia since they needed Italy's co-operation if they were to present a united front to Germany. This led to the **Stresa Front** and the **Hoare–Laval Pact** being formed in 1935.

The plain truth was that in 1935 Britain was not physically ready for serious military action. It had allowed its armed forces to run down. The army's troop numbers had fallen from three and a half million in 1919 to less than 200,000 in 1930. Defence spending which had stood at £700 million in 1920 had dropped to £115 million in 1935. The effects of this are evident in the accompanying source.

> We had an important meeting of the Chiefs of Staff this afternoon to draw up our report as to the measures to be taken in view of the Mediterranean situation. I was surprised to find how very unready the other two Services were and how long it would take them before they could give any effective resistance to Italian action by land or air. The Naval situation is bad enough, as you are well aware … Our feeling is that everything possible should be done to avoid precipitate hostilities with Italy until we are more ready. It would be a serious business if the great League of Nations, having at last agreed to act together, was able to be flouted militarily by the nation whom it was trying to coerce. The Navy will, of course, do its best provided you give us time and enough warning, but it would be a dangerous prospect for us to go to war with Italy with the British Fleet immobilised and the Home Fleet on leave and scattered. War is not a light measure which we can go into blindfold trusting to luck.

APPEASEMENT

starts from the conviction that the main duty of government is to avoid war. To that end all reasonable measures short of war should be considered. If this means granting an aggressor some of his demands in order to satisfy him, that is preferable to armed conflict.

THE STRESA FRONT, 1935

was an agreement signed at Stresa between Britain, France and Italy. It produced little beyond a general re-commitment to the Locarno principles and a mild reprimand of Germany for its disregard of Versailles in rearming. In fact the main outcome of Stresa was that it encouraged Mussolini to think that France and Britain would not actively oppose his take-over of Abyssinia.

Q Why was Britain not prepared to act more firmly over Abyssinia?

Source E From the First Sea Lord, Admiral Sir A. Ernle Chatfield to Sir Robert Vansittart, Head of the Foreign Office, 8 August 1935.

Chatfield's major concern was that military weakness made it impossible for Britain to contemplate war with Italy. But there was an influential section of opinion which opposed the idea of war not on grounds of military weakness but because they ruled out war on Britain's part altogether. A major voice in this regard was the leader of the Labour Party, Clement Attlee. Referring to the Italian crisis in particular but expressing a general approach to international questions, Attlee told the Commons:

Source F From a speech of Clement Attlee in the House of Commons, May 1935.

> We stand for collective security through the League of Nations. We reject the use of force as an instrument of policy. Our policy is not one of seeking security through rearmament but through disarmament. Our aim is the reduction of armaments, and then the complete abolition of all national armaments under the League.

THE HOARE–LAVAL PACT, 1935

appeared to justify Mussolini's judgement at Stresa. Samuel Hoare and Pierre Laval, the respective British and French Foreign ministers, negotiated a settlement, which, with the aim of ending hostilities in Africa, proposed that two-thirds of Abyssinia be ceded to the Italians, leaving the native people with the remaining impoverished third.

When the details of the concessions to Italy in the **Hoare–Laval Pact** became fully known there was uproar in parliament. To limit the political damage, the Prime Minister, Stanley Baldwin, asked Hoare to resign. In his resignation speech in the Commons, Hoare claimed to have been deeply disturbed by the thought that Abyssinians might have gained a false expectation of Britain's capacity to help them. He referred to the weakness of the British forces and the unwillingness of any other country to join Britain in a military engagement. In the circumstances there had been no alternative to the Pact with France.

> I have been terrified that we might lead Abyssinia on to think that the League could do more than it can do, that in the end we should find a terrible moment of disillusionment in which it might be that Abyssinia would be destroyed altogether as an independent State. There is the British Fleet in the Mediterranean, there are the British reinforcements in Egypt, in Malta and Aden. Not a ship, not a machine, not a man has been moved by any other member state.

Source G From a speech by Sir Samuel Hoare in the House of Commons, December 1935.

What is notable about Sources E to G is their common refusal to contemplate war as a possible or permissible extension of British policy. In Attlee's case it was a moral argument; in Chatfield's it was an argument from strategic necessity; for Hoare it was the demand of international realities.

Attlee's assertion is an interesting example of a basic paradox in British attitudes at this time. He declared his support for the League of Nations and collective security, but at the same time he rejected the use of force and appealed for disarmament. Attlee's position was contradictory. If collective security was to be workable, it had to encompass the use of force, albeit internationally organised and employed only as a last resort. The inability of other anti-war groups to appreciate this was expressed in such events as the **'King and Country' debate** in 1933 and the **Peace Ballot** of 1935.

ACTIVITY

Having read section 3, give your view on whether the belief in collective security was realistic or unrealistic. Points to consider:

▼ Was there a genuine alternative to the policy followed by Hoare over the Abyssinian question?
▼ How important was the absence of the USA from the League?
▼ How grave a weakness was the League's lack of an army?

---

4 Appeasement and the Coming of War

Appeasement is most closely associated with the name of Neville Chamberlain but it is important to remember that the policy had already begun under Ramsay MacDonald and Stanley Baldwin, his predecessors as National government Prime Ministers. They had been opposed to rearmament, had not challenged Italian aggression in Abyssinia, had failed to resist the German re-occupation of the Rhineland, and together with the French had adopted a non-interventionist policy towards the **Spanish Civil War**.

Those critics who believed that the National government's foreign-policymakers had been weak and ineffectual charged them with being '**guilty men**'. The substance of the accusation was that Baldwin

---

The German Re-occupation of the Rhineland, 1936

The Versailles Treaty had stipulated that the areas on both banks of the Rhine should be demilitarised. This was in response to the demands by France that its eastern frontier should be made safe from German aggression. However, in 1936 Hitler sent in troops to reclaim the region. He fully expected the French and British to resist and had given instructions for his troops to withdraw should this happen. In the event, apart from formal diplomatic protests, France and Britain did nothing.

THE PEACE BALLOT, 1935

In a house-to-house canvass organised by the League of Nations Union, eleven and half million people answered a series of questions regarding their views on disarmament. Most responded strongly in favour of Britain's remaining a member of the League of Nations and backed the notion of an 'all-round reduction of armaments'. To arguably the most important question, whether they supported international armed resistance against an aggressor, nearly seven million replied yes, more than two million said no, with another two million abstaining.

ISSUES:
How responsible was Britain for the outbreak of a European war in 1939?
Need Britain have gone to war in 1939?

THE 'KING AND COUNTRY' DEBATE, 1933

In February 1933 the Oxford Union voted by a large majority in favour of the resolution 'That this House will in no circumstances fight for its King and Country'. While the opinion of Oxford University students was unimportant in itself, the debate was interpreted by many as evidence of the powerful pacifism that prevailed in the country at large.

GERMAN AGGRANDISEMENT UNDER HITLER, 1933–39

1933 Germany withdrew from disarmament talks at Geneva and from the League of Nations;

1935 Hitler re-introduced conscription and began to expand Germany's armed services in defiance of 1919 restrictions;

1936 German troops re-occupied the Rhineland; Rome-Berlin Axis laid basis for military co-operation with Fascist Italy; the Axis was expanded into **anti-Comintern Pact** with the inclusion of Japan;

1938 the 'Anschluss' incorporated Austria into the German Reich; Sudetenland area of Czechoslovakia occupied by Germany;

1939 remainder of Czechoslovakia seized; the Nazi-Soviet Pact; Germany invaded Poland.

THE ANTI-COMINTERN PACT, 1936

The Comintern was the Soviet organisation for promoting international Communist revolution. In 1936, the Axis powers – Germany, Italy and Japan – declared their common opposition to the Comintern and the USSR. Although Germany still had designs on regaining the Chinese territory lost at Versailles, it was ready to give the Japanese a free hand in their conquest of China. The anti-Comintern Pact lapsed with the signing of the Nazi-Soviet Pact in August 1939.

The Spanish Civil War, 1936–39

In 1936 General Franco led his Nationalist forces, representing Catholic conservative Spain, in rebellion against the Republican government, which had the support of a combination of anarchists, regional separatists and Communists. A bitter three-year conflict followed. Italian and German forces aided Franco's armies, while the USSR gave support to the Republicans. Although a significant number of left-wing volunteers joined the International Brigade to fight for the Republic and a smaller number on the right went to support Franco, the British government remained officially neutral throughout the struggle, which was eventually won by the Nationalists.

Figure 18 Map showing German aggrandisement between 1933 and 1939.

and Chamberlain and their Foreign Office advisers, by their failure to prevent German rearmament, their acceptance of the German occupation of the Rhineland, and their capitulation to German demands over Czechoslovakia at Munich, had convinced Hitler that

Britain lacked the will to resist on any issue. Thus he had no need to hesitate about occupying **Poland** in 1939, as there was no more reason for Britain to defend the Poles than there had been to defend the Czechs a year earlier. Britain's gesture towards upholding the Versailles settlement, by guaranteeing to protect Poland, failed because it came too late; it contradicted the previous British policy. Had the guarantee been given earlier, it would have warned Germany that there were limits to British patience. However, in the circumstances, Britain's commitment to Poland in 1939 was arbitrary, since in moral terms Poland's case was no stronger than Czechoslovakia's had been.

The Munich Settlement, 1938

The Sudetenland was overwhelmingly German, but under the Versailles Treaty it had been made a part of the newly created state of Czechoslovakia. Hitler eagerly exploited the demand of the three million Sudeten Germans for 'self-determination', the right to be reincorporated into Germany. He subjected the Czech government to a set of impossible demands. A series of meetings between Hitler and Chamberlain in 1938 culminated in the Munich agreement of September. Britain, France and Italy acknowledged Germany's claims and the Czechs were forced to accept the loss of the Sudetenland. This averted the immediate threat of war. However, the following year Hitler ignored the Munich settlement and ordered the German occupation of Bohemia and Moravia, a seizure that effectively destroyed the Czechoslovak state.

The 'guilty men' charge included the condemnation of Britain's leaders for undermining Soviet-British relations, which if properly developed could have acted as a counter-weight to the growth of Germany. From the time of the Nazis' coming to power in Germany in 1933, Stalin had endeavoured to persuade Britain and France into forming a defensive alliance with the USSR against the Third Reich. But his overtures were ignored. This led him to interpret the Munich agreement as a cover under which the capitalist powers of Western Europe had plotted to attack the Soviet Union. To pre-empt the threatened assault Stalin had entered into **the Nazi-Soviet Pact** in 1939. This alliance gave Hitler a free hand to expand westward since he had now secured Germany's Eastern front. So, concludes the argument, appeasement had made eventual war with Germany more, not less, likely.

How was appeasement applied in relation to Germany?

THE 'GUILTY MEN'
The term was first used as the title of a pamphlet published in 1940 by a group of radical critics of the National government's appeasement policy. The group, which used the pseudonym 'Cato', included Michael Foot, later to be a leader of the Labour Party.

POLAND
In March 1939, Germany ignored the Munich agreement and took over the rest of Czechoslovakia. It was at this point that Britain gave formal guarantees that it would protect Poland in the event of a German invasion, which now looked certain. The guarantees were essentially a gesture since Britain simply did not have the physical means to defend Poland in 1939. Nonetheless, it was in accordance with these guarantees that Britain declared war on Germany six months later.

THE FAILURE OF APPEASEMENT

1935 –36 Italy's attack on Abyssinia – the Hoare–Laval Pact allowed Italy to keep a large area of Abyssinia;

1936 German re-occupation of the Rhineland went unchallenged by France and Britain;

1936 –39 the Spanish Civil War – Britain remained neutral despite German and Italian assistance for Franco;

1938 March in defiance of the Versailles settlement German troops entered Austria and incorporated it into the Third Reich. Britain and France took no action; **September** at Munich Britain accepted Germany's seizure of the Sudetenland region of Czechoslovakia;

1939 March German forcibly took over the remainder of Czechoslovakia – this effectively marked the final failure of appeasement; Britain gave Poland protective guarantees against Germany; **September** The guarantees were honoured when Britain declared war on Germany following Hitler's occupation of Poland.

The Nazi–Soviet Pact, 1939

In August Ribbentrop and Molotov, the respective German and Soviet foreign secretaries, signed an agreement pledging their countries to remain at peace with each other for ten years. In secret proposals they also agreed that Germany and the Soviet Union would carve up Poland between them. This the two countries promptly proceeded to do. In the event, the ten-year peace did not even reach two years; in June 1941 Hitler unleashed 'Operation Barbarossa' against a stunned Stalin and the USSR.

When Chamberlain spoke to the nation on radio of his readiness to sacrifice the Sudetenland rather than risk war, his insularity was accepted by the majority of the British people as being the only proper response.

> How horrible, fantastic, incredible it is that we should be digging trenches and trying on gas-masks here because of a quarrel in a far-away country between people of whom we know nothing.

Source H From a BBC broadcast by Neville Chamberlain, 27 September 1938.

Figure 19 'Europe Can Look Forward to a Christmas of Peace'. Low's cartoon ironically depicts Hitler as a benign Father Christmas filling his sack with 'presents' for himself. Austria has already gone in and he is now dropping in Czechoslovakia. Poland is next.

5 The Debate Over Appeasement

ISSUES:
Was there a genuine alternative to appeasement?
Did appeasement deserve the fierce criticism it received?

For a generation after 1939 appeasement was a dirty word. The dominant view was that the failure to halt the expansion of Nazi Germany had been the result of a series of craven surrenders on the part of France and Britain. However, in the 1960s historians began to reconsider appeasement. They queried whether it could be simply dismissed as a policy of cowardice. Might it not have been that the political situation in Europe in the 1930s made some form of appeasement the only option? Revisionist scholars, taking their cue from A.J.P. Taylor's seminal study *The Origins of the Second World War* (1961), pointed out that appeasement was not an aberration in British foreign policy but was part of a logical progression of thought that went back at least to 1919. Basic to it was a profound horror of war, arising from memories of the ghastly struggle of 1914–18. Moreover there was a general belief, strengthened by newsreels of the terrible effects of the Japanese bombing of China, that a future war would be still more appalling since the civilian population would be at the mercy of aerial bombardment. Stanley Baldwin put this chillingly:

> I think it is well also for the man in the street to realise that there is no power on earth that can protect him from being bombed. Whatever people may tell him, the bomber will always get through.

Source I From a speech of Stanley Baldwin in the Commons, November 1932.

Since war was too horrible to contemplate, its avoidance became a demanding necessity. None of the political parties felt free to advocate a rearmament programme. Furthermore, in a time of economic depression, it was not easy to argue the merits of arms expenditure at the expense of welfare provision. Stanley Baldwin put this point very strongly:

> I put before the whole House my own views with *appalling frankness* … Supposing I had gone to the country and said that we must rearm, does anybody think that this pacific democracy would have rallied to the cry? I cannot think of anything that would have made the loss of the election from my point of view more certain.

Source J From a speech of Stanley Baldwin in the Commons, 12 November 1936.

Between the wars Britain had a general trust in the League of Nations and in collective security as the best safeguards against international threats. When, therefore, Chamberlain became Prime Minister, he did not initiate appeasement; it already existed as the received wisdom of the day. It is important to stress that Chamberlain was hugely popular immediately after Munich. Thanksgiving prayers

Q Why was Neville Chamberlain so popular in Britain after Munich?

were said in Westminster Abbey and Canterbury Cathedral, praising him as a saviour of world peace. Newsreel commentaries thanked God for Neville Chamberlain, to which cinema audiences responded with spontaneous applause.

Another defence of appeasement has been made by reference to Britain's military position in the 1930s. The truth was that Britain was overstretched; its overseas and imperial defence requirements were such that it could not fully meet its commitments. In this predicament, it was impossible for Britain to resist Germany by armed force. The British chiefs-of-staff frequently confided to the interwar governments that Britain was incapable of simultaneously defending its interests in the Far East, in the Mediterranean, and in Europe. Britain on its own did not have the resources to prevent the re-occupation of the Rhineland, the Anschluss, or the rape of Czechoslovakia. In such a predicament, avoidance of open conflict was the only option. As events showed when Britain did go to war in 1939, it was quite incapable of genuinely defending Poland.

Q Could Britain have resisted Germany militarily before 1939?

Given these factors, it is arguable that appeasement was not a choice but a necessity. It is this line of thought that informs the writings of the revisionist historians. One of their interesting emphases is on the ambiguous attitude of the political left towards war and disarmament. Many on the left who condemned Chamberlain and the other appeasers for not standing up to the aggressors had themselves vociferously opposed rearmament in the interwar period. In Britain, for example, the annual Labour Party Conference consistently passed resolutions condemning expenditure on arms. Yet when war came in 1939 the Party was very prompt to blame the government for Britain's not being prepared.

Another key consideration is that until the post-Munich period moderate political opinion was markedly sympathetic towards Germany. The harshness of the Versailles settlement in regard to Germany was commonly acknowledged as giving that country the right to redress its legitimate grievances. As even Winston Churchill acknowledged, it was arguable that the re-occupation of the Rhineland, the incorporation of Austria into the Third Reich, and the reclamation of the Sudetenland were all in keeping with the principle of self-determination which the Allies had made the basis of the peace talks in 1919.

Q What influence did British distrust of the USSR have on appeasement?

There was also an ideological dimension to the problem. Since 1917, Bolshevik Russia had espoused the cause of the violent overthrow of the capitalist nations of Europe. We now know that there had been no possibility of this. The Soviet Union did not have the strength, even if it had had the will. But at the time the threat seemed real enough and it was taken seriously in western Europe. That was why many in Britain welcomed the growth of a strong, anti-

Communist Germany. They saw it as a barrier to the spread of Bolshevism westward. The perceived Soviet menace predisposed Britain to being conciliatory towards Nazi Germany.

Summary of the Reasons for Britain's Appeasement of Germany

▽ The memories of the slaughter of 1914–18 created a powerful anti-war feeling in Britain.

▽ Many people put their faith in the League of Nations and backed the concept of collective security.

▽ A growing belief between the wars that Germany had been harshly treated in the Versailles settlement.

▽ A similar belief that according to the principle of self-determination Germany had the right to recover the German territories taken from it.

▽ Fear of Soviet Russia made Britain more tolerant of Nazi Germany.

▽ The same fear made it attractive to have Germany as a buffer state in central Europe.

▽ Anglo-French mutual suspicions made effective co-operation difficult.

▽ The cost of Britain's existing defence commitments discouraged further military expenditure.

▽ The USA's detachment from Europe meant Britain could not rely on American support.

▽ The armed services chiefs warned the government in the mid-1930s that Britain was already overstretched militarily and was incapable of fighting a major European war.

▽ The severe economic Depression made welfare spending a priority before rearmament.

Twenty years after the war's end, England's most provocative historian listed a set of reasons as to why war had come about:

> What caused the Second World War? There can be many answers: German grievances against the peace settlement of 1919 and the failure to redress them; failure to agree on a system of general controlled disarmament; failure to accept the principles of collective security and to operate them; fear of communism and, on the Soviet side, of capitalism, cutting across ordinary calculations of international policy; German strength, which destroyed the balance of power in Europe, and the resentment of German generals at their previous defeat; American aloofness from European affairs; Hitler's inordinate and unscrupulous ambition – a blanket explanation favoured by some historians; at the end perhaps only mutual bluff.

Why did Britain go to war in 1939?

Source K From *English History 1914–45* by A.J.P. Taylor, 1965.

ACTIVITIES

▼ Using the summary of Britain's appeasement policy towards Germany as a base, examine the debate over the issue. Who has the stronger case – the proponents of the 'guilty men' argument or the later revisionists?

▼ Re-read A.J.P. Taylor's survey of the reasons for war in 1939. Which of the reasons he gives do you regard as the most important? It would help if you put the list in ascending order of significance. Are there any points that you would add to his list?

▼ Working on Britain's Foreign Policy, 1918–39

Your first aim should be to develop a clear understanding of the development of British policy between the wars. Use the various boxes in the text and the Summary to gain an idea of the order of events. A sound chronology is basic to a study of history. The Issue and Activity boxes should help you highlight the principal areas of debate in regard to collective security and appeasement. Questions that will assist your re-reading are:

▽ What were British aims at the Versailles peace talks and how far were they achieved?

▽ What was meant by the principle of collective security? How did Britain try to put the principle in practice?

▽ What were the supporters of appeasement attempting to achieve? What have been the main criticisms of this policy?

Summary – Britain's Foreign Policy, 1918–39

Year	Conflict	Treaties and Agreements	Aim
1919		Treaty of Versailles	to establish stability in Europe by limiting French and German influence in post-war world
1918–20	British forces invaded Russia		to regain war supplies given to imperial Russia; to assist Whites against Reds
1921		Trade agreement with Bolshevik Russia	to ease relations with Russia
1922	British forces sent to Chanak		to support Greeks against a resurgent Turkey

Year	Conflict	Treaties and Agreements	Aim
1924		Labour government recognised USSR	to improve trade prospects
		Conservative government withdrew recognition	to snub USSR over the Zinoviev Letter
1925		Locarno Treaty	to guarantee Versailles border settlements and pledge Britain to the maintenance of peace
1929		Labour government recognised USSR	to restore Anglo-Soviet relations
1935	Italy's attack on Abyssinia	Hoare–Laval Pact	to resolve Abyssinian issue by granting concessions to Italy
1936	Spanish Civil War	Non-Intervention Agreement in regard to Spanish Civil War	to avoid being drawn into Spanish conflict
1938		Munich Agreement	to avoid war by appeasing Hitler by granting German claims to Sudetenland
1939	Britain declared war on Germany	Franco-British guarantees to Poland	to protect Poland against German aggression

Answering Essay Questions on Britain's Foreign Policy, 1918–39

The following is a question which requires you to make a historical judgement by comparing two distinct but connected events. To be in a position to answer it, re-read sections 4 and 5 of this chapter and also section 1 of chapter 2.

'War with Germany was unnecessary in 1914, unavoidable in 1939.' How far do agree with this assertion?

The question asks you to compare the reasons for Britain's going to war in 1914 with those that applied in 1939. A good start would be for you to write two separate lists of causes or reasons, something along the lines of the following (numbered for convenience):

1914

1 German aggression
2 British reluctance to contemplate a German-dominated Europe
3 Mutual rivalry as expressed in the Anglo-German arms race
4 Britain's fear that it was losing its naval supremacy
5 Britain's membership of the Triple Entente
6 The popular desire in Britain for war
7 Britain's treaty obligations to Belgium
8 Britain's sense of prestige and honour
9 Britain's need to protect its economic interests
10 The Liberal government's fears of a Conservative challenge

1939

1 German aggression
2 British reluctance to contemplate a German-dominated Europe
3 Germany's tearing up of the Munich agreement
4 Britain's commitment to the defence of Poland
5 Britain's sense of prestige and honour

You may of course add to or subtract from the list, according to your own knowledge or judgement. The implication in the quotation is that Britain had a choice in 1914 but not in 1939. Do the points of comparison and contrast in your lists substantiate this or challenge it? Is it important that in both cases Britain declared war on Germany? Does this mean that choice applied in both cases? Did Germany intend war with Britain in either 1914 or 1939? If not, and the weight of evidence suggests it did not, then could war be said to be unavoidable on either occasion? How important do you regard the British commitment to Belgium and Poland to have been? Both were based on formal treaties. Did this make them equally binding? How realistic is it to suggest that Britain could have stayed aloof from European affairs in 1914 anymore than in 1939? There are writers who now argue that Britain could, indeed should, have stayed out of both wars. Are their views worth considering?

Sub-questions such as these should provide you with a basis on which to structure an answer. Remember, it does not matter whether or not you agree with the assertion in the question. Your task is to build a logical argument based on your own judgement.

Answering Source-Based Questions on Britain's Foreign Policy, 1918–39

Read back over sections 4 and 5 of this chapter.

The Roots of Appeasement

Source F From a speech of Clement Attlee in the House of Commons, May 1935.

We stand for collective security through the League of Nations. We reject the use of force as an instrument of policy. Our policy is not one of seeking security through rearmament but through disarmament. Our aim is the reduction of armaments, and then the complete abolition of all national armaments under the League.

I put before the whole House my own views with *appalling frankness* … Supposing I had gone to the country and said that we must rearm, does anybody think that this pacific democracy would have rallied to the cry? I cannot think of anything that would have made the loss of the election from my point of view more certain.

Source J From a speech of Stanley Baldwin in the Commons, 12 November 1936.

How horrible, fantastic, incredible it is that we should be digging trenches and trying on gas-masks here because of a quarrel in a far-away country between people of whom we know nothing.

Source H From a BBC broadcast by Neville Chamberlain, 27 September 1938.

▼ QUESTIONS ON SOURCES

Comprehension questions:
1. In what ways does Source F reveal Clement Attlee's views on rearmament? **(5 marks)**
2. Why, according to Baldwin in Source J, would Britain not have supported rearmament in 1936? **(5 marks)**
3. What, according to Source H, is Britain's responsibility towards Czechoslovakia? **(5 marks)**

Stimulus questions:
4. What were the main arguments of those who opposed British rearmament in the 1930s? **(8 marks)**
5. What part did the horror of war play in shaping British attitudes towards appeasement? **(8 marks)**

Cross-referencing question:
6. To what extent do these three sources share a common view of Britain's responsibilities in foreign affairs? **(10 marks)**

Evaluation question:
7. How valuable are these three sources to a historian who is studying attitudes towards appeasement in the 1930s? **(10 marks)**

Lead-out question involving historical judgement:
8. Did those in the National government who followed appeasement policies towards Nazi Germany have any other genuine alternative? **(15 marks)**

Points to assist you in approaching these questions

These three statements were delivered by three party leaders, Baldwin and Chamberlain of the National government, and Attlee of the Labour Party – a very representative spread. Each individual speech dismisses the notion of force as a genuine option. Attlee does so on moral grounds, Baldwin on the grounds that Britain would not support the arms expenditure that such a policy would entail, and Chamberlain on the grounds that it is highly unreasonable to ask the British people to contemplate fighting for a cause that does not concern them. But what should be stressed is that Attlee at this stage totally rules out war 'as an instrument of policy'. With Baldwin it is a matter of political expediency; he is concerned that if he advocated the necessary rearmament he would lose the next election. However, your own knowledge will tell you that both Baldwin and Chamberlain did have a genuine desire, that went beyond the merely political, to avoid war. Taken together these sources do indicate a strong common attitude uniting the leaders in their attitude towards Britain's involvement in military conflict. Subsequently, after the evident failure to deter German aggression, appeasement was roundly condemned. This should not hide the fact that, as the sources indicate, until 1938 appeasement was the prevailing attitude among the leaders of the major parties.

Further Reading

Books in the Access to History series
Britain: Foreign and Imperial Affairs 1919–39 by Alan Farmer lucidly covers British foreign policy between the wars.

General
There are valuable up-to-date assessments of the foreign policies of Lloyd George, Ramsay MacDonald, Baldwin, and Neville Chamberlain in *Modern British Statesmen 1867–1945* edited by Richard Kelly and John Cantrell (Manchester UP, 1997). For the interwar years *The Origins of the Second World War* by A.J.P. Taylor (Penguin, 1991) should be consulted since all later studies are essentially reactions to what Taylor wrote. Of the huge number of important books on appeasement, the following are recommended: *British Politics and Foreign Policy in the Age of Appeasement* by R.J.Q. Adams (Macmillan, 1993), *Eden* by David Carlton (Allen Lane, 1981), *Chamberlain and the Lost Peace* by John Charmley (Hodder & Stoughton, 1989), *The Origins of the Second World War* by Richard Overy (Longman, 1987), and *The Roots of Appeasement* by Martin Gilbert (Weidenfeld & Nicolson, 1966). A helpful short summary is *Appeasement* by Kenneth Robbins (Blackwell, 1997). A book which offers many fascinating insights into the attitudes of the protagonists is *Churchill and Appeasement* by R.A.C. Parker (Macmillan, 2000).

BRITAIN AT WAR, 1939–45

CHAPTER 5

POINTS TO CONSIDER

War is arguably the greatest trauma that a nation's people collectively undergo. In the twentieth century war became 'total war'. It was so demanding of human and material resources that every country that fought a major war was fundamentally changed by the experience. This chapter traces the impact that the Second World War had on Britain.

Six years of struggle, a longer period than for any of the other victor nations, altered the British social, political and economic landscape. Sometimes the changes merely hastened trends that were already established; in other cases the changes were entirely unprecedented. Each of the chapter sections describes an aspect of Britain's wartime experience. A study of Churchill's Coalition is followed by a survey of the main military features of Britain's war effort. The last two sections deal with the social and economic changes. Although for exam purposes you may not need to have a detailed knowledge of all these aspects, you are encouraged to read what is said about them. Six years is a concentrated period and the overlap between separate developments is particularly marked.

1 Churchill's Coalition Government, 1940–45

ISSUES:
What was Winston Churchill's personal contribution to Britain's survival in the Second World War? What criticisms have been made of his handling of the war?

Neville Chamberlain was not a convincing leader in wartime. The failure of his appeasement policy hung over him. When the Norwegian campaign, the first major engagement of the war for Britain, went badly in April 1940 he was roundly condemned by all parties in parliament, including a large section of his own Conservatives. He resigned to be replaced by Winston Churchill, 'the man of the hour'. The outbreak of war with Germany put Churchill in a strong position. Throughout the 1930s he had consistently warned against the growing dangers of an expansionist Nazi Germany and had urged Britain to rearm. Far from having been the warmonger that his critics had described him as, events now appeared to have vindicated his call for rearmament and his denunciation of appeasement. He was ideally placed to succeed Chamberlain. As Prime Minister at the head of a Coalition, Churchill remained in office throughout the war against Germany.

Q In what circumstances did Churchill become Prime Minister in 1940?

-Profile-

WINSTON CHURCHILL
(1874–1965)

In many ways Churchill was a radical, but he was loathed by the Left because of his strike-breaking and fierce anti-Bolshevism. He was too individualistic to be entirely at ease in any one party. In 1904, after only four years as a Unionist MP, he left the party to join the Liberals. His radical approach to social questions made him the great ally of Lloyd George in their creation of the pre-1914 social service state. Twenty years later, having established an impressive record as a Liberal social reformer, he returned to the Conservative fold, but in a strange relationship. He called himself a 'constitutionalist' and despite being Chancellor of the Exchequer in Baldwin's government between 1924 and 1929 did not formally rejoin the Conservatives until 1929. Churchill remained out of office for the next ten years. His demand that Britain rearm, and his outspoken attacks on appeasement and on the idea of independence for India made him unpopular with the Conservative establishment and he despaired of ever playing a major role in politics again. It is certainly hard to think that, had the Second World War not intervened, he would have reached the pre-eminence he then did.

Clement Attlee described him as 'the greatest citizen of the world of our time'. As well as making history Churchill also wrote it. His deep historical sense was evident in his many books and in his brilliant speeches in which he used his speech impediment to great effect. One example was his deliberate mis-pronunciation of the word 'Nazi', with a long 'a' and a soft 'z', in order to show his contempt for the movement to which it referred. His feel for the dramatic and his ability to use elevated language without losing the common touch is evident in the extract from his first broadcast to the nation as Prime Minister:

1874	born the son of Randolph Churchill, a leading Tory radical;
1898	fought in the Sudan under Kitchener;
1900	taken prisoner by the Boers in South Africa; entered the Commons as a Conservative MP;
1904	left the Conservatives to join the Liberals;
1908 –09	President of the Board; of Trade – showed himself to be a progressive social reformer;
1910 –11	Home Secretary;
1911	used troops against striking Welsh miners;
1911 –15	First Lord of the Admiralty;
1916	served on the Western Front;
1917 –18	Minister of Munitions;
1919	Fiercely anti-Bolshevik, he supported British intervention in Russia;
1921 –22	Secretary for the Colonies;
1924	left the Liberals and declared himself a 'Constitutionalist';
1924 –29	Chancellor of the Exchequer;
1926	strongly opposed the General Strike;
1929	formally rejoined the Conservatives;
1939 –40	First Lord of the Admiralty;
1940 –45	Prime Minister and Minister of Defence;
1945	his party heavily defeated in the General Election;
1947	helped to define the Cold War by his 'iron curtain' speech;
1951 –55	Prime Minister;
1965	died.

This is one of the most awe-inspiring periods in the long history of France and Britain. It is also beyond doubt the most sublime. Side by side, unaided except by their kith and kin in the Great Dominions and by the wide Empires which rest beneath their shield – side by side, the British and French peoples have advanced to rescue not only Europe but mankind from the foulest and most soul-destroying tyranny which has ever darkened and stained the page of history. Behind them – behind us – behind the Armies and fleets of Britain – gather a group of shattered States and bludgeoned races: the Czechs, the Poles, the Norwegians, the Danes, the Dutch, the Belgians – upon all of whom the long night of barbarism will descend, unbroken even by a star of hope, unless we conquer, as conquer we must, as conquer we will.

Source A From a BBC broadcast by Winston Churchill, 19 May 1940.

Churchill wrote in his war memoirs that on becoming Prime Minister in 1940 he felt that the whole of his previous life had been a preparation 'for this hour and this trial'. As Lloyd George had done in 1916, he devoted himself totally to the task of winning the war. Every other consideration took second place. Despite the deep depression from which he frequently suffered, the 'black dog' as he called it, he never wavered in his conviction that Britain would prevail. His inexhaustible capacity for work, his nerve-tingling oratory, and his extraordinary gift for inspiring others were used to rally the nation to a supreme effort. He later wrote that the British people were the lions; he merely provided the roar. Yet such was his personal contribution to Britain's survival during the darkest days of war that A.J.P. Taylor described him as 'the saviour of his country'.

This is very much the traditional picture of Churchill in wartime. His chief biographer, Martin Gilbert, paints him as an inspiring leader guiding a united nation through peril to victory over a deadly enemy and, in so doing, establishing himself as an outstanding world figure. But there have been challenges to that view. Interestingly these have come not from the left but from the right. Revisionist historians, such as Alan Clark and John Charmley, have advanced interesting alternative interpretations. They criticise him on two counts. One is that Churchill as a war leader clung to the notion of victory when he had the opportunity to make peace with Germany. The irony of that charge is that there was at least one moment when Churchill appeared to give serious thought to negotiating a settlement with Germany. Although he suppressed the fact in his memoirs, it is now known that in late May he discussed a compromise peace with a small group of his Cabinet. He even said that he might consider pulling Britain out of the war, but only after it had fought on for a time so as to win better terms.

However, whatever consideration Churchill may have given to these ideas, he certainly did not act upon it. Nothing came of the War Cabinet discussions. Although Halifax was keen to pursue the notion of a settlement, Churchill, sure of Attlee's support, overruled him and thereafter would not entertain talk of negotiations with Germany. That is why revisionists are able to sustain the accusation that Churchill, despite being a dedicated imperialist, prolonged the struggle for five years thereby weakening Britain to such an extent that it was no longer able to keep its empire after the war was over.

The other charge also has an irony. Throughout his career Churchill opposed socialism yet, critics say, it was during his Coalition government that measures were introduced that prepared the way for the socialist policies followed by British governments after 1945 (see page 136).

A third gloss on the Churchill record has been provided by David Carlton, who has argued that what motivated Churchill during the later war years was the same thing that had inspired him since 1917 – hatred and fear of Russian Communism. Carlton's argument is that, despite being Stalin's ally, Churchill, as his private correspondence has revealed, believed that by 1944 the Soviet Union was as great a threat to British interests as ever Nazi Germany had been.

Source B From 'Churchill's Secret War with Stalin', article by David Carlton in *The Daily Telegraph*, 11 February 2000.

Churchill became obsessed with the Communist threat and thereafter saw the struggle to defeat Germany as no more than a second-order crusade. Increasingly he devoted attention to frustrating Soviet expansionist aims. Accordingly he struck a brutal but realistic bargain with Stalin in 1944 with respect to Bulgaria, Romania and anti-communist POWs, but Britain was able to intervene in Greece to prevent communists seizing power.

The 'brutal bargain' between Stalin and Churchill to which Carlton refers was the agreement by which the Soviet Union was given a free hand in Bulgaria and Romania and allowed to deal as it chose with any Soviet citizens who, after being captured by the Germans, had fought against the USSR. In return the Soviet Union would not enforce a Communist takeover in Greece. This is an aspect of what may be called Churchill's appeasement of Stalin at the end of the war. In order to limit Soviet ambitions, Churchill, at the **Yalta Conference**, joined with the USA in accepting the USSR's right to remain in control of the territories in eastern Europe that it had taken in its push westwards against Germany. By a bitter irony this included Poland, the country whose independence Britain had gone to war in 1939 to defend.

ACTIVITIES

Paul Addison has written 'Churchill was a profoundly egocentric statesman for whom parties were vehicles for ambition rather than causes to be served.'

▼ Explain in your own words what you think Addison meant by this. What evidence is there in this chapter to support or challenge this view?
▼ How acceptable do you find the revisionists' criticisms of Churchill's record as wartime leader?

---

2 Outline of the Military Struggle, 1939–45

It is possible to gain a basic understanding of Britain's part in the Second World War by outlining the major campaigns and developments. Always refer to the maps in this book or in a historical atlas so that you can locate the key places mentioned.

The Second World War was in fact two wars, one in Europe, the other in the Far East. The European conflict began with the German invasion of Poland in September 1939 and lasted until May 1945 when a shattered Germany surrendered unconditionally to the Allies. The Far-Eastern struggle started in December 1941 when Japan, already occupying China and parts of south-east Asia, launched an attack on the US Pacific base at Pearl Harbor. It ended with the surrender of Japan in August 1945 after two of its cities had been subjected to atomic bombing a few days earlier.

The Phoney War, September 1939–April 1940

Although it had declared war on Germany, Britain was not yet in a position to take the offensive. The British busied themselves digging shelters, filling sandbags, trying on gas-masks and organising the evacuation of children from the urban areas to the countryside. Much went on behind the scenes to prepare the armed services for war, but essentially it was a matter of waiting for Germany to make the first move. American journalists dubbed this period of relative calm 'the phoney war'.

THE YALTA CONFERENCE, FEBRUARY 1945 was attended by the USSR, Britain and the USA. It met to consider details of the surrender terms to be presented to Germany and to make preliminary arrangements for a post-war settlement. The discussions were continued at the Postsdam conference in July and August. These revealed the widening differences between the former Allies, which hardened into the Cold War divisions.

Figure 20 Photo of Londoners sleeping in an underground station. At the beginning of the war people were forbidden for safety reasons to congregate in the stations, but the authorities soon relented when they realised the usefulness of these underground areas as ready-made shelters for large numbers of people.

Norway, April 1940

The war began in earnest for Britain in April 1940 when Germany, anxious to gain vital iron-ore deposits, invaded Norway after taking Denmark as a stepping stone. The British responded by sending a task force to Norway but it was too small to prevent the Germans overrunning the country. It was this failure that led to the resignation of Chamberlain and his replacement by Churchill at the head of a Coalition government (see page 105).

Dunkirk and the Fall of France, May–June 1940

Worse was soon to follow. Early in May, Hitler ordered the launching of the long-expected western offensive. Within a matter of weeks his forces had swept through the Low Countries and occupied northern France. The British Expeditionary Force (BEF) found itself pinned onto the beaches along the Channel ports. For a time it was feared that the BEF would be destroyed but in a desperate nine-day rescue effort, organized by the Royal Navy and involving an 'armada' of small private vessels, over 300,000 British and French troops were evacuated from Dunkirk. Churchill referred to it as 'a miracle of deliverance' but added that wars are not won by retreats. Seven weeks after the offensive had been launched, Paris had fallen and the French had surrendered.

The Battle of Britain, August–October 1940

In preparation for the invasion of Britain, the Luftwaffe (German Air Force) was instructed to gain control of the skies over the Channel and southern Britain. But in the six days, 13–18 August, the Germans had 236 planes shot down while British losses were only 95. This led the Luftwaffe to redirect its attacks onto London rather than the RAF airfields. Despite being stretched to the limit the British pilots, whose average age was 22, and ground crews sustained their resistance. Between 30 August and 7 September, the RAF lost 185 planes to the Luftwaffe's 225. On 15 September, in the last major engagement of the battle the aircraft losses were German 56, British 26. Early in October, Hitler suspended the invasion plan indefinitely. Churchill, in tribute to the RAF's heroism, declared that 'never in the field of human conflict was so much owed by so many to so few'. Typically, the pilots of Fighter Command used the line to describe their unpaid mess bills.

Total Planes Lost During the Battle of Britain
British 915 (fighters)
German 1,733 (fighters and bombers)

The Blitz, September 1940–May 1941

The Battle of Britain led to a change of Luftwaffe strategy. It switched to a form of terror tactics by attacking civilian targets in a sustained series of nightly raids on London and other selected cities. These were at their most intensive between September 1940 and May 1941; for some 76 consecutive nights London suffered heavy bombing. The normal pattern of life and work was disrupted but the morale of Londoners largely held. Although intermittent German raids continued after May 1941 their numbers noticeably fell as the Luftwaffe turned its attention to planning for Germany's attack on the USSR.

Main Areas Attacked During the Blitz
London
Belfast
Birmingham
Bristol
Coventry
Hull
Manchester
Plymouth

Figure 21 Churchill inspecting the war damage in Battersea caused by German raids, September 1940. Incendiary bombs were responsible for the high degree of devastation.

Operation Barbarossa, 1941

Tearing up the Nazi-Soviet Pact, Hitler unleashed a massive attack on Russia in June. Code-named Barbarossa, the attack proved to be the turning point of the war. Unable to gain a quick victory, Germany found itself involved in a savage war in the east that drained it of men and resources and brought about its first major military defeats. The great benefit of Barbarossa to Britain was that it ended any real possibility of a German invasion.

The North African Campaigns, 1940–43

The entry of Italy into the war on Germany's side in June 1940, following the fall of France, extended the conflict to north Africa. Despite early successes for the Italian troops their attempt to push British forces out of Egypt failed. By early 1941 such was the Italian disarray that Germany had to come to its ally's aid. This marked the entry into the desert war of Rommel's Africa Corps. After two years of fighting in which fortunes swung to and fro, British forces led by General Montgomery had amassed superior resources. In the Battle of El Alamein in October 1942 Rommel's army was defeated and forced to withdraw. The German retreat westwards was blocked by an Anglo-American force under General Eisenhower, which had landed in Morocco and Algeria. Rommel, caught between the two Allied armies, put up a skilful resistance but was eventually overcome by greater numbers. In May 1943, over 300,000 German and Italian troops surrendered in Tunisia. This opened the way for Allied landings in southern Italy two months later, the first direct challenge to German control of western Europe since 1939. The tide of the war had turned.

Pearl Harbor, December 1941

The conflict of 1939–45 truly became a world war in December 1941 with the entry of the USA. As part of its strategy to gain a free hand in extending its control of east Asia, Japan launched an intended knockout strike on the US Pacific fleet at Pearl Harbor in Hawaii. However, the attack, far from forcing the USA out of the Pacific, did the very opposite. In declaring war on the Japanese empire President Roosevelt committed the American people to wage unceasing war until 'the day of infamy' had been avenged. A development of immense significance was Germany's decision to support its Axis partner by also declaring war on the

USA. This brought America with its vast resources into the European war as Britain's ally. The development that Churchill had been praying for since 1939 had at last occurred.

Stalingrad, 1942–43

As part of their push south-eastward to seize the oil fields of the Caucasus, the German forces invading Russia besieged the city that bore the Soviet leader's name – Stalingrad. The city was not of major strategic value but Stalin, choosing to define it as a symbol of Russian resistance, demanded that it be defended to the death. Hitler responded in like manner. Ignoring the appeals of his generals at Stalingrad, who urged a withdrawal, he instructed his army not to retreat one millimetre. The result was that the German besiegers became the besieged. Deprived of supplies and reinforcements, they were battered and starved into submission. Their surrender in February 1943 was a catastrophe from which Germany never recovered. Stalingrad was singly the most important campaign of the war in Europe. Its outcome destroyed the sense of invincibility in Hitler's armies and gave hope of final victory to Britain and the Western Allies.

The Allied Reconquest of Europe, 1944–45

By the summer of 1944, after months of preparation, the Allied forces were ready to open the long-awaited second front in Europe. On D-day, 6 June, British, American and Canadian troops stormed and took the Normandy beaches. They then began the process of pushing the German forces out of the occupied areas of northern Europe. By September 1944, Paris and Brussels had been liberated. The Germans fought on courageously but they were now caught in a closing three-pronged claw made up of the Allied armies advancing eastwards towards the Rhine, pushing up through Italy towards southern Germany, with Soviet armies moving westwards into Germany on a series of fronts. After one last desperate resistance in the Battle of the Bulge in the Ardennes in early 1945, Germany had nothing left. To avoid capture by the Russians who had entered Berlin, Hitler committed suicide on 30 April in his Berlin bunker. On 7 May the German government agreed to an unconditional surrender.

NAVAL AND AIR STRATEGY, 1939–44

Since 1939 the crossing of the Atlantic had been a perilous affair for British convoys. The success of the U-boats threatened to starve Britain of food and materials. What helped to save the situation was the breaking of the German Enigma Code by 'Station X' at Bletchley Park in Buckinghamshire. Provided with vital information concerning German naval movements, the Royal Navy was able to protect Allied convoys and exact a heavy toll of German vessels.

This victory in the 'Battle of the Atlantic' coincided with the beginning of a sustained Anglo-American air offensive, which aimed to destroy Germany's economy. The Allied day and night raids were often costly in men and planes but they achieved the main objective of softening up Germany prior to a major land invasion.

Figure 22 Map showing the main features of the Second World War.

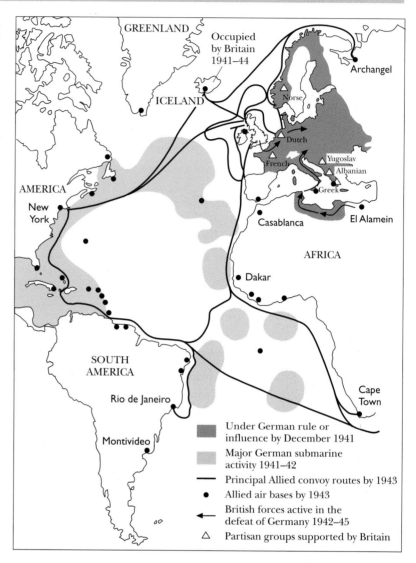

GREENLAND

Occupied by Britain 1941–44

Archangel

ICELAND

Norse

Dutch

Yugoslav

French

Albanian

AMERICA

Greek

New York

Casablanca

El Alamein

AFRICA

Dakar

SOUTH AMERICA

Cape Town

Rio de Janeiro

Montivideo

	Under German rule or influence by December 1941
	Major German submarine activity 1941–42
——	Principal Allied convoy routes by 1943
•	Allied air bases by 1943
←	British forces active in the defeat of Germany 1942–45
△	Partisan groups supported by Britain

Number of VIs fired –
10,000
3,676 hit London
2,600 failed to reach their target
1,878 were shot down by anti-air batteries
1,846 were destroyed by fighters
Number of people killed by the VIs – 6,184
Number of V2s launched – 1,115, killing 2,754 people

Germany's V1 and V2 campaigns, June 1944–February 1945

The Normandy landings coincided with what proved to be Hitler's last throw of the dice – his use of terror weapons against Britain. The attacks by the V1 flying bomb (a pilotless jet-propelled plane loaded with explosives), which began in June, were followed in September by the launching of the V2 (an armed rocket). The weapons caused widespread death and damage in and around London and led to the evacuation of one and a half million people. But, owing to Allied bombing of the launch sites and later the overrunning of them by Allied land forces, the destruction was never on the scale Hitler had originally planned.

The War in the Far East, 1941–45

Since British attention was naturally concentrated on the struggle in Europe the war in the Far East seemed a secondary affair. Those who fought in it sometimes referred to it bitterly as 'the forgotten war'. Yet arguably it was as important as the western struggle. The initial advantage lay with Japan. By the spring of 1942, it had driven Britain from Burma and Malaya, captured Singapore, and seized the Dutch East Indies. These striking gains, together with its control of China, which it had first invaded in 1931, seemed to give it enormous power. But the more territory Japan took, the greater became the difficulty of retaining it. The defeat of the Japanese in the naval Battle of Midway in June 1942 marked a turning point; the initiative was no longer with them. The Allies began to gain mastery of the western Pacific. Japan's dedicated resistance meant that it became a bitter protracted war; the Americans suffered heavy casualties as they drove the Japanese from island to island with the ultimate objective of a full-scale invasion of Japan itself.

With the end of the European war in May 1945, the Allies were free to devote their full attention to the defeat of Japan. When that defeat did come it occurred in a remarkable way that few had foreseen. By July the 'Manhattan Project', which employed the leading scientists from the Allied countries, had developed an atomic bomb of immense destructive force. The American decision to use this new weapon gained the approval of Clement Attlee's Labour government. On 6 August, the Japanese city of Hiroshima was devastated by the first atomic bomb to be dropped. On 8 August the USSR declared war on Japan. A day later a second atomic bomb was dropped – on Nagasaki. Eight days later Japan surrendered.

ACTIVITY

From what you have read in this section, how would you explain Britain's survival and eventual victory? It would help if you listed the key developments and turning points in what you see as their order of importance. For example, was control of the skies more important than victory at sea or on land?

ISSUES:
Was the war won on
the home front?
How well was civilian
morale maintained
during the war?
To what extent did the
war turn Britain into a
collectivist state?

3 The Home Front, 1939–45

a) The Effects of the Bombing on Britain

In twentieth-century warfare, the line between combatant and non-combatant became increasingly blurred. The concept of total war and the technology of aerial bombardment made the terrorising of the civilian population both legitimate and possible. Yet one reason why the London Blitz proved bearable is that, grim though the bombing was, it never reached the scale anticipated in the gloomier pre-war forecasts. German and Japanese cities were later to experience Allied bombardment that carried civilian suffering way beyond that undergone in British cities. The death toll of 60,000 Britons killed as a result of bombing during the war was truly fearful but it was smaller than expected.

There was, however, greater destruction of property. Three and a half million houses were bombed out. The social impact of this was shown in the record of 60 million changes of address in Britain between 1939 and 1945. Damage to factories and production centres in cities such as London and Coventry was severe, but the use of makeshift premises and the dispersal of industrial plant meant that production was not severely curtailed. Interestingly, worker absenteeism fell during the Blitz and again during the V1 and V2 attacks in 1944-45, which suggested that the systematic bombing had strengthened rather than weakened civilian morale. There was some panic, particularly at the beginning of the Blitz, but this was not widespread and a mixture of resolution and resignation appears to have been the general response. The normal pattern of life and work was disrupted but not destroyed. As Source C illustrates, people adjusted to the undoubted horror of it all and the sense of a shared common danger tended to maintain morale.

Source C From a private diary entry of a London journalist, 18 October 1940.

> So we have got accustomed now to knowing we may be blown to bits at any moment. The casual scraps of news we get about results of raids bring this home better than statistics. Two girls go into a telephone box to send word they may be late home, as there is a raid on. Bombs fall close by. Both killed. A woman of 94 with six daughters in a large expensive house are taking shelter in the basement when the house is hit. Two of the daughters die. What a picture! A family creeps out of its garden dugout to get some supper. They sit down at table. Next minute they are all dead. We know this may happen to any of us. Yet we go about as usual. Life goes on.

b) The War's Influence on Social Attitudes

ISSUE:
Did the war narrow or enlarge class divisions?

An interesting feature of the collective war effort in Britain was the way it increased social perception. The shared experience of the dangers of war and developments, such as evacuation, helped make people aware of each other in ways that had not happened before. Knowledge of 'how the other half lives' led to a questioning of the class differences that existed. Privilege and deprivation would, of course, continue after the war but, insofar as the twentieth century became the 'age of the common man', the impact of the Second World War was a major factor in making it so. This is not to argue that everybody pulled together as suggested by the Ministry of Information propaganda films or the patriotic BBC broadcasts. Britain was far from being a united nation during the war. One example of this was the flourishing **black market**. Another was the frequency of industrial disputes. Although these fell in number with the outbreak of war, by 1942 they were back at pre-war level.

Table 19 Industrial strikes 1939–45.

	Working Days Lost	Number of Strikes	Number of Strikers
1939	1,356,000	940	337,000
1940	940,000	972	299,000
1941	1,079,000	1,251	360,000
1942	1,527,000	1,303	456,000
1943	1,808,000	1,785	557,000
1944	3,714,000	2,194	821,000
1945	2,835,000	2,293	531,000

One of the first responses in Britain to the outbreak of war in 1939 was **evacuation**. This proved to be a remarkably revealing social episode. Considerable research has been undertaken by social historians into the effects of evacuation and there is a large measure of agreement that the majority of children suffered significant psychological disturbance as a result of being uprooted from home, family and environment. The sense of loneliness and disorientation is movingly described in Source D.

BLACK MARKET
The term refers to the illegal selling of rationed food and goods, which enabled people to buy more than their allowance permitted. It became a highly organised and lucrative activity. Every city and town had its black marketeers (known as 'spivs') and a large and eager clientele. How widespread the system was is suggested by the fact that during the war over 100,000 people were prosecuted by the Ministry of Food for black market offences. Another 130,000 were fined or imprisoned during the post-war rationing period.

EVACUATION
At the outbreak of the war, the government, fearing large-scale air attacks on major urban centres, organised a migration of primary school children from the danger zones to the relatively safer rural areas. Although four million were planned for, only one and a half million actually made the move. During the phoney war period most evacuees drifted back home, only to migrate again when the Blitz began late in 1940. A further evacuation occurred in 1944 at the time of the rocket attacks on London.

Next day they labelled me, addressed me and packed me off to the country.

I paraded with the other children from Tollington School outside Hornsey station as heavily loaded as a soldier in full marching kit. A gas mask in a white tin box stuffed with sticky plaster, anti-burn cream and iodine pulled me down one side: a haversack crammed with sandwiches and apples balanced me on the other. Brown paper parcels hung from my belt like grenades. In my pocket were labels displaying my school, home address and destination; in one hand I carried a brown suitcase containing clothes, in the other a wad of comics.

Our teachers marshalled us into queues and classes. Mothers sidled alongside, tying knots, straightening caps, tucking loops of hair beneath peaks. 'Look after yourself, darling,' my mother said. 'Don't forget to eat your sandwiches … And don't forget to send that card as soon as you can'. 'All right,' I said, feeling the stamped, addressed card already smeared with chocolate. 'I won't forget.'

She had a handkerchief in her hand now; so did some of the other mothers as the queues shuffled towards the carriages. The mistresses fed us into compartments and the doors closed. I had a last glimpse of the mothers, some already walking away with heads bowed, some waving handkerchiefs, mine with handkerchief pressed to her face. There was a sudden thrust of pain, a blade of parting flesh, a momentary appreciation of fireside security and maternal love, and then steam curtained the window.

They took us by bus from the station at Abbotsley, Huntingdonshire, to the school hall. There pyramids of buns, bottles of fizzy lemonade and worried groups of foster mothers awaited us. With a dark leggy boy called Kenneth Francis – an ancient enemy – I was led away by a sadly pretty housewife with pale cheeks and straight hair to a council house clean and scented with the varnish smells of new furniture and hot-pot cooking.

That evening Kenneth and I, briefly at peace, walked up the long vegetable garden and sat in a sloping field of clover. There we rolled and shouted, sucked the honeyed petals of clover, embraced the countryside and sneered at the soiled grassland we had left behind. We walked down a lane between hedges loaded with blackberries and garlanded with bryony. The lane led to a stream where tiny fish darted and trembled in hollows pressed in the mud by cattle hooves, where water boatmen skated and wild irises grew and – or so it was said – a kingfisher sprinted through the evening air.

Suddenly the white council house was remote, the country cruel, home the other side of the world. We went to strange beds and lay with fists clenched. Our toes found tepid hot water bottles and our fingers silk bags of old lavender inside the pillows. An owl hooted, wings brushed the window. I remembered the London sounds of distant trains and motor cycles, the creaking limbs of the mountain ash, next door's dog, the droning radio, the fifth stair groaning and the ten-thirty throat clearing; I remembered the familiar wallpaper where you could paddle a canoe through green rapids, a shadow like a nose on the ceiling and the curve of the bedstead rail which had seemed as permanent as evening cocoa. We sobbed in awful desolation but never again mentioned those first war tears to each other.

Source D From *Wartime Reminiscences* by Derek Lambert, 1960.

The writer conveys the mixture of regimentation, confusion and misery that accompanied evacuation at the point of departure. Equally striking is his description of his initial reaction to the strangeness of his foster home. The homesickness he recalls was the lot of most evacuees. What Source D clearly shows is that a different way of life was being learned; town and country were meeting for the first time. This latter point is also illustrated in Source E. The sense of shock, evident in the various reports of the Women's Institute (WI), at the habits of the evacuees suggests that for the first time the middle and wealthier classes were learning how the other half lived. The WI's recording of the malnourishment and lack of social graces of the evacuees helped create an awareness of the poverty and deprivation from which large sections of the urban population suffered.

Walthamstow. 'Bread and lard are a usual breakfast for a number of children when at home.'

Grimsby. 'Their chief food at home was in most cases fish and chips, more often the latter without the fish. Milk puddings were unheard of and some did not even know what a pudding was.'

Manchester. 'Few children would eat food that demanded the use of teeth – in almost every case could only eat with a teaspoon. Practically all disliked fresh vegetables and pies and puddings of fresh fruit were quite unknown to them.'

Liverpool. 'One little girl of five and a half remarked one day that she would like to have beer and cheese for supper. Most of the children seemed under-nourished when they arrived, yet some were troublesome to feed, not liking stewed fruit, vegetables and jam. Children had been used to receiving a penny at home to buy their own dinners. One used to buy broken biscuits, the other Oxo cubes. Most of them seemed quite unaccustomed to ordinary everyday food and preferred a "piece" or bag of chips on the doorstep.'

Newcastle. 'Those from the most neglected homes had no idea of eating at table, but were expert in making anything into a sandwich, fingers being preferred to forks. Soup seemed to be unknown to some of the children. One mother admitted they never had soup, while two boys (10 and 12) attempted it with a knife and fork … '

Lambeth. 'The children did not seem to have much idea of proper meals; they used to whine for a bit of bread … A large number, even from apparently well-off homes, were quite unused to sitting down to table or to using knives and forks. They were used to having their food handed to them to take out, or eat anywhere.'

Source E From 'Town Children Through Country Eyes', a Pamphlet of the National Federation of Women's Institutes, 1940.

Evacuation proved to be a remarkable social experiment. Designed as a protective measure for the young children of the cities, it led to a rethinking in social attitudes. In many instances, criticism and revulsion among the better off turned into sympathy and brought a new sense of social concern. It was no coincidence that a major Education Act, aimed at widening educational opportunity for all children was introduced in 1944 (see page 134). However, social concern was not a universal response. While acknowledging that such experiences as evacuation opened the eyes of many to the deprivation existing in Britain, a number of historians have stressed that there was an equal likelihood that it confirmed the prejudices of some:

For conservative social observers, it [evacuation] confirmed the view that the bulk of the problems were caused by an incorrigible underclass of personally inadequate 'cultural orphans' for whom a Welfare State could do little. Evacuation thus shows us that the ideological consensus of wartime, so stressed by … some historians was something of a myth.

Source F From an article by John Macnicol, quoted in *Britain 1918–1951* edited by Peter Caterall, 1994.

During the war many female volunteers swelled the ranks of the women's branches of the armed forces and the auxiliary domestic units such as the Land Army. This development, together with the large number of women who went to work in factories, appeared to give women increased status. Yet within a few months of the war's end 75 per cent of the female workers had left their jobs to return to their traditional role in the home. This makes it questionable whether the war had permanently altered traditional patterns of social behaviour.

What impact did the war have on women workers?

ACTIVITY

Having read this section comment on the suggestion that evacuation proved to be an unintended but extraordinarily productive social experiment. Do make appropriate use of the Sources D, E and F.

c) The Growth in the Authority of the State

A striking feature of war in the twentieth century was the encouragement it gave to centralist tendencies in government. Faced with the strains of total war, nations without exception showed a readiness to accept extension of State control as a means of creating the maximum war effort. This was as evident in democratic countries as in totalitarian regimes. Britain's Coalition government moved so far towards regulation that the post-war Labour government inherited an established pattern of centralised control (see page 136).

COLLECTIVIST

Collectivism is the notion that in a society the individual is less important than the group. Therefore, in times of need, the rights of the individual must be subordinated to the greater good of the group. All wartime nations witnessed a rapid growth of central state power in accordance with this principle.

Extension of State Power in Britain During the War

Regulations were introduced imposing: food and fuel rationing, conscription, limitations on press freedom, and suspension of legal freedoms. New government departments were established covering such areas as: food supply, information, economic warfare, civilian aviation, and town and country planning. The Ministry of Labour and National Service was empowered to:

▼ conscript men and women into the armed services
▼ direct workers to specific jobs in particular areas
▼ control rates of pay and hours of employment
▼ subject employers to Ministry control.

THE EMERGENCY POWERS ACT OF 1939

Such persons may be detained whose detention appears to the Secretary of State to be expedient in the interests of public safety or the defence of the realm.

The Secretary of State, the Minister of Labour, has the authority to oblige any person in the United Kingdom to perform any service required in any place. He may prescribe the remuneration of such services and the hours of work. He may require such persons to register particulars of themselves; he might order employers to keep and produce any records and books.

Britain, in effect, became a **collectivist** state during the Second World War. Rationing, conscription, direction of labour, and the suspension of many traditional legal and constitutional freedoms: these were accepted by the British public, if not with a will at least without open signs of resistance. The Minister of Labour, Ernest Bevin, was authorised under the terms of **the Emergency Powers Act** to marshal such labour resources as he thought necessary, to direct them to work in such areas as he chose, and to have total control over pay and hours of employment; the employers themselves were equally subject to his direction. These were unprecedented powers for a British minister and the fact that they were exercised with discretion and moderation did not lessen their significance.

Source G From the Emergency Powers (Defence) Act, August 1939.

How was the growth in State power justified?

Libertarians were unhappy about the arbitrary powers of detention. However, as had happened during the First World War, when a similar extension of government authority had occurred, the argument of national security carried the day. Necessity justified the increase in government power. Legal niceties took second place to the struggle for survival. As its title was meant to convey, the Act was an emergency measure not a permanent enlargement of State power. To survive the war, the nation had to be organised at its most effective. If this required a massive spread of government power, that was the price that had to be paid. This in essence was the case put forward by government and parliament and accepted by the mass of the people.

ACTIVITY

Read section 3c again and then list the principal ways in which the powers of the State were increased as a direct result of the war.

ISSUE:
Did the war strengthen or weaken the economy?

4 The Economic Impact of the Second World War

The most immediate effect of the war was that it ended the Depression. Even before hostilities began in 1939, the threat of war in the late 1930s (see page 93) had led Britain to embark on a major rearmament programme. This recreated a huge demand for industrial products, which in turn led to a demand for workers. The problem was no longer a surplus of labour but a shortage. By 1941 an extra two million workers were needed to cope with the demands of war. Women were brought in to bridge the gap. By 1943, nearly half of the females in Britain between the ages of 14 and 59 were employed in war work. In addition half a million young women had joined the armed services or the auxiliary services such as the Land Army.

PAYE (PAY AS YOU EARN)
is a sophisticated form of government robbery by which the tax due from workers is extracted from their wages before they have received them.

LEND LEASE
was an arrangement that operated from 1941 under which Britain imported war materials from the United States with no obligation to pay for them until the war was over. Between 1941 and 1945 Britain received $30 million worth of supplies under this scheme.

The Impact of the War on Britain's Finances

Government expenditure rose from £1.4 billion in 1939 to £6.1 billion in 1945

Income tax (levied from most workers by **PAYE**)
25% of earnings in 1939, 50% of earnings in 1945

Government borrowing by direct loans and **lend lease** from the USA (in 1945 Britain owed £3 billion to overseas creditors)

the National Debt rose from £500 million in 1939 to £3,500 million in 1945

the Balance of Payments deficit in 1945 was £875 million.

A far-reaching effect of the 1939–45 war was that it made the idea of government direction of the economy seem perfectly logical and reasonable. The six-year struggle was a national effort led by a Coalition government, which introduced a range of measures that would have been unacceptable in peacetime. Conscription, rationing, price and wage regulation, and import-export controls were among the restrictions that had been imposed. Thousands of farmers were dispossessed of their land during the war for failing to conform to the production levels laid down by the government. All this helped to create an atmosphere in which it was accepted that government knew best. In 1944 the government formally announced that it was now responsible for the 'maintenance of a high and stable level of employment'. A.J.P. Taylor wrote that the war 'produced a revolution in British economic life, until in the end direction and control turned Great Britain into a country more fully socialist than anything achieved by the conscious planners of Soviet Russia'.

By an interesting coincidence it so happened that a powerful theory was available to justify the government's intrusion into the running of economic affairs. Every so often a particular financial or economic theory arrives to dominate its time and appears to oblige governments to structure their policies in accordance with it. For most of the period between the late 1930s and the late 1970s, **Keynesianism** provided the basic frame of reference.

Keynes maintained that the only agency with sufficient power and influence to keep demand at a high enough level was the government itself. He urged, therefore, that the government should use its budgetary and revenue powers to raise capital, which it could then reinvest in the economy to keep it at a high level of activity. This artificial boost to the economy would lead to genuine recovery and growth. Companies and firms would have full order books and the workers would have jobs and earnings. Those earnings would be spent on goods and services with the result that the forces of supply and demand would be stimulated. Keynes argued that the government should be prepared to overspend in the short term even if this meant borrowing to do so. It would eventually be able to repay the debts by taxing the companies and workers whose profits and wages would rise considerably in a flourishing economy.

The six years of government-directed war effort, during which Keynes was an influential figure at the Treasury, helped to give strength to his arguments. What is interesting is that although Keynes thought in terms of limited government action, it was the notion of government being an *essential* part of economic planning that became widely accepted. The Labour governments under Clement Attlee after 1945 were to benefit from this new conviction.

BALANCE OF PAYMENTS (OR TRADE BALANCE) is a measurement of the profit or loss on trade in a given period. When exports are greater in value than imports there is a balance of payments surplus. When imports exceed exports in value there is a balance of payments deficit. For Britain in the twentieth century deficits were a recurrent problem.

Q How was the increase in government power justified?

KEYNESIANISM John Maynard Keynes, a Cambridge academic, believed that depressions, such as the one that had afflicted the economy in the 1930s, were avoidable if particular steps were taken. His starting point was demand. He calculated that it was a fall in demand for manufactured products that caused industrial economies to slip into recession. If demand could be sustained, decline could be prevented and jobs preserved.

Q According to Keynes, what role should government play in the economy?

ACTIVITY

Read section 4 and consider the issues it raises. Try the following questions to test your understanding:

▼ What evidence is there to support A.J.P. Taylor's suggestion that the 1939–45 war 'produced a revolution in British economic life'?
▼ What were the main features of Keynesianism?

▼ Working on Britain at War, 1939–45

Your aim should be to gain as clear an idea as possible of the consequences of war on British society. Do not try to remember all the details of the military engagements, but do familiarise yourself with the broad strategies so that you are able to explain victory and defeat. An appreciation of the scale of the military struggle is essential to understand the impact it had on society and the economy. Churchill is interesting and important, so you should make the effort to understand why historians find him so significant a figure.

Answering Structured Writing and Essay Questions on Britain at War, 1939–45

Types of question	Examples of typical questions
Structured	1 In what ways did Churchill bring a new approach to the running of the war effort when he took over from Chamberlain in 1940?
	2 Describe the ways in which Germany, between 1940 and 1945, tried to break British civilian morale by aerial attacks. What methods were used by Britain to counter these?
	3 Describe the steps taken by the Coalition government to protect the civilian population during the 1939–45 war.
	4 Describe the methods used by Britain to raise money to sustain the war effort.
Causes	5 Explain why Churchill became Prime Minister in May 1940.
	6 Explain why Britain and the Allies were able to win the Battle of the Atlantic.
	7 Explain why there was so little resistance to the increase in State power that occurred during the Second World War.

Types of question	Examples of typical questions
Historical judgement	8 Examine the validity of the claim that Churchill prolonged the war with Germany unnecessarily.
	9 To what extent did wartime evacuation 'change social attitudes in Britain'?
	10 How far do you agree that Britain's victory over Germany in the Second World War was won on the home front?

Answering Source-Based Questions on Britain at War, 1939–45

It is worth recalling the different types of source-based questions that you have met in earlier chapters (see page 51):

Types of question	
comprehension	a basic understanding of what the source says
cross-referencing	the ability to put a source in its historical setting
evaluation	the ability to judge the importance and reliability of a source
analysis	the ability to explain the significance of a source in relation to its wider historical background

There is a further category – questions that ask you to *synthesise*, that is to make connections between different sources and to draw conclusions about their value. This type of question carries high marks, so it is well worth your becoming confident in handling them.

The following sources offer a set of views on the effects of the war on Britain. Study them and then consider the questions that follow.

The war is a spur to a higher level of social attainment, destroying what is moribund, and bringing out the best qualities in our people.

Source H From Benefits of War by A.M. Low, 1943.

[The War] produced a revolution in British economic life, until in the end direction and control turned Great Britain into a country more fully socialist than anything achieved by the conscious planners of Soviet Russia.

Source I English History 1914–45 by A.J.P. Taylor, 1965.

Source J From *The People's War* by Angus Calder, 1969.

> The effect of the war was not to sweep society on to a new course, but to hasten its progress along the old grooves.

Source K From *Britain and the Second World War* by Henry Pelling, 1970.

> Those who attribute social change after 1945 to the war have failed to avoid the commonest of historical pitfalls, the fallacy of *post hoc, ergo propter hoc* [what follows is caused by what precedes].

▼ QUESTIONS ON SOURCES

1. How do Sources H, I, J and K differ from each other in their value as interpretations of the impact of the 1939–45 war on British society? **(15 marks)**

Here are some ideas to help you prepare an answer.

A lively controversy has been generated among modern historians over the changes produced in British society by the Second World War. The four extracts represent some of the major lines of thought. Writing as a contemporary of the war, A.M. Low sees it as positively beneficial; the war elevated social aspirations, helped to clear away obsolete ideas, and encouraged the population to show its finer characteristics.

Twenty years after the end of the war, A.J.P. Taylor compares its impact on Britain with the experience of revolutionary Russia. He makes the contentious claim that Britain underwent an economic revolution during the course of the war and that the degree of central control and direction assumed by the government created a nation more truly socialist than that of Soviet Russia. In contrast, Angus Calder's conclusion is that, far from causing a revolution, the Second World War merely hastened Britain's progress along the path already taken. Dismissing the concept of revolution altogether, Henry Pelling argues that there is no necessary causal connection between the war and social change in Britain; using the Latin tag, he accuses those who see such a connection of having fallen into the obvious error that merely because one event follows another it can be assumed that the one caused the other. Does the fact that Low was writing during the war weaken or strengthen the value of what he says? Does it mean that Source H has a different value from the other sources since they were written after the events?

The sources are obviously short extracts from longer works. As they stand they are assertions. The evidence for their claims is not provided. How does this affect their value?

Further Reading

Books in the Access to History series

Britain: Foreign and Imperial Affairs 1939–64 (chapter 1) by Alan Farmer is very helpful on developments between 1939 and 1945 while *Britain: Domestic Politics 1939–64* by Paul Adelman (chapter 2) offers a number of illuminating points on wartime politics under Churchill.

General

War & Society in Britain 1899–c.1948 by Rex Pope (Longman, 1991) is a short informed introduction that students would find helpful. The 1939–45 struggle is covered in *The Second World War* by Martin Gilbert (HarperCollins, 1997) and in *The Second World War* by John Keegan (Hutchinson, 1989). On a particular theme, there is a brief and fascinating reappraisal of the Battle of Britain in *The Battle* by Richard Overy (Penguin, 2000). The disagreements over Churchill's role in the war are best studied in *The Churchill Coalition and Wartime Politics 1940–45* by Kevin Jefferys (Manchester UP, 1991), *Churchill: the End of Glory* by John Charmley (1993), and *The Road to 1945* by Paul Addison (1992). The social impact of the wars is best approached by reading *The People's War* by Angus Calder (1969), and *Britain in the Century of Total War: War, Peace and Social Change* (Penguin, 1968) by Arthur Marwick. The same author's latest ideas on the same theme are in his book, *A History of the Modern British Isles 1914–1999* (Blackwell, 2000). There is a collection of essays specially written for students on many of the themes in this chapter in *Britain 1918–1951* edited by Peter Caterall (Heinemann, 1994). A fascinating study of life on the home front is *Austerity in Britain: Rationing Controls and Consumption 1939–1955* by Ina Zweiniger-Bargielowska (OUP, 2000).

POST-WAR BRITAIN, 1945–64

POINTS TO CONSIDER

Following a landslide victory in the 1945 election, Labour came into power with a large majority. During the next six years it introduced the welfare state and nationalised a significant part of the industrial economy. Yet, despite gaining an unprecedentedly large popular vote in the 1951 election, Labour lost marginally to the Conservatives who went on to govern for the next 13 years. During that time they continued in all major respects the policies begun by the previous government. This was because the social and economic policies of the 1945–51 Labour government set a pattern that was largely followed by all succeeding governments down to 1979. This chapter describes the domestic achievements of Clement Attlee's post-war governments, examines the historical debate on those achievements, and then considers how the Conservative administrations that followed dealt with the issues and policies they inherited from Labour. There is a case for saying that the 1945-51 period was one of the most formative of the whole century, so it would leave a sad gap in your knowledge if you were to overlook it.

ISSUE:
What social and economic objectives did the post-war Labour government of 1945–51 set itself?

1 The Labour Party in Power: the Attlee Years, 1945–51

The 1945 Election Result			
	Votes	**Seats**	**% Vote**
Conservative	9,988,306	213	39.8
Liberal	2,248,226	12	9.0
Labour	11,995,152	393	47.8
Communist	102,780	2	0.4
Others	751,514	20	3.0

Table 20 The 1945 election result.

a) Labour's Landslide Victory in the 1945 Election

The scale of the Labour Party's victory in 1945 surprised even itself. Ten years earlier it had gained 37.9 per cent of the overall vote but had won only 154 seats (see page 77). In 1945 it gained ten per cent more of the vote, increased its support by three and a half

million, and won 393 seats. This gave it a massive majority of 180 over
the Conservatives. In hindsight, the reasons are not difficult to find.
Churchill's great popularity as a wartime leader did not carry over
into peacetime. In the minds of a good part of the electorate his
Conservative Party was associated with the grim depression years of
the 1930s and with the failure either to prevent war or to prepare for
it adequately.

In 1945 there was also a powerful feeling in Britain that effective
post-war social and economic reconstruction was both vital and
deserved, and that the tired old Conservative establishment that had
dominated the interwar years would be incapable of providing it.
People could remember clearly how a generation earlier the Lloyd
George Coalition and the Conservative governments of the 1920s
had failed to deliver 'the land fit for heroes' that the nation had been
promised. Robert Pearce, a modern analyst, captures the public
mood in 1945:

> Periods of warfare – that is to say of violence, brutality and general
> mayhem – are often followed by outbreaks of tender idealism whose
> most common symptom is the vision of a fairer society. As in 1918,
> with 'a fit country for heroes to live in', so in 1945, when the Labour
> party was closely associated with hopes for better housing and a
> welfare state … Labour did not have to win the election but merely
> avoid losing it.

Source A From *Attlee's Labour Governments 1945–51* by Robert Pearce, 1994.

The Labour Party had been created specifically to protect the
interests of ordinary people. Now its hour had come. Despite its own
failure to handle the financial crisis of 1931 during its brief period of
minority government, the Labour Party was not associated in the
minds of the electorate with the mistakes of the preceding 25 years.
It was, therefore, judged to be best fitted to undertake the task of
reconstruction in 1945.

Another important factor was the Conservatives' poor election-
eering. Confident of victory Churchill misread the mood of the
nation. On one notorious occasion he suggested that the Labour
Party's proposed reform programme would require 'a Gestapo' to
enforce it. He also failed to appreciate the reputation that had been
gained by the leading Labour figures who had served in his own
wartime Coalition. The ministerial record of such men as Attlee,
Cripps, Bevin, Dalton and Morrison had destroyed any doubts there
might have been about their ability or loyalty.

Summary of Reasons for Labour's Landslide Victory in 1945

▼ A broad feeling that the interwar political establishment had not understood the needs of ordinary people and had outlived its time.

▼ The mismanagement of the economy by Conservative politicians.

▼ The inglorious appeasement policy of the National government which had failed to prevent war occurring.

▼ The memories of the failure of the interwar governments to provide 'a land fit for heroes'.

▼ The attractive image of the Labour Party as representing the progressive spirit of the times.

▼ Churchill's inability to carry his wartime popularity into peacetime.

▼ The Conservative Party's ill-judged and unconvincing election campaign.

▼ Leading Labour figures had gained invaluable experience as ministers in the wartime Coalition and had gained the respect of the electorate.

---

b) The Leading Members of Attlee's Governments

▼ Ernest Bevin – Foreign Secretary, 1945–51

▼ Herbert Morrison – Lord President of the Council and Deputy Prime Minister, 1945–51; Foreign Secretary, 1951

▼ Hugh Dalton – Chancellor of the Exchequer, 1945–47

▼ Aneurin Bevan – Minister of Health, 1945–51; Minister of Labour, 1951

▼ Stafford Cripps – President of the Board of Trade, 1945–47; Chancellor of the Exchequer, 1947–50.

Ernest Bevin

ranks alongside Churchill and Attlee as one of the most influential British statesman of the age. Between the wars, as a right-wing Labour Party member and trade unionist, he fought against the Communist infiltration of the unions and the party. He held ministerial office continuously for over ten years after 1940, playing a critical role as Minister of Labour under Churchill in organising the war effort. As Foreign Secretary in Attlee's government, he established the basic lines of British foreign policy which lasted throughout the Cold War period.

Stafford Cripps

was regarded as the most intellectually gifted member of Attlee's government. His strong pro-Communist leanings became more acceptable after the USSR entered the war in 1941. He took the post of Minister of Aircraft Production between 1942 and 1945. Cripps was sent on special missions to India in 1942 and 1946 and helped prepare the way for Indian independence. His lean features and joyless manner seemed perfectly fitted to his role as Chancellor of the Exchequer calling on the nation to make sacrifices and put up with shortages during the period of **austerity**.

AUSTERITY
describes the hard times the British experienced in the late 1940s. In addition to the restrictions and rationing imposed on them, people had to endure a particularly severe winter in 1946–47, which exhausted coal stocks and led to fuel shortages and regular and dispiriting cuts in domestic and industrial electricity supplies.

Herbert Morrison

served with distinction as Home Secretary throughout the war and as Attlee's second in command showed the same dedication after 1945. Morrison had a running feud with Aneurin Bevan whose left-wing views he regarded as dangerous. Having lost to Attlee in the leadership election in 1935, Morrison seemed to be permanently sidelined within the party. He served as Deputy Prime Minister between 1945–51 and, after a brief spell as Foreign Secretary in 1951, as deputy leader of the party between 1951 and 1955.

Hugh Dalton

had been Minister of Economic Warfare and President of the Board of Trade under Churchill. He made a major contribution to the planning of Labour's nationalisation programme. A loud, self-opinionated academic whom Attlee tolerated only because of his talents, Dalton had to resign as Chancellor of the Exchequer in 1947 after incautiously leaking some of his Budget plans.

Aneurin Bevan

was the dominant figure on the left of the Labour Party in Attlee's time. He came from a Welsh mining background and represented the Ebbw Vale constituency continuously from 1929 to his death in 1960. Like Churchill, he overcame a speech impediment to become an outstanding parliamentary orator. His greatest achievement as a minister was the creation of the National Health Service (NHS), which came into operation in 1948. He was defeated for the leadership of the party after Attlee's retirement in 1955 by Hugh Gaitskell.

CLEMENT ATTLEE (1883–1967)

-*Profile*-

In his own time and for years afterwards, Clement Attlee tended to be underrated. He suffered by comparison with Winston Churchill. Attlee's unprepossessing physical presence and limited skills as a public speaker did not create the grand image. Churchill described him as 'a modest little man with much to be modest about'. However, in the 1970s, Attlee began to be reassessed. Stress was laid upon his skill in surviving six years of one of the most difficult periods of twentieth-century government. Nor was it merely survival. His record as Prime Minister was truly remarkable. Nationalisation, the welfare state, NATO, Indian independence: these were the striking successes of this unassuming man. His ordinariness was, indeed, a positive virtue in that he came to typify the very people whose well-being he did so much to advance. Attlee's achievements would have been impressive at any time, but when it is appreciated that they were accomplished in a post-war period dominated by the most demanding of domestic and international crises they appear even more striking.

In an interview in 1960, Attlee summed up his own practical, down-to-earth style of conducting government business:

> A Prime Minister has to know when to ask for an opinion. He can't always stop ministers offering theirs; you always have some people who'll talk on everything. But he can make sure to extract the opinion of those he wants when he needs them. The job of the Prime Minister is to get the general feeling – collect the voices. And then, when everything reasonable has been said, to get on with the job and say, 'Well, I think the decision of the Cabinet is this, that or the other. Any objections?' Usually there aren't.

Source B From *A Prime Minister on Prime Ministers* by Harold Wilson, 1977.

1883	born in London into a comfortable middle-class family;
1901 –04	read law at Oxford;
1907	became manager of a boys' settlement in London's East End;
1914 –18	served as an officer in the war;
1919	became Mayor of Stepney;
1922	elected Labour MP for Limehouse;
1930 –31	served in Ramsay MacDonald's Labour government;
1935 –55	leader of the Labour Party;
1940 –45	Deputy PM in Churchill's Coalition government;
1945 –51	Prime Minister;
1955	retired as party leader and went to the House of Lords;
1967	died.

ISSUE:

How far was the Attlee government's introduction of the welfare state the implementation of socialist principles?

c) Labour's Creation of the Welfare State

In 1942, the wartime Coalition government had produced the groundbreaking Beveridge Report, which laid down a comprehensive plan for State welfare provision (see page 203). The Report naturally aroused an eager response from the Labour Party. But the fact was all the parties accepted the Report's basic objectives. They agreed that social reconstruction was a post-war necessity in Britain. This showed how much ground had been made in Britain by collectivism, the notion of the people and the nation acting together with a common purpose. This in turn was evidence of the influence of the moderate socialism that the Labour Party espoused. Yet Churchill did not regard the Report as socialist; his reluctance to put the Report into practice was on the grounds of cost rather than principle. It is noteworthy that the Labour members of his War Cabinet supported him in 1942 and 1943 in defeating Commons motions demanding legislation to implement the Report.

However, in office after 1945 with a massive majority, the Labour government turned its attention to implementing the main proposals in the Report. Labour's strategy for an integrated social-welfare system took the form of four major measures, which came into effect in July 1948. In a Prime Ministerial broadcast Attlee explained in plain terms what the intention was:

> The four Acts which come into force tomorrow – National Insurance, Industrial Injuries, National Assistance and the National Health Service – represent the main body of the army of social security. They are comprehensive and available to every citizen. They give security to all members of the family.

Source C From a BBC broadcast by Clement Attlee, 4 July 1948.

The National Insurance Act of 1946

built upon the Act of 1911 (see page 11) by creating a system of universal and compulsory government-employer-employee contributions to provide against unemployment, sickness, maternity expenses, widowhood and retirement.

The Industrial Injuries Act of 1946

provided cover for accidents occurring in the workplace.

The National Assistance Act of 1948

established National Assistance Boards to deal directly and financially with cases of hardship and poverty.

The National Health Service Act of 1946

brought the whole population into a scheme of free medical and hospital treatment. Drug prescriptions, dental and optical care were included. Under the Act the existing voluntary and local authority hospitals were co-ordinated into a single, national system, to be operated at local level by appointed health boards.

THE FAMILY ALLOWANCES ACT, 1945

provided a weekly payment of 5 shillings (25p) for every child after the first. The money was paid directly to the mother and did not require a means test.

Source D From a speech of Ernest Bevin in the House of Commons, 18 July 1949.

THE EDUCATION ACT, 1944 (THE BUTLER ACT)

preceded the Attlee programme. It was introduced by R.A. Butler, and may be regarded as the first organised attack on one of Beveridge's five giants – Ignorance. It provided compulsory free education within a tripartite secondary education system. At the age of 11 pupils were to take an examination ('the 11-plus') to determine whether they were to attend a secondary-modern, a secondary-grammar, or a secondary-technical school.

Two other measures need to be added to the four listed by Attlee – **the Education Act** of 1944 and **the Family Allowances Act** of 1945. These were introduced before Labour came into office but were implemented by Attlee's government.

So significant was the Labour government's introduction of the welfare state that it has been described as a social revolution. However, as the Labour landslide victory in the 1945 General Election showed, it was the view of the electorate that after six years of war effort the nation was ready for such a revolution. The Beveridge Report had shown the way. Interestingly, Attlee's government, when introducing the welfare measures, was careful to point out that, far from representing revolutionary socialism, the welfare state was a responsible act of social reconstruction.

> From the point of view of what is called the welfare State and social services, I beg the House not to drag this business into a kind of partisan warfare. This so-called welfare State has developed everywhere. The United States is as much a welfare State as we are only in a different form.

In saying this Bevin was hoping to take the question out of the political arena, arguing that the welfare state was not peculiar to Britain. In the light of such views, it is perhaps best to see Labour's impressive achievement in the field of social services not as an entirely new departure but as the implementation of welfare policies that represented progressive thinking in all parties. But the fact remains that it was Labour under Attlee that found the commitment and consistency of purpose to turn good intentions into workable and permanent structures, often in the face of determined opposition, such as that of the British Medical Association (BMA) to the NHS. How well the various schemes actually worked remains a matter of dispute. Some writers – Sources E and F are examples – regard them as having, in practice, fallen far short of their original aims.

The BMA

Professions are notoriously reluctant to put the public first. The majority of consultants and senior doctors, fearing a loss of privileges and reduction in income, initially refused to co-operate with Aneurin Bevan, who was responsible for the introduction of the NHS. In the end he had to buy off the BMA. In return for a guarantee that they would not lose financially and would be allowed to keep their private practices, the doctors agreed to enter the NHS. Bevan remarked bitterly that he had won them over only by 'stuffing their mouths with gold'.

Half a century after the Beveridge Report it is clear that the Second World War raised expectations that were never fulfilled. Some of the most radical ideas of the period, like Beveridge's plan for subsistence level benefits, were never implemented. The class structure proved more enduring, and the power of the state more limited, than radical reformers imagined. Social reform had little impact upon women. Yet revisionists should beware of revising away the 1940s. The welfare reforms of the period were an impressive attempt to create a post-war settlement based on new conceptions of social justice. They did succeed in raising the living standards of the poor, and the social status of the working class as a whole.

Source E From 'A New Jerusalem' by Paul Addison in *Britain 1918–1951* edited by Peter Caterall, 1994.

The NHS failed to improve the general medical service available to the bulk of the population. The middle classes benefited to some extent but the lower classes continued to experience a humiliating standard of care. The middle classes were liberated from doctors' fees and they enjoyed the services of the better practitioners, while the lower classes, especially after the introduction of the **prescription charge** in 1952, continued to receive an inferior service, but for a higher level of payment through taxes and direct charges.

Source F From 'Doctors, public service and profit' by Charles Webster in *Britain 1918–1951* edited by Peter Caterall, 1994.

PRESCRIPTION CHARGES

At various times in the 1950s and 1960s, Labour governments, when hard-pressed financially, introduced charges on medical prescriptions. These were always controversial since they contravened Bevan's founding principle that the NHS should be free at the point of treatment. A number of leading Labour government ministers, including Bevan himself and Harold Wilson, resigned in protest when such charges were brought in.

Figure 23 Cartoon showing 'Matron' Bevan forcing the doctors to take the nasty medicine of the NHS.

ACTIVITY

Points for you to debate, based on your reading of section 1c.

▼ Did the fact that the welfare state fell short of its expectations diminish the original achievement in setting it up?

▼ Did Bevan's compromise with the BMA mean that the NHS was 'fatally flawed from the start'?

▼ How accurately does Figure 23 depict the relationship between the BMA and Aneurin Bevan?

ISSUE:

How extensive was the Labour governments' restructuring of the economy?

CHIEF INDUSTRIES AND INSTITUTIONS NATIONALISED UNDER LABOUR

1946 the Bank of England, coal, civil aviation, cable and wireless;
1947 road transport, electricity;
1948 gas;
1949 iron and steel.

Q Why did the Labour governments experience serious financial problems?

---

d) The Economy under Labour, 1945–51

From its earliest days the Labour Party had held the principle that government had the right to direct the key aspects of economy in order to create efficiency and social justice. When it came into office with an overwhelming majority in 1945 the times were ripe for it to fulfil its aims. In its election manifesto, *Let us Face the Future*, the party promised to implement an ambitious programme for the **nationalisation** of Britain's major industries. These were specified as the fuel and power industries, iron and steel, and inland transport, which included rail, road and air services.

What prevented Attlee's governments from going further down the road of reform was the sheer scale of the financial problem they inherited. By the end of the war Britain had debts of £3,500 million, and a balance of payments deficit of £875 million. To meet this crisis, Hugh Dalton, the Labour Chancellor of the Exchequer, negotiated a loan of $6,000 million from the USA and Canada. The government's hope was that in accordance with Keynesian theory the loan would provide the basis of an industrial recovery. But such recovery as did occur was never enough to meet expectations. Part of the problem was that the American dollar was so strong at the end of the war that

---

Nationalisation

Clause IV of the Labour Party's constitution committed it to achieving 'the common ownership of the means of production, distribution and exchange'. This involved bringing the major private industries under public control after compensating their former owners. (In effect, public control meant government control.) Labour believed that nationalisation would bring greater productivity and efficiency. In office from 1945 to 1951, Labour made nationalisation a major part of its programme.

it dominated international commerce. The consequence was that Britain began to suffer from what was known as the '**dollar gap**'.

What made the situation still worse was that Britain had agreed with the USA, its Cold War ally, to increase its spending on defence from £2.3 billion to £4.7 billion. Despite demobilisation in 1945, Britain as one of the occupying forces in Europe and as a member of the United Nations Security Council, continued to maintain a large peacetime army. In 1950 this stood at nearly one million men. In addition to the expense entailed by this was the extra expenditure Britain had shouldered when Attlee's government in 1948 committed Britain to the development of its own atomic weapon. By 1951 the nation was spending 14 per cent of its GNP on defence. Faced with these costs, the Labour government's only recourse under Dalton and his successor, Stafford Cripps, was to adopt a policy of austerity. Controls on imports were imposed to keep dollar spending to a minimum. But this led to shortages and rationing. In an effort to ease the situation the pound sterling was devalued in 1949 from $4.03 to $2.80.

The hard times were not made easier by the fact that this period of austerity coincided with Labour's creation of the welfare state, which placed further heavy financial burdens on an already strained economy. Moreover, Britain's financial problems would have been even greater had it not been for the relief provided by the **Marshall Plan**, which operated from 1948.

ACTIVITY

Having studied section 1, attempt the following questions.

▼ Why did the Labour government make nationalisation a major part of its economic programme?

▼ Why was the government so heavily burdened with financial difficulties between 1945 and 1951?

---

2 The Debate Over the Labour Governments' Achievements

The record of Attlee's governments showed that despite working throughout under the shadow of serious economic difficulties they achieved a high degree of activity and success. This was a tribute to their enthusiasm and to the administrative and political skills of their leading ministers.

THE DOLLAR GAP

Since sterling was weaker than the dollar, the goods that Britain desperately needed from North America had to be paid for in dollars. This drained Britain of a substantial part of the loan it had negotiated while at the same time making it harder to meet the repayments.

How did Labour attempt to deal with Britain's financial problems?

THE MARSHALL PLAN

After 1945 the world's trading nations all experienced severe balance of payments difficulties. Worried that this would destroy international commerce, the USA, the only economy with sufficient resources, adopted a programme in 1947 to provide dollars to any country willing to receive them in return for granting trade concessions to the United States. Whatever America's self-interest may have been, it is difficult to see how Europe could have recovered without a massive inflow of American capital. Under the Plan, which bore the name of the US Secretary of State, George Marshall, Europe received $15 billion, Britain's share being ten per cent of that.

What did Labour
achieve during its six
years of office, 1945–51?

Main Achievements of the Attlee Governments, 1945–51

▽ It introduced a nationalisation programme.

▽ It created the welfare state.

▽ It helped convince the USA of the need for the Marshall Plan.

▽ It granted independence to India (see page 237).

▽ It organised a housing programme that created one million homes by 1950.

▽ It played a key role in the formation of NATO, and as ally to United States in the Cold War (see page 226).

So large was Labour's majority in the 1945 election that its opponents feared it would enable the new government to usher in sweeping socialist changes into Britain. It is true that during the next six years many significant and lasting reforms were introduced, but the Labour governments made no attempt either to disrupt the capitalist system in Britain or to destroy the social structure. That indeed was the complaint of the left-wing critics of Attlee's government, who argued that Labour, with its unassailable majority, was in a position to bring about a genuine transformation of British society. But instead, they asserted, it threw away the opportunity by settling for half measures. Its nationalisation programme was not really an attempt to take central control of the economy. It was restricted to non-profit making concerns and made no effort to take over the private banks or insurance companies. Another left-wing charge was that, by borrowing heavily from the USA in order to meet its financial difficulties, Attlee's government lost its freedom of action in foreign policy. Dependent on America, Britain found itself locked itself into a lasting Cold War hostility towards the Soviet Union.

A powerful argument from an opposite political viewpoint was that the Labour government had indeed thrown away a historic opportunity to reform Britain – not, however, by doing too little but by doing too much. Writers such as Corelli Barnett have claimed that what Britain needed after the war was the reconstruction of its industrial base. Priority should have been given to financial recovery and investment in the nation's **infrastructure**. This, runs Barnett's argument, would have provided the means for Britain to re-establish itself as a major manufacturing economy, able to respond to the post-war international demand for commodity goods. But, instead, Britain made a priority not of industrial recovery but of social welfare. However, welfare was costly and Britain, being practically bankrupt at the end of the war, had to borrow heavily to fund it. Saddled with large debts, Britain was able to achieve only low economic growth. To strengthen his case, Barnett quoted the example of West Germany,

INFRASTRUCTURE
refers to the interlocking systems and installations which enable a nation's industrial economy to operate. These include such essential facilities as transport, power supply, sewerage and communications.

which, by delaying its welfare state until it had achieved industrial recovery, put itself on the path to an economic miracle.

The Labour government of this period laid down the policies that were to be followed in all essentials by successive Labour and Conservative governments during the next 35 years. Until Margaret Thatcher came into power in 1979 and deliberately challenged this **consensus**, there was a broad level of agreement on what were the major domestic and foreign issues and how they were to be handled.

Whatever the later questions concerning the Labour governments' performance there was little doubt among contemporaries that something momentous had occurred. They were conscious that Labour had created the welfare state, that it had carried into peacetime the notion of State-directed planning, which had always been one of its basic socialist objectives, and that in so doing it had established Keynesianism as the basic British approach to economic planning (see page 123). R.A. Butler, a leading Conservative, put the Labour reforms into historical perspective by describing them as 'the greatest social revolution in our history'. What gives particular significance to Butler's words is that the Conservative Party came in all major respects to accept that revolution.

ACTIVITY

Show that you understand the arguments about the Attlee government's achievement by writing down three lists: a) achievements, b) left-wing criticisms, c) right-wing criticisms. Do you think the achievements outweigh the criticisms from whatever quarter?

Q

How important historically were Attlee's governments?

CONSENSUS

is the notion that between 1945 and 1979 there was substantial common ground between the major parties on basic issues. Conservative and Labour economic policies were based on Keynesian principles, their welfare policies on the Beveridge Report, their foreign policies on the pro-American alliance, and their imperial policies on the principle of independence for Britain's former colonies. This common area of agreement did not prevent serious political rivalry, but, when in government, the Labour and Conservative parties followed fundamentally similar policies.

---

3 The Conservatives in Power, 1951–64

ISSUE:
Was the period 1951–64 one of growth or stagnation?

The 1950 Election Result			
	Votes	**Seats**	**% vote**
Conservative	12,502,567	298	43.5
Labour	13,266,592	315	46.1
Liberal	2,621,548	9	9.1
Others	381,964	3	1.3

Table 21 The 1950 election result.

Table 22 The 1951 election
result.

The 1951 Election Result			
	Votes	**Seats**	**% Vote**
Conservative	13,717,538	321	48.0
Labour	13,948,605	295	48.8
Liberal	730,556	6	2.5
Others	198,969	3	0.7

**CONSERVATIVE
PRIME MINISTERS,
1951–64**

1951 Winston Churchill
–55
1955 Anthony Eden
–57
1957 Harold Macmillan
–63
1963 Alec Douglas-Home
–64

a) The Conservative Victory in 1951

The election figures for 1951 reveal one of the extraordinary characteristics of British electoral politics. It is possible for a party to poll more votes than its opponents yet still be defeated. The Labour Party won the largest number of votes ever gained up to that point in electoral history. Yet because of the way its support was distributed across the constituencies it gained fewer seats than the Conservatives. After six years of government Labour had in fact more than held its share of the vote. Thus it was not a matter of an unpopular government being swept from office by a disillusioned electorate. The explanation of Attlee's losing office in 1951 is not so much Labour decline as Conservative recovery. While Labour had gained an added two million votes between 1945 and 1951, the Conservatives had added nearly four million. This, together with the fact that the Conservative vote was more evenly spread, gave Churchill's party a considerable boost. The Conservatives had already cut the overall Labour majority to five in the 1950 election and although Attlee's government carried on for another 18 months it became increasingly difficult for it to govern effectively. Weariness had also set in. Attlee, Bevin and Morrison, for example, had been in office continuously since 1940. The government had also been weakened by Aneurin Bevan's resignation in April 1951 over the decision of Hugh Gaitskell, the Chancellor of the Exchequer, to make NHS patients pay prescription charges.

There were, of course, more positive aspects to the victory of the Conservatives. Their heavy and unexpected defeat in 1945 had left them shell shocked. However, by the late 1940s their fortunes had begun to improve. Much of this was due to the re-organisation of the party undertaken by Lord Woolton, the Conservative Party Chairman. It was also at this time that the younger Tory MPs, such as R.A. Butler, began to bring new ideas and confidence to the party. The nationalisation issue gave them a cause round which they could rally and on which they could attack the government.

Although the Conservatives consistently voted against the early nationalisation programme, their challenge was unimpressive. Down to the Iron and Steel Bill, introduced in 1948, they had offered only

Why did the
Conservatives win
the 1951 election?

token resistance. The principle of public ownership itself was rarely discussed; most of the debates were taken up with considering the methods by which nationalisation would be introduced and what compensation should be paid to the dispossessed owners. But the proposal to nationalise iron and steel enabled the Conservatives to rally in defence of the steel manufacturers. Of all the concerns to be nationalised, the steel industry was the only one showing a profit at the time of its takeover. This encouraged a determined struggle against the Bill amongst owners and shareholders and allowed the Opposition in parliament to develop an attack upon nationalisation as an abuse of government power.

R.A. Butler

As Minister of Education in Churchill's Coalition, Butler had been responsible for the Education Act of 1944 (see page 134). He played a major part in restoring the Conservative Party's morale during the Attlee years and went on to hold a number of ministerial offices, including those of Chancellor of the Exchequer (1951–55) and Home Secretary (1957–62). Although he never achieved the leadership of the party he was one of the most progressive Conservatives of the period and gave his name to the term '**Butskellism**'.

BUTSKELLISM
The word, first coined in 1954 by *The Economist*, joined together the names of Butler, seen as representing the Conservative left, and Hugh Gaitskell, regarded as a key figure on Labour right. It suggested the common ground between the major parties on such matters as finance, the economy and the welfare state.

Q Had the Conservatives been converted to 'welfarism'?

The narrow Conservative victory in 1951 was followed by larger majorities in the elections of 1955 and 1959. This gave the Conservatives 13 unbroken years of government between 1951 and 1964. The distinctive characteristic of the policies followed in this period was how closely they coincided with those introduced by the Attlee governments. In the words of a modern historian, Dilwyn Porter, 'Attlee's patriotic socialists gave way to Churchill's social patriots'. Just as Labour had moved to the right by accepting capitalism and the mixed economy, so the Conservatives moved to the left by accepting Keynesianism and the managed economy.

In opposition the Conservatives had opposed every nationalisation measure and many of the welfare proposals. Yet, in government themselves after 1951, they fully denationalised only one industry – steel – and built upon the welfare programme which they had inherited. Labour could justly claim that it had converted the Conservative Party to welfarism. This was certainly the story of the next 13 years. Successive Conservative governments put increasing amounts of revenue into the National Health Service and the social security system (see page 168).

KEY EVENTS AND DEVELOPMENTS, 1951–55

▼ rationing was ended;
▼ the steel industry was denationalised;
▼ the Conservative Party committed itself to building 300,000 houses a year;
▼ faced with financial and economic difficulties R.A. Butler, the Chancellor of the Exchequer, began the 'stop-go' process of regulating the economy (see page 147);
▼ the accession of Elizabeth II ushered in a new 'Elizabethan age';
▼ Britain detonated its first atomic bomb in 1953;
▼ end of the Korean war, 1953 (see page 227).

ISSUE:

Why was Eden's premiership so short-lived?

ACTIVITY

After reading this section, show that you have grasped the major points by writing down two or three paragraphs explaining why the Conservatives came to power in 1951.

Points to consider:

▼ Labour's problems – financial and economic difficulties (check back to page 136) – tight majority after 1950 – weary after long period of government – right–left divisions.
▼ Conservatives – recovered from shock of 1945 defeat – influx of young enthusiastic MPs – Woolton's reforms – attack on nationalisation provided a cause around which the party could rally.

b) Churchill's Government, 1951–55

Churchill was 77 when he became Prime Minister for the second time. He was too old and frail to be much more than a figurehead. What sustained him was his reputation. For some months in 1953 he was out of action altogether following a stroke. Nobody seemed to notice. Yet his government was responsible for a number of important developments.

c) Anthony Eden's Government, 1955–57

The 1955 Election Result			
	Votes	**Seats**	**% Vote**
Conservative	13,286,569	344	49.7
Labour	12,404,970	277	46.4
Liberal	722,405	6	2.7
Others	346,554	3	1.2

Table 23 The 1955 election result.

Eden had been Foreign Secretary from 1935 to 1938, when he had resigned over the National government's appeasement policy, and again from 1940 to 1945. A handsome man who set the hearts of Tory ladies aflutter, he had long been regarded as the heir apparent to Churchill as Conservative leader. However, he had to wait far longer than he had expected since Churchill did not finally retire until 1955. The election that Eden called soon after becoming Prime Minister in 1955 produced an increased Conservative majority. This was the only real success of his short administration. Having had to wait so long, Eden was a man in a hurry. Irritated by criticism in the

Tory press that his domestic policies 'lacked the smack of firm government', he was determined to achieve success in foreign affairs, which he had always regarded as his special area of expertise. This drew him into the ill-fated Suez affair (see page 230), the strain of which broke his health and led to his early retirement.

(see page 230)

ISSUE:
Did Macmillan follow 'the middle way' in his policies?

d) Harold Macmillan's Government, 1957–63

HAROLD MACMILLAN (1894–1986)

-Profile-

Macmillan's appearance was that of a typical English gentleman. Yet by birth he was half Scottish, half American. He had a gallant service record in the 1914–18 war, an experience which gave him a particular respect for the working class. This was deepened by his witnessing, as MP for a Durham constituency, the grim effects of the Depression in the North-East. He expressed his unorthodox Conservatism in 1938 in his book, *The Middle Way*, which may be regarded as an early appeal for consensus politics. He argued for the acceptance of Keynesianism and pressed the case for extending the direction by the State of a broad range of services. Having held key posts in Churchill's 1940–45 Coalition and in the 1951–55 government, he became PM in 1957. Although he was Chancellor of the Exchequer at the time of the Suez affair in 1956, Macmillan was generally regarded as not being deeply implicated in the government's failure. This left him well placed to heal the wounds in the party. He was the first PM to commit Britain to entering the EEC and was an outspoken supporter of independence for the African colonies. He proved himself a keen Cold Warrior by supporting the USA in its conflicts with the Soviet Union.

   Despite his seemingly relaxed style Macmillan worked extremely hard and could be ruthless on occasion: in 1962 in the 'Night of the Long Knives' he dismissed half his Cabinet. Despite considerable unhappiness in his private life he maintained an 'unflappable' air in public. He had a dry sense of humour and took particular delight in the satirists' portrayal of him as 'Supermac', originally intended as an ironic reference on his government's uncertain economic performance. His own comment on this was famously that under Conservatism Britain had 'never had it so good'. The last years of his premiership were marred by **the Profumo affair**.

1894	born into the Macmillan publishing family;
1917	badly wounded in action;
1924	elected as Conservative MP;
1930s	opposed appeasement policy;
1938	published *The Middle Way*;
1940 –42	Minister of Supply;
1942 –45	Minister with special responsibility for the war in North Africa;
1951 –54	Minister for Housing and Local Government;
1954 –55	Minister of Defence;
1955	Foreign Secretary;
1955 –57	Chancellor of the Exchequer;
1957 –63	Prime Minister and leader of the Conservative Party;
1984	became the Earl of Stockton;
1986	died.

THE PROFUMO AFFAIR, 1963

was a sexual scandal involving the Minister for War, John Profumo, whose liaison with a prostitute created a national security risk since she included members of the Soviet embassy among her clients. Profumo lied in the House of Commons about the relationship. The scandal did not by itself bring down the government, but the fact that the Prime Minister believed Profumo's original denial of impropriety suggested that Macmillan was losing his political grip.

KEY EVENTS AND DEVELOPMENTS, 1957–64

1957 the government reduced Britain's conventional armed forces and expanded its nuclear deterrent programme;
the UK's first hydrogen bomb tested;
the Homicide Act removed the death penalty except for five specific offences;
the Rent Act put six million properties on the market by abolishing rent control but caused a general rise in rents;

1958 life peerages were introduced, allowing selected men and women to enter the House of Lords;

1959 an increased majority for Conservatives in the general election;
Britain was a founding member of EFTA;

1962 Commonwealth Immigration Act – for the first time restrictions were placed on the number of immigrants allowed into Britain from Commonwealth countries;
the government set up the National Economic Development Council;
Macmillan and President Kennedy negotiated the Nassau Agreement by which the USA undertook to supply Polaris nuclear missiles for Britain's submarines;
Britain supported the USA in the Cuban Missile crisis;

1963 Nuclear Test Ban Treaty, signed by Britain, the USA and the USSR, ended the testing of nuclear weapons in the atmosphere;
Britain's first application to join the EEC was vetoed by France;
Macmillan's government was embarrassed by the Profumo affair;
Alec Douglas-Home became PM on Macmillan's retirement.

Figure 24 Cartoon of Harold Macmillan as 'Supermac'. Macmillan takes on the form of Superman, the popular comic-book hero who could do anything. Macmillan became the butt of the political and social satirists who flourished in the late 1950s and 1960s in the press and the theatre, and in particular in the BBC programme, 'That Was The Week That Was'.

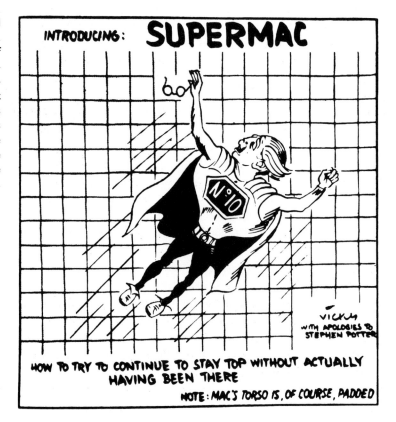

The 1959 Election Result			
	Votes	**Seats**	**% Vote**
Labour	12,215,538	258	43.8
Conservative	13,749,830	365	49.4
Liberal	1,638,571	6	5.9
Others	255,302	1	0.9

Table 24 The 1959 election result.

e) The Conservatives and the Economy, 1951–64

The deflationary policies of the Labour government before 1951 did have beneficial effects in the short term. The cost of British goods dropped and exports picked up. There was also a major uplift in the international economy in the 1950s, largely a result of the Marshall Plan, which led to increased demand for British products. Yet Britain's recovery was not as pronounced as it might have been. Compared with what was happening in Europe and the USA, the British economy appeared sluggish. Nevertheless the Conservative governments of 1951–64 made no serious attempt to change the main lines of Britain's economic and financial strategies. They continued to operate a **mixed economy**. This is an aspect of the consensus politics that operated in Britain between 1945 and 1979, sometimes referred to as 'Butskellism' (see page 141). The Conservatives continued with Labour's twin aims of trying to maintain full employment while at the same time achieving economic growth, all this against a background of heavy debt repayment.

The governments of the time followed a loose form of Keynesianism (see page 123). They hoped to avoid the extremes of **inflation and deflation** by a series of adjustments to meet particular problems as they came along. If inflation rose too quickly, measures to slow it down would be introduced. These invariably involved a raising of interest rates to discourage borrowing and an increase in import controls to limit purchases from abroad, thereby reducing the trade gap. The annual budgets were an important part of the mechanism. As a check on overspending or too rapid a rise in wages, taxes might be increased. Treasury officials spoke of such moves as preventing the economy from 'overheating'.

Alternatively, if there was a fall in demand for goods, which meant difficulties for manufacturers and retailers, the Chancellor of the Exchequer of the day might introduce 'a give away' budget in which taxes and interest rates were lowered. This, it was hoped, would encourage more spending and thus result in a demand-led recovery.

A common criticism voiced by both parties when in opposition was that budgets were too often used as short-term measures to buy votes

ISSUE:

Was there any real difference between Labour and Conservative governments in the economic policies they followed in the post-war period?

THE MIXED ECONOMY

Politicians often present their arguments as if there is a clear choice between a state-regulated economy with government controls, and a market economy without them. In fact, no such choice exists. After 1945 Britain operated a mixed economy – mixed in its combination of public ownership and private enterprise, and mixed also in the sense that even in the areas where the free market supposedly operated there was very considerable state intervention.

Q

What economic policies did the Conservative governments follow in the period 1951–64?

INFLATION AND DEFLATION

Inflation refers to the decline in the value of money over a period of time. More money is needed to buy the same quantity of goods. Deflation is the opposite process whereby money increases in value over a span of time. Neither inflation nor deflation is bad in itself. It is when the process occurs too rapidly or is too long sustained that problems set in. In Britain in the second half of the twentieth century inflation was seen as the major threat to financial and economic stability.

Figure 25 Vicky's cartoon depicts a situation in which the Conservative government, behind its slogans advocating economic freedom, had set out on the path towards a planned economy. Selwyn Lloyd, the Chancellor of the Exchequer, thumbs a lift on Harold Wilson's Labour scooter, knowing that they are both going the same way. This is another illustration of the underlying consensus between the parties on essential issues.

Q Did the budgets in this period illustrate the lack of a consistent economic policy?

INTEREST RATE

refers to the percentage interest that has to be paid back on a loan. The belief was that a rise in the interest rate discouraged borrowing by making it more expensive. Between 1939 and 1997 it was the government itself that fixed interest rates.

in general elections. An interesting illustration of vote-catching was the Conservative budgets of the late 1950s and early 1960s. In his 1959 budget the Chancellor of the Exchequer, Derick Heathcoat Amory, made an effort to boost support for the government in the forthcoming election by introducing a range of tax cuts. This was at a time when the prevailing high inflation suggested that financial restraint would have been a more appropriate policy. The result was increased consumer spending which led to still higher inflation and a wider trade gap. Faced with this, Heathcoat Amory changed tack and adopted deflationary measures which included tax and **interest rate** rises, cuts in public spending, and an attempt to put a limit on wage increases.

Successive Conservative Chancellors continued with these restrictive measures until the 1964 election loomed. To regain lost popularity Macmillan's government in 1963 returned to an expansionist budgetary policy; taxes and interest rates were again lowered. The consequence was another boom in consumer spending. Since the sudden demand for goods could not be met from British stocks there was a rapid increase in the import of foreign manufactures. The net result was that by the end of 1964 Britain had a balance of payments deficit of over £800 million.

What such a train of events suggested was that Britain lacked a consistent economic strategy. The series of adjustments made by governments did not really add up to an integrated plan. Policy lagged behind events; it did not direct them. This is what led commentators to coin such terms as **stop-go** and **stagflation** to denote the failure of governments to develop policies that produced a consistently performing economy. All this pointed to the difficulty of managing a modern economy, which is always vulnerable to the play of unforeseeable circumstances. When Harold Macmillan was asked by a reporter what he regarded as the most difficult feature of government planning, he replied 'events, dear boy, events'.

> **STOP-GO**
> When domestic consumption and prices rose too quickly, the government put on the 'brake' by increasing taxes and raising interest rates, thus making it more difficult to borrow money. When production and exports declined, the government pressed the 'accelerator' by cutting taxes and lowering interest rates, thus making it easier to borrow money.

4 The Debate on the Conservatives' Performance, 1951–64

a) The Case for the Prosecution

There is no doubt that in 1964 Britain was more prosperous than it had been in 1951. Yet critics argued that this would have occurred regardless of who was in power. The greater prosperity was largely the result of an upturn in the international economy. The charge was that Britain should have been more prosperous still. It ought to have seized the opportunity offered by the worldwide demand for manufactures to enter into a period of industrial growth such as had happened in Germany, the USA and Japan. But the Conservative governments had dithered. They had accepted the broad Keynesian principles of a directed economy but had not shown the will or competence to carry them through. They had not developed coherent economic policies but had simply employed 'stop-go' tactics to prevent the economy swinging too wildly between deflation and inflation. Apart from a wish to keep the value of sterling, they had no structured financial strategy. They had used budgets and tax adjustments not in a responsible way but as a technique for buying votes at election time. A major error was the government's failure to invest in industrial research and development. It had shown equal misjudgement in not making efforts to improve Britain's poor employer-worker relations. The result of all these shortcomings was 'stagflation'; by the mid-1960s Britain had one of the poorest growth rates among the advanced industrial nations.

> **ISSUE:**
> Did the period 1951–64 mark '13 wasted years'?

> **STAGFLATION**
> is a word combining stagnation and inflation. It refers to the situation in which industry declined but inflation still persisted, with the result that the economy received the worst of both worlds.

It could be argued that the government's record in foreign affairs was equally unimpressive (see page 230). Critics, taking their cue from the American statesman, Dean Acheson who had asserted that Britain had lost an empire but not yet found a role, pointed to a series of reverses that Britain had suffered in its foreign relations. Its humiliation over Suez in 1956 had indicated that Britain was no longer strong enough to act independently in foreign affairs. This confirmed that the days of British imperialism were over, which in turn accelerated the process already begun of granting independence to the African colonies. Decolonisation in the 1950s and 1960s was, therefore, not an act of generosity; Britain was simply not in a position to keep them.

A similar inability to act independently was evident in the Nassau agreement of 1962. Britain's buying of Polaris missiles from the Americans in order to maintain itself as a nuclear power was tantamount to admitting that it no longer possessed an independent deterrent. It was the Anglo-American talks at Nassau that led to the final great diplomatic embarrassment suffered by Macmillan's government – the French rejection of Britain's application to join the EEC on the grounds that the British were not 'sufficiently European minded' (see page 243).

b) The Case for the Defence

Under Conservative governments wages were higher, rationing had gone, people were healthier, better housed, and a greater number of them were better educated. Given Britain's heavy defence burdens these were major achievements. Moreover, while Labour criticised the Conservative governments over points of detail it did not advance a fundamentally different policy. Both parties were committed to maintaining Britain's position as a world power. Indeed, the real debate over this was not between the parties but within the Labour movement. The left did have an alternative; it wanted the scrapping of the greater part of Britain's defence budget and the unilateral abandonment of nuclear weapons. But this never became mainstream Labour Party policy. Notwithstanding their constant bickering, the two main parties did not offer true alternatives. Strength is given to this argument by observing what happened after 1964. Despite his appeal to modernity and his mocking of the Conservatives as political dinosaurs, Harold Wilson in office behaved as a conservative in the key areas of economics and foreign affairs.

ACTIVITY

You have the heard the prosecution and defence cases. Now consider your verdict.

▼ Working on Post-War Britain, 1945–64

Given the historical significance of the post-war Labour measures it is important that you grasp how they laid the basis for the modernisation of Britain. The three areas to concentrate on are the 1945 landslide victory, the creation of the welfare state and the nationalisation programme. You will have gathered from the chapter that the Conservative governments that followed were very close to Labour in many of their policies. This consensus is a key feature of post-war British politics and you would do well to make sure you understand where the policies of the parties coincided.

Answering Structured Writing and Essay Questions on Post-War Britain, 1945–64

Types of question	Examples of typical questions
Structured	**1** In what ways did the post-war Labour government reform the system of social welfare in Britain? **2** Describe the main nationalisation measures introduced by Attlee's governments between 1945 and 1951. **3** Describe the steps taken by the post-war Labour government to deal with the financial problems that faced Britain after 1945. **4** Describe the budget policies adopted by Macmillan's government between 1957 and 1964.
Causes	**5** Explain why the Labour Party won a landslide election victory in 1945. **6** Why did Aneurin Bevan meet strong resistance from the medical profession to his plans for a National Health Service? **7** Account for the electoral recovery of the Conservative Party by 1951. **8** Explain why the Conservative Party was in office for so long after 1951. **9** Why was Anthony Eden's Conservative government, 1955–57, so shortlived?
Historical judgement	**10** Examine the validity of the claim that the Attlee governments achieved 'a revolution in Britain'. **11** 'Thirteen wasted years.' How far do you agree with this verdict on the period of Conservative government between 1951 and 1964?

Answering Source-Based Questions on Post-War Britain, 1945–64

Study the following source material and then answer the questions which follow.

Source G From a description of the 1945 General Election by a Labour activist in the North of England.

I will always remember July 26 as a sunny day – though I don't really know if it was. My friends and I had not expected Labour to win. We remembered 1935 and we had heard of 1931. We thought the Tories were too smart and that they would always kid the masses. We told ourselves that the young did not know the 1930s and the old ones would thank Churchill for a good war. But my heart was in my mouth as every result came in. I thought I was dreaming.

Source H From the entries for 1945 in the diary of the writer, Martin Belloc Lowndes.

I have never known the middle-class people with whom I am in touch to be more amazed than at the result of the election. They are trembling with fear. Certain people connected with the government – I should say the *late* government – cannot believe that they are really out. Sir John and Lady Anderson gave a lunch party. Three of the guests came on here afterwards and told me about it. They said nobody who was there seemed to realise what was going to happen.

Source I From *Attlee's Labour Governments 1945–51* by Robert Pearce, 1994.

'All our enemies having surrendered unconditionally, or being just about to do so', wrote former Prime Minister Winston Churchill, 'I was instantly dismissed by the British electorate.' He was not the only one to be shocked by the result of the 1945 General Election.

Political commentators were equally amazed. Almost everyone, including Labour's leaders, had predicted a comfortable Conservative victory. Yet, in retrospect, it is hard to understand such views … .

The election result no longer seems even mildly surprising. Indeed, it has been said that, by the time of the campaign, Labour did not have to win the election but merely avoid losing it.

▼ QUESTIONS ON SOURCES

1. Study Source G
With reference to source G and your own knowledge, explain the reference to '1931' in the context of the 1945 election. **(3 marks)**
2. Study Source H
With reference to your own knowledge, explain how useful Source H is as evidence about the 1945 election. **(7 marks)**

3. Study Sources G, H and I and use your own knowledge.

Outline the reasons why those who feared a Labour victory in 1945, and those who wished for it, were taken by surprise by the actual election result. **(15 marks)**

Points to note about question 3

The vital point to realise here is that the question concentrates on the surprised reaction to the election result, not on the election itself. There are two aspects to the surprise – the fact of a Labour victory at all, and the fact that it was a landslide. Source G deals with the surprise among Labour supporters; they thought that a combination of the Tories' ability to trick the masses, Labour's handicap dating from its 1931 crisis, and respect for Churchill among young and old, would carry the day for the Conservatives. Source H expresses the bewilderment of the middle-class Conservative supporters who were terrified by the thought of what might not happen with Labour in power. You will notice that, unlike Source G, Source H describes only the sense of surprise; it does not give reasons why the Conservatives had thought they would win. Source I provides a measured analysis of why contemporaries should not have been so surprised. It is able to provide what they were not aware of at the time – that it was quite possible for the electorate to admire Churchill as a wartime leader but not feel obliged to vote him back into office in peacetime.

Further Reading

Books in the Access to History series

Britain: Domestic Politics 1939–64 by Paul Adelman (chapters 3 to 8) provides an excellent analysis of the Attlee government and of the 13 years of Conservatism that followed.

General

Recommended books which cover the whole period are: *A History of the Modern British Isles 1914–1999* by Arthur Marwick (Blackwell, 2000), *The People's Peace, British History 1945–90* by Kenneth Morgan (Oxford University Press, 1999), who is one of the leading authorities in this field, *Hope and Glory: Britain 1900–1990* by Peter Clarke (Penguin, 1996), which is a highly entertaining text, *From Blitz to Blair A New History of Britain Since 1939*, edited by Nick Tiratsoo (Phoenix, 1997), which contains a stimulating set of essays by left-wing writers, and *Post War Britain* by Alan Sked and Chris Cook (Penguin, 1992), which takes a right of centre approach. An excellent short study of the post-war revolution is *Attlee's Labour Governments 1945–51* by Robert Pearce (Routledge, 1994). A valuable collection of articles on the 1951–64 Conservative years is to be found in *The Age of Affluence 1951–64* edited by Vernon Bogdanor and Robert Skidelsky (Macmillan, 1974). An important and controversial book explaining Britain's decline is *The Audit of War* by Corelli Barnett (Macmillan, 1986). This could be usefully compared with *Britain's Decline: Problems and Perspectives* by Alan Sked (Blackwell, 1987). The definitive text on the post-45 consensus is *Consensus Politics From Attlee to Major* by Dennis Kavanagh and Peter Morris (Blackwell, 2nd edition 1994). A witty and informative study of the party leaders of the period is *A Question of Leadership: From Gladstone to Thatcher* by Peter Clarke (Penguin, 1992). Among individual biographies which students would enjoy are *Attlee* by Robert Pearce (Longman, 1998), *RAB: the Life of R.A. Butler* by Anthony Howard (Cape, 1987) and *Harold Macmillan* by Alistair Horne (Macmillan, 1990).

THE AGE OF CONSENSUS, 1964–79

CHAPTER 7

POINTS TO CONSIDER

The period 1964–79 was notable for its consensus politics. Successive Labour and Conservative governments tended to follow very similar policies. This was principally because they were beset by economic problems for which they had few clear answers. To explain these problems, the chapter begins with a study of 'Britain in decline', a contemporary reference to Britain's apparent inability to match the growth rates of the world's major industrial economies. You are encouraged to read this opening section so that you can then put the governments of the period into perspective by appreciating the difficulties they faced.

Introduction

A number of critical developments gave shape to Britain between 1945 and the end of the century. It is helpful to list these. (They are numbered for clarity but the order is not meant to suggest their relative importance.)

1. The introduction of the welfare state.
2. A significant rise in the standard of living of the people.
3. Continuing heavy defence commitments and expenditure.
4. The shift from a manufacturing to a service economy.
5. The decline in trade union strength which reflected the decrease in the number of industrial workers in the staple industries.
6. Inflation and recession as recurring features of the economy.
7. Significant levels of immigration which changed Britain into a multi-racial society.
8. The weakening of parliament as an institution, in the face of growth of power of central government.
9. Class shifts and political realignments that altered electoral voting patterns.
10. The retreat from Empire and the abandonment of Britain's economic ties with the Commonwealth.
11. A loss of sovereignty entailed by Britain's entry into the EEC.

These were the issues which dominated politics in the second half of the twentieth century. The distinctive feature of the years before 1979 was how close the political parties were in their response to these issues. Although Labour and the Conservatives rowed fiercely with each other as government and opposition, once each party was in office it seldom made major changes to the policies it inherited from the other.

Governments and Prime Ministers, 1964–79		
	Labour	**Conservative**
1964–70	Harold Wilson	
1970–74		Edward Heath
1974–76	Harold Wilson	
1976–79	James Callaghan	

ISSUES:
Why was Britain's economic growth rate in this period slower than that of its main industrial competitors?
Were the trade unions a barrier to economic growth?

1 'Britain in Decline' – the Economy 1964–79

A factor that should be stressed at the outset is that Britain in the second half of the twentieth century was moving into a new historical stage of its economic development. It was changing from an industrial economy to a post-industrial economy. Manufacturing industries were shrinking while the service and finance industries were expanding. The transition was not smooth or consistent and so caused considerable social disruption. This, indeed, was the root cause of Britain's post-war difficulties. The nation was having to adjust to a major change in its economic and social structure. For all the talk of Keynesianism and planning, the truth was that central and local government had only a marginal influence in shaping this transition. It was a case of responding to developments rather than directing them.

Such were Britain's difficulties in this period that some observers used such terms as 'Britain in decline' to describe it. They meant by this (as is shown in Table 25) that Britain had failed to match the growth rates achieved by the industrial economies of Western Europe, Japan and the USA.

Q What are the grounds for regarding the period as one of decline?

Country	% Growth
Austria	4.3
Germany	3.4
Italy	3.4
France	4.1
USA	2.8
Japan	5.8
Britain	1.9

Table 25 Annual percentage growth rates, 1960–79.

One explanation for Britain's relatively poor performance is that it spent too much on defence and too little on investment in industry. The figures in Table 26 support this argument.

	1963–65	1966–70	1971–75	1976–79
Japan	0.9	0.9	0.7	0.6
Holland	1.9	2.3	2.0	1.6
Italy	2.6	2.4	2.1	1.9
West Germany	10.8	10.3	6.9	6.2
France	26.2	22.5	18.4	19.6
USA	40.6	31.9	27.7	25.4
Britain	34.5	25.6	28.9	29.3

Table 26 Percentage of research and development budget spent on defence.

ACTIVITY

How would you explain the gap between the high spending by Britain and the USA on defence, as shown in Table 26, and the low spending of most other countries? (You need to check the material on foreign policy in Chapter 10.)

a) Industrial Relations

In explaining Britain's economic difficulties in this period some analysts lay particular stress on its poor record in industrial relations. The argument runs that Britain's trade unions had become a powerful obstructive force which used strike action or go-slow tactics to force weak employers into granting irresponsible wage claims and into preserving jobs that ought to have been scrapped. This led to overmanning, rates of pay unrelated to productivity, and a general refusal to co-operate in industrial modernisation. It is certainly true that employer-worker relations were troubled throughout the 1960s and 1970s and that industrial action (stoppages and go-slows) were a serious problem. There was a feeling that strikes were often politically motivated and were led by union officials intent on damaging the economy rather than protecting their members' rights. Harold Wilson described a strike by the National Union of Seamen in 1966 as a deliberate attempt to destroy 'the economic welfare of the nation'.

In retrospect this can be seen as a distortion based on a misunderstanding of union strength. Trade unions react to economic circumstances; they do not create them. Unions cannot be powerful in a weak economy. They are basically a conservative force. The fact was that for reasons outside union control British manufacturing and its

Q Why did Britain experience strained industrial relations in this period?

Q How responsible were the trade unions for Britain's industrial problems?

related industries were in long-term decline. To protect their members' interests the only course open to the unions was to fight a rearguard action to keep job losses to a minimum and to obtain adequate redundancy settlements. Much of this was done undramatically through responsible employer-union negotiation. It was only when this broke down and there was confrontation that the general public took notice. And then, largely because of the way the disputes were presented in a predominantly anti-union press, the unions were seen as culprits. That made them easy scapegoats.

Both Labour and Conservative governments in this period made moves towards introducing statutory rules into industrial relations but neither party was prepared to risk unpopularity by pushing too hard on the issue. Labour could not afford to antagonise its chief supporters and financial backers, the trade unions, by interfering with their customary right to bargain with employers. This was what prevented Harold Wilson's government (1964–70) from persevering with its attempts to outlaw unofficial strikes, as laid out in its 1969 White Paper, *In Place of Strife* (see page 161).

For their part, the Conservatives could not easily reconcile the thought of impositions on employers and workers with their belief in a free market. Edward Heath's government (1970–74) did put into law restrictions on the unions similar to those proposed in *In Place of Strife*, only to find itself involved in a running battle with the unions. In 1972 alone, strike action accounted for the loss of 23 million working days. The climax of the struggle came in 1974 with an industrial crisis and a three-day week (see page 165).

Table 27 Unemployment in Britain, 1949–79.

Year	Number (thousands)	Year	Number (thousands)	Year	Number (thousands)
1949	413	1959	621	1969	595
1950	404	1960	461	1970	628
1951	367	1961	419	1971	868
1952	468	1962	566	1972	929
1953	452	1963	878	1973	785
1954	387	1964	501	1974	628
1955	298	1965	376	1975	1,152
1956	297	1966	564	1976	1,440
1957	383	1967	603	1977	1,567
1958	536	1968	631	1978	1,608
				1979	1,464

Year	Stoppages	Days Lost (thousands)	Year	Stoppages	Days Lost (thousands)
1949	1,426	1,807	1964	2,524	2,277
1950	1,339	1,389	1965	2,354	2,925
1951	1,719	1,694	1966	1,937	2,398
1952	1,714	1,792	1967	2,116	2,787
1953	1,746	2,184	1968	2,378	4,690
1954	1,989	2,457	1969	3,116	6,846
1955	2,419	3,781	1970	3,906	10,980
1956	2,648	2,083	1971	2,228	13,551
1957	2,859	8,412	1972	2,497	23,909
1958	2,629	3,462	1973	2,873	7,197
1959	2,093	5,270	1974	2,922	14,750
1960	2,832	3,024	1975	2,282	6,012
1961	2,686	3,046	1976	2,016	3,284
1962	2,449	5,795	1977	2,627	9,985
1963	2,068	1,755	1978	2,349	9,306
			1979	4,583	29,474

Table 28 The number of strikes and working days lost through industrial disputes, 1949–79.

ACTIVITIES

1. How would you explain the particularly high number of stoppages between 1970 and 1974 and in 1979, as shown in Table 28?

2. What connections can be made between the unemployment figures in Table 27 and the stoppage figures in Table 28?

b) Consumerism

While taking note of the difficulties that Britain experienced, it has also to be pointed out that the period was one of a continuous rise in living standards, of which a main feature was the rise in the purchasing power of the population (see page 213). This was what Harold Macmillan had in mind when he said in 1957 that the British people had 'never had it so good'. However, critics of Britain's post-war economic policy asserted that this was achieved by ignoring reality. The fact was that wages and purchases were increasing at the very time that the basic economy was going into decline. Britain's poor growth rate when compared with its competitors showed this. The unavoidable conclusion was that Britain was paying itself wages and salaries that it was not really earning. Furthermore, since the goods on which earnings were spent were mainly imported products, consumerism did not necessarily help British manufacturing industries. The consequence was inflation and recurrent balance of payments crises.

c) The International Oil Price Rise, 1973

In 1973, a major development occurred internationally that showed how susceptible the British economy was to events in the outside world. Until the early 1970s the large multi-national companies had controlled the production and distribution of oil and had supplied the Western world with a steady supply of relatively cheap fuel. However, from the early 1960s **OPEC** members began to establish greater control over their own oil industries. How strong OPEC had become was shown dramatically in 1973 when its Arab members chose to use oil as a weapon in their long-running conflict with Israel.

In retaliation for the West's support of Israel in the Arab-Israeli war of that year, the Arab members of OPEC drastically reduced their oil supplies to those Western countries which they believed had sided with Israel. At the same time OPEC sharply raised the price of its oil exports. Between 1972 and 1980 the cost of oil increased from $2 to $35 per barrel. The main target was the United States, but pressure on the USA in turn increased pressure on all the other Western states whose economies were heavily dependent on oil. It was not simply fuel but all the many oil-based products, such as plastics, that became greatly more expensive. The result was rapid and severe inflation throughout the industrial world. In the decade after 1973 Britain suffered a severe recession.

OPEC (THE ORGANISATION OF PETROLEUM EXPORTING COUNTRIES)

Within a decade of its formation in 1961, this body came to represent all the leading oil-producing nations, including the strategically vital Arab states of Bahrain, Iraq, Kuwait, Libya and Saudi Arabia. This gave OPEC a strength and status that allowed it to resist Western domination and negotiate on equal terms with the foreign oil companies.

The Immediate Effects in Britain of the Oil Price Rise

▼ The balance of payments deficit rose to £1 billion.
▼ The annual inflation rate rose to 16 per cent.
▼ The value of sterling dropped to $1.57.
▼ The interest rate was raised to 15 per cent.
▼ A record budget deficit.
▼ Between 1974 and 1976 the unemployment figures doubled to 1.44 million.

Oil was a major cause of the inflation and the economic difficulties that followed in the 1970s. By a strange irony it was also oil that then appeared to offer economic salvation. North Sea oil, which was first discovered in 1974, began to come on stream by the late 1970s. By 1980 Britain had reached the point where it was exporting more oil than it imported. This rapid development held out the promise of Britain's being able to achieve a major improvement in its balance of trade.

Summary of Chief Reasons for Britain's Economic Difficulties, 1951–79

▼ Costly military and defence commitments.
▼ The legacy of two world wars which had left Britain financially exhausted.
▼ The high costs of running a welfare state.
▼ Troubled industrial relations, which lessened productivity and prevented modernisation.
▼ The problems Britain faced going through a testing transition from an industrial-based economy to a service-based one.
▼ The heavy costs Britain incurred by joining the EEC in 1973.
▼ The oil price rise that began in 1973.

ACTIVITY

Use the summary box to check your understanding of section 1, and then examine the contention that Britain in the period 1951–79 was 'the sick man of Europe'.

---

2 Harold Wilson's Governments, 1964–70

ISSUE:
How progressive were the Wilson governments?

It was possible to argue that the Conservative Party's choice of a peer, Lord Home, to replace Harold Macmillan in 1963 showed how little it had really modernised itself. But although Alec Douglas-Home, as he quickly restyled himself after renouncing his peerage, usually came off worse in his duels with Harold Wilson in the Commons, his party suffered only the narrowest of defeats in the 1964 election.

The 1964 Election Result			
	Votes	**Seats**	**% Vote**
Conservative	12,001,396	304	43.6
Labour	12,205,814	317	44.1
Liberal	3,092,878	9	1.2
Others	348,914	0	1.3

Table 29 The 1964 election result.

Why did the Labour party win the 1964 election?

Labour's ability to win an electoral victory, albeit a marginal one, after 13 years in the wilderness suggested that the tide had turned in its favour. It presented a more youthful image, not simply in that Wilson was a younger man than Home or Macmillan but in that Labour seemed more in tune with young people and their idea of a progressive Britain. The notion of 'the swinging sixties' may have been largely a creation of the media but astute Labour politicians acknowledged its reality and were anxious not to appear unfashionable. Wilson also cleverly played on the contrast between himself as the plain straight-speaking Yorkshireman and Home as the huntin'-shootin'-fishin' aristocrat who was out of touch with real people and their wants. Wilson tapped into the mood of the day by speaking of Britain's need to respond to the 'white heat of the technological revolution'. The situation was similar in many ways to 1945 when Labour had successfully presented itself as the force of progress standing against the effete political establishment.

Yet the voters did not turn overwhelmingly to the Labour Party in 1964, any more than it had to the Conservatives in 1951. However, the figures show that while Labour, compared with 1959, had slightly increased its share of the vote from 43.8 per cent to 44.1 per cent, the Conservatives had slipped six points from 49.4 per cent to 43.6 per cent. This was just enough to give Labour an overall majority of four seats. The critical factor was the falling away of support for the Conservatives. Their decline indicated that after 13 years of Conservatism a significant number of electors wanted a change. The Conservatives' decision to move closer to the principle of the planned economy had opened them to the charge that they were losing their traditional moorings and were ceasing to offer a distinct alternative to the Labour Party.

What difficulties confronted Wilson's government?

Wilson's first two years of office were relatively successful. The creation of a new Department of Economic Affairs under George Brown, which drew up a 'National Plan', and a new Ministry of Technology, suggested that the government was intent on modernising. The electorate were sufficiently impressed to give Labour a majority of 110 over the Conservatives in the 1966 election. But matters did not go

Table 30 The 1966 election result.

The 1966 Election Result			
	Votes	**Seats**	**% Vote**
Labour	13,064,951	363	47.9
Conservative	11,418,433	253	41.9
Liberal	2,327,533	12	8.5
Others	452,689	2	1.7

KEY EVENTS AND DEVELOPMENTS, 1964–70

1964 the newly created Ministry of Technology and Department of Economic Affairs drafted a National Plan;
IMF loaned the UK £1 billion;

1965 Southern Rhodesia made a Unilateral Declaration of Independence (UDI);
Redundancy Payments Act provided financial settlements for laid-off workers;
Race Relations Act;

1966 election extended the Labour majority to 110 over the Conservatives;
prices and incomes freeze introduced;
industrial Reorganisation Corporation set up;
three-month seamen's strike.

1967 a special parliamentary officer – the Ombudsman – appointed to protect ordinary citizens from misuse of authority by government departments;
dockers' strike;
the idea of a National Economic Plan dropped;
France vetoed Britain's second EEC membership application;
the pound devalued;
the Abortion Act legalised the termination of pregnancy for health reasons;
the Sexual Offences Act permitted homosexual acts in private;

1968 the Immigration Act prohibited new immigrants from settling in Britain unless they had family connections already established;
Race Relations Act;

1969 Open University established;
In Place of Strife introduced but then withdrawn;
voting age lowered from 21 to 18;
the death penalty abolished;

1970 Conservatives gained a majority of 30 in general election.

well from that point on. Uncertainty about the wisdom of Wilson's financial strategy caused tensions between the left and right of the party. Lengthy strikes by the seamen's and the dockers' unions enlarged Britain's balance of payments deficit. This was one of the reasons why the IMF had to be asked for another large loan. So serious were Britain's financial difficulties that late in 1967 Wilson was forced to take the step he had been determined to avoid since taking office three years earlier – the devaluation of the pound. He went on television and in solemn tones informed the nation of what he had been reluctantly forced to do.

Perhaps if devaluation had been introduced earlier and in a less theatrical way it could have passed off as technical financial adjustment. But by delaying the measure and then turning it into a drama Wilson unwittingly made devaluation appear as a great political and economic failure by the government. That is how it was perceived by many inside as well as outside the Labour Party. The trade unions were angered by Wilson's attempt to lay most of the blame for the government's financial plight on the strikers, a tactic he had tried the previous year when condemning the seamen's actions. When the government subsequently introduced '**In Place of Strife**', a set of

> **'IN PLACE OF STRIFE', 1969**
> was a White Paper (a formal statement of the government's intentions) which proposed a series of legal restrictions on the right of workers to strike. After introducing it in Cabinet, Barbara Castle, the Employment Secretary, was obliged to abandon it in the face of strong opposition led by James Callaghan, the Labour Party treasurer, who pointed out the dangers of alienating the trade unions which still provided the bulk of the party's funds.

proposals aimed at preventing future strikes, the trade unionists in the party rebelled and forced it to be withdrawn.

Source A From Harold Wilson's speeches in the House of Commons, 20 June and 20 July 1966.

> It is difficult for us to appreciate the pressures which are put on men in the highly organised strike committees in the individual ports by this tightly knit group of politically motivated men [the striking seamen's leaders], who are now determined to exercise back-stage pressures, endangering the security of the industry and the economic welfare of the nation … Sterling has been under pressure for the past two and a half weeks. After an improvement in the early weeks of May, we were blown off course by the seven weeks' seamen's strike.

George Brown

was a prominent and outspoken figure on the right of the Labour Party. He was deputy leader between 1960 and 1970 but his relations with Harold Wilson, who defeated him in the leadership contest in 1963, were never entirely happy. He tried to make a success of the new Department of Economic Affairs, which he led from 1964 to 1966, but he too often clashed with the Treasury over financial questions. His lack of tact proved a handicap when he became Foreign Secretary (1966–70). The British media were quick to seize on his indiscretions. Fond of a drink or two, Brown was often described by the newspapers as being 'tired and emotional', a euphemism for drunk. He became a peer in 1970. A study of Brown's career during the Wilson years helps to show the internal dissensions and rivalries that afflicted the Labour Party in this period.

Q

Why did Wilson's government prove a disappointment to many of its supporters?

In 1970 at the end of Harold Wilson's first government there was a general feeling that it had not lived up to expectations. The sharpest sense of disappointment was among traditional Labour supporters. They felt that the government had promised much but delivered little. Compared with the last Labour government, that of Clement Attlee, it had an unimpressive record of reform. It had entered office claiming to be a modernising reforming government, but in practice had appeared different from its Conservative predecessors only in style not in content. While its list of reforms looks impressive they did not add up to substantial change. Although certain sections of industry had been improved, it could not be said that the streamlining of British industry overall had been achieved. A leading social analyst, Peter Townshend, dismissed Labour's attempts at reform as 'hot compresses on an ailing body politic'.

For some this is a harsh verdict since it does not take sufficient account of the social reforms, which in retrospect appear ground-breaking. The legalising of abortion, the decriminalising of homosexual acts, and the abolition of the death penalty may be said to mark an important stage in the modernising of Britain. These, of course, were and remain controversial issues. There were those who were unhappy with these expressions of what became known as 'the permissive age'. Roy Jenkins, Home Secretary between 1965 and 1967, attempted to put the best gloss on things when he suggested that a more appropriate term than the permissive age would be the 'civilised age'.

But even those who accepted the value of such reforms tended to see them as isolated achievements. It was the left of the Labour Party and the young people who had had the highest hopes of Harold Wilson who by 1970 were the most disillusioned. They found that the character of politics had not changed in the way they had expected. 1964 had not marked a new departure but a continuation of the same. It was simply the party labels that had changed. The specific charges of the left-wing critics are worth listing. They complained that Wilson's government had either introduced or presided over:

▽ rising unemployment
▽ inflation
▽ wage controls
▽ attempted restriction of trade union freedoms
▽ immigration controls
▽ reintroduction of prescription charges
▽ retention of Britain's nuclear weapons
▽ support of the USA's involvement in the Vietnam War.

Despite these criticisms from the left, Wilson believed that Labour's basic support was solid. The result of the election he called in 1970 took him by surprise. He had not realised that his undistinguished economic policies, and his apparent failure to control the unions, had lost his government a significant degree of support among moderate voters. There was a five per cent swing from Labour to Conservative, enough to put Edward Heath into office with a Commons' majority of 30.

ACTIVITY

It has often been said that in British politics governments are finally judged on their economic record. How justified do you find the criticisms, referred to in section 2, of the economic performance of Harold Wilson's government? How highly would you rate its record on social reform? Cross reference to Chapter 9 will help you in this.

The 1970 Election Result			
	Votes	**Seats**	**% Vote**
Conservative	13,145,123	330	46.4
Labour	12,179,341	287	43.0
Liberal	2,117,035	6	7.5
Others	903,299	7	3.1

Table 31 The 1970 election result.

ISSUE:
Why was there con-
frontation between the
government and the
unions?

KEY EVENTS AND DEVELOPMENTS, 1970–74

1970 the Industrial Relations Act tightened the law against industrial strikes;

1971 the ailing Rolls-Royce company was nationalised and subsidies were granted to other private companies in difficulties;

1971 the TUC voted against unions registering under the Industrial Relations Act;

1972 the miners' strike began a series of industrial stoppages – over 23 million working days were lost – the miners eventually won a 21 per cent pay rise; the government introduced a pay freeze;

1973 the UK formally entered the EEC; the government declared a 'state of emergency' and introduced a three-day working week to save fuel supplies; OPEC's actions led to a rapid rise in world oil prices and mounting inflation;

1974 the miners struck again for higher wages and to protect jobs; Heath called a general election over the union issue but was defeated.

3 The Heath Government, 1970–74

Edward Heath was not dissimilar in 1970 from Harold Wilson in 1964; he entered office with the aim of following expansive policies only to end with these largely unachieved. He declared that he was adopting 'a new style of government' and that his aims were 'to reduce the rise in prices, increase productivity and reduce unemployment'. By the time of his defeat in 1974 he had been successful in none of these. The rapid inflation that followed the oil price rise in 1973 made the holding down of prices impossible. The wage demands of the unions, which in the majority of cases were accepted by the employers, and the large number of days lost through strikes, resulted in a decline rather than a growth in productivity. These factors meant that unemployment could not be reduced. Indeed, 1972 marked the highest figure for joblessness since the Depression in the 1930s.

Edward Heath

was one of the talented young Conservatives who helped regenerate the party in the early 1950s. In 1960 Harold Macmillan gave him the task of negotiating the UK's entry into the EEC. This work became the defining characteristic of his career. In 1965 he became the first elected leader of the Conservative Party but this democratic distinction did not prevent his only period as Prime Minister from being widely regarded as a failure. After two election defeats in 1974 (he lost three elections out of four within a space of nine years) he was beaten in the party's 1975 leadership contest by Margaret Thatcher with whom he had strained relations for the rest of his long career. He did not hold office again but remained in politics as a backbench MP. In 2000 he entered his 51st year as a member of the House of Commons.

Despite Edward Heath's good intentions and considerable efforts, his four years in office were overshadowed and eventually ended by the problem of industrial relations. He had originally hoped that rather than confront the unions he could sit down with them and solve common problems together. He offered them a package in which in return for their co-operation in imposing a wages policy they, along with the **CBI**, would become directly involved in government economic planning. But the unions were suspicious – not without good reason. One of the government's first measures was the 1970 Industrial Relations Act. This built upon what Labour's *In Place of Strife* had proposed in 1969 but not followed through. It restricted the right of workers to strike by introducing a new concept of 'unfair industrial practice'. A National Industrial Relations Court (NIRC), with authority to judge the validity of strike action, was created and unions were required to put themselves on a government register if they wanted to retain their legal rights. The TUC resisted by urging its members not to register or co-operate with the government.

It was the National Union of Miners (NUM) which forced the issue. In 1972, in a joint bid to gain a wage increase and to highlight the increasing number of pit closures that threatened its members' livelihood, the NUM called a strike during which it effectively used pickets to bring the movement of coal to a standstill. This seriously disrupted fuel and electricity supplies and reduced many industries to a three-day working week. Hoping to defeat the miners, the government introduced a series of restrictions on the use of fuel, which recalled the austerities of the 1940s. However, when the miners' dispute was eventually settled in 1973, the NUM gained a 21 per cent wage increase – a figure nearly three times the amount that the employers had originally offered. Emboldened by its success, the NUM again went on strike early in 1974 in pursuit of a further wage demand. This was too much for Heath. He called an immediate election on the issue of who ran the country – the miners or the government. The answer of the electorate was not what he had expected. The election gave Labour a majority of four over the Conservatives. With the support of the 14 Liberal MPs, Harold Wilson was able to embark on his second period of government.

The 1974 Election Result (February)			
	Votes	**Seats**	**% Vote**
Conservative	11,868,906	297	37.9
Labour	11,639,243	301	37.1
Liberal	6,063,470	14	19.3
Northern Irish Parties	717,986	12	2.3
Scottish Nationalists	632,032	7	2.0
Plaid Cymru	171,364	2	0.6
Others	260,665	2	0.8

Table 32 The February 1974 election result.

> **Q**
>
> Why did Heath experience major difficulties with the unions?

> **THE CBI (CONFEDERATION OF BRITISH INDUSTRY)**
>
> An organisation representing Britain's leading manufacturers and industrialists. Officially it was politically neutral, but it tended in most cases to side with the Conservative Party.

ACTIVITY

Between 1964 and 1974 both the Labour and Conservative governments experienced very strained relations with the unions. Why was this? Who was to blame – the government or the unions? Try to see both sides of the case.

ISSUE:
**Did this government
simply continue
Heath's policies?**

4 Labour in Office, 1974–79

The 1974 Election Result (October)			
	Votes	**Seats**	**% Vote**
Labour	11,457,079	319	39.2
Conservative	10,464,817	277	35.8
Liberal	5,346,754	13	18.3
Northern Irish Parties	702,094	12	2.4
Scottish Nationalists	893,617	11	2.9
Plaid Cymru	166,321	3	0.6

Table 33 The October 1974 election result.

From the beginning Harold Wilson's second government suffered from three crippling restrictions. One was the thinness of its overall majority in the Commons. After the second election in 1974, it had a majority over the Conservatives of 42 but its overall majority was a mere three seats. This made Labour heavily dependent on the Liberal MPs and gave the Liberal Party an influence on government it had not enjoyed since Lloyd George's day. There was justice in this. Having picked up votes from disillusioned Conservative and Labour supporters, the Liberals had done remarkably well in the 1974 elections, and their 13 seats were poor reward for polling half as many votes as the Labour Party and the Conservatives taken separately.

The second problem was that the Labour governments of 1974–79 held office at a time when Britain began to suffer the worst effects of the rapid inflation that followed the oil price rise of 1973. In 1976, the government had to negotiate a loan of £4 billion from the **IMF**. The terms of the loan required Britain to make major cuts in its public expenditure. By 1979 the government had reduced its spending programme by £1 billion. This helped stabilise the financial situation but at the cost of increased unemployment which reached 1.6 million in 1978. One effect of this was that the trade unions became embittered and their traditional loyalty to the Labour Party weakened. This helps to explain the economic crisis that occurred at the end of 1978 that led to the '**winter of discontent**'.

Labour's third abiding problem – its struggle to come to terms with the unions – was closely related to inflation. The credit the government had gained from repealing the Industrial Relations Act was lost by its inability to persuade the workers to co-operate consistently with it. In many respects this was a repeat of the troubles that had stalked the Heath government. The bitter aspect for Labour was for a time after 1974 Wilson seemed to be on co-operative terms with the

IMF (THE INTERNATIONAL MONETARY FUND)
was a scheme intended to prevent countries going bankrupt. It began operating in 1947 and by 1990 had been joined by over 150 countries. Each of the member states deposited into a central fund from which it could then draw in time of need. The aim was that nations with serious balance of payments difficulties would be able to ease them without having to resort to drastic deflationary measures.

unions. His harmonious relations with Jack Jones, the moderate leader of the influential Transport and General Workers Union, promised much. The problem was that Wilson had led the nation to believe that Labour would break from the 'stop-go' economic policies associated with the Conservatives. But the effects of the 1973 oil price crisis (see page 158) destroyed any hopes he had of doing that. The pressures of rising prices and the need to conform to IMF demands for public spending cuts forced him and his successor in 1976, James Callaghan, to adopt similar policies.

The public service workers were the group that felt most victimised by this and it was their sense of grievance that produced the 1978–79 winter of discontent, which was instrumental in destroying Callaghan's government in the 1979 election. It is arguable that Callaghan had made matters worse during his period of government by appearing to allow things to drift. His relaxed style of leadership had its attractions but it was not ideally suited to a critical situation where a more dynamic approach seemed necessary. Yet the problems he inherited were so serious that it is difficult to see how he could have solved them, given the constraints within which he had to work.

> **THE WINTER OF DISCONTENT**
> was the term used by journalists to describe the crisis that contributed to the defeat of the Labour government in the 1979 election. The government's attempts to fight inflation by cutting public expenditure and discouraging wage increases met resistance from the public-sector unions. A series of strikes among public-service workers in the winter of 1978–79 caused considerable disruption in some areas. This was seized upon by journalists who presented isolated cases of uncollected refuse in the streets and unburied bodies in cemeteries as if they were nationwide occurrences.

ACTIVITY

Re-read sections 3 and 4. Explain in your own words why the Wilson and Callaghan governments of 1974–79 were as troubled by their relations with the trade unions as the Heath government had been.

Year	Conservatives	Labour
1964–70	for the first time elected a leader of the party – Edward Heath	in office under Wilson – not able to achieve its objective of relating Britain to 'the white heat of the technological revolution'
1970–74	in office under Heath – economic plans destroyed by industrial relations crises	internal party divisions continued
1974–79	Heath ousted from the leadership by Margaret Thatcher	in office under Wilson and Callaghan – overwhelmed by the inflationary effects of the oil price rise

Table 34 Party difficulties, 1964–79.

ISSUES:
Were there any funda-
mental differences
between the major
political parties in this
period?
What were the main
features of the post-
war consensus?

5 The Age of Consensus, 1945–79

Government in this period was a matter of adapting to the needs of the time. The striking example of this was the ability of both the Conservative and Labour Parties to adjust their respective political approaches in keeping with the changing economic situation. What the period 1945–79 shows is that the Marxist left wing of the Labour Party and the reactionary right wing of the Conservative Party had been marginalised. In power, the parties governed from the centre and were essentially moderate in their policies. It was the moderate Attlee and Bevin who shaped the Labour Party in this period, just as it was the progressive Butler and Macmillan who gave the essential form to Conservatism. This is evident in the way successive governments adopted the existing political agenda. It was rare that a government seriously attempted to undo the work of its predecessor. Rather than destroying the welfare policies of the post-war Labour governments, the Conservatives in the years 1951–64 built upon them. Every year they spent more public money on welfare provision.

Figure 26 Graph showing government expenditure on the NHS.

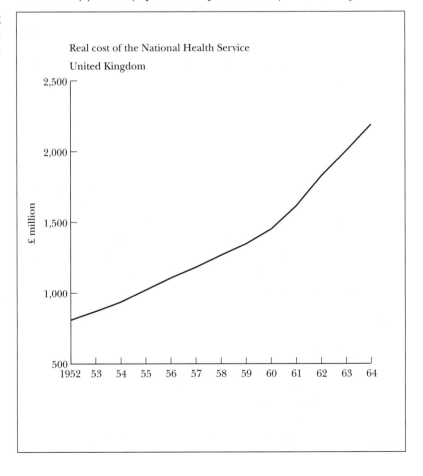

Similarly, the management of the economy by the Labour administrations of the 1960s and late 1970s was the same in all key respects as that followed by the Conservatives between 1951 and 1964. To take particular examples – welfare, education, immigration, finance, employment, industrial relations: on these key issues the policies pursued by Labour and Conservative governments concurred. The same was true of the conduct of foreign policy; genuine differences between the parties were few. A consistent broad line of British foreign policy, pro-American, anti-Soviet, and anti-imperialist, was discernible from 1945 to the early 1990s (see page 225).

The basic governmental approach was practical rather than theoretical. Changes which originally had been opposed on party grounds were accepted if they subsequently proved workable or if there was thought to be no alternative to them. It was the growth of corporatism (government-directed economic planning) during the war that prepared the way for the welfare state measures of the 1945–51 period. Once these were in place no subsequent government attempted to remove them. After 1945 it was generally accepted that in economic matters demand management along broad Keynesian lines was the best way of running a modern industrial society, and that in social matters the mechanism of the state was the best means of securing the welfare of the citizen.

A fascinating feature of all this was that the sharpest political debate took place not between the parties but within them. This was especially true of the Labour Party. Throughout the period the centre had a running battle with the left wing, which demanded that Britain give up its independent nuclear deterrent. Resolutions were passed at the party's annual conferences committing it to unilateral disarmament. But at no point when in government did the Labour Party ever make a serious move towards fulfilling that commitment. Indeed, the opposite was often the case. Harold Wilson's government increased the amount of government spending on nuclear development.

The Conservative right bemoaned the failure of their party when in office to maintain its commitment to protect and conserve traditional British institutions. It pointed to the readiness of the various Conservative governments after 1951 to:

What were the main complaints of the right?

▼ extend bureaucracy
▼ retreat from empire
▼ increase public spending
▼ embrace the policy of comprehensive schooling
▼ subsidise both private and public industries
▼ permit continued immigration
▼ expand social welfare provision
▼ countenance the loss of sovereignty involved in entering Europe.

Such policies, the right argued, were barely distinguishable from the programme of the Labour Party.

The equivalent grievance of the Labour left was that their party, contrary to its traditions and its constitution, was never socialist in practice. In office, Labour governments instead of undermining the capitalist system subordinated the interest of the working classes to its demands. Among the betrayals of socialism listed by the left were the party's:

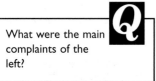

What were the main complaints of the left?

▼ retention of Britain's independent nuclear deterrent
▼ abandonment of nationalisation
▼ imposition of immigration controls
▼ pro-American foreign policy
▼ acceptance of the UK's membership of the capitalist EEC.

It may be that both left and right exaggerated the degree to which their respective parties had modified their principles. However, the frequency with which they made such charges lends weight to the idea that British politics was essentially moderate in operation. If parties are judged by what they did when in power, a far greater convergence between them can be seen than the cut and thrust of their political debate would suggest. Although they were reluctant to admit it, the parties engaged in consensus politics; that is to say, not creating policies which they then urged the electorate to support, but constructing programmes based upon their perception of what the electorate wanted. This is sometimes called the reactive style of politics – not leading but following.

One reason for this was the consistently narrow gap that divided the parties in terms of their electoral support. As Figures 27 and 28

Figure 27 Graph illustrating the number of seats won by the three major parties in the general elections held between 1955 and 1979.

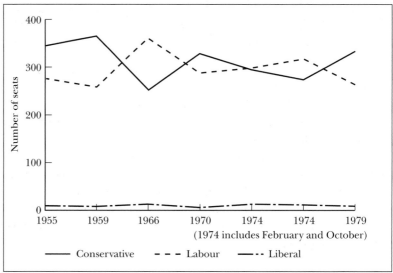

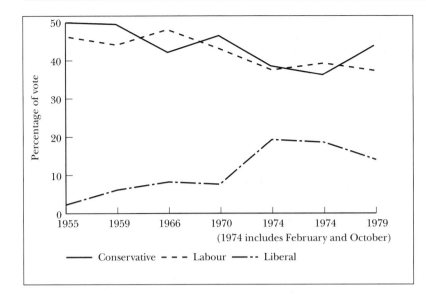

Percentage of vote

1955   1959   1966   1970   1974   1974   1979
(1974 includes February and October)

——— Conservative   – – – Labour   —·–· Liberal

ACTIVITIES

Much of this chapter has been taken up with suggesting how 'consensus politics' operated in post-war Britain. To show that you have grasped this notion go back over the chapter and make a broad survey of the period, noting the key issues on which the parties agreed or disagreed.

Examine Figures 27 and 28. In what ways do they help us to understand why consensus politics was such a marked feature of the period 1955–79?

show, support fluctuated within very narrow bands. Election results were decided by very slight shifts of opinion. (1935 was the last occasion any party won more than 50 per cent of the overall vote.) Large parliamentary majorities were the exception rather than the rule. This made parties wary of advocating or pursuing policies that might seriously alienate the electorate. To avoid this, parties in office always governed from the centre and followed essentially moderate programmes. To do otherwise was to risk making themselves unelectable.

▼ Working on The Age of Consensus, 1964–79

Your aim should be to get a clear picture of developments in these 15 years during which Britain wrestled with major economic and financial problems and struggled to come to terms with the legacy of the war. The chapter is broken down into the separate ministries and it is best to develop an understanding of the chronology by reference to the various governments. The linking theme of the chapter is the political consensus that operated in this period, which can be seen in the measures that were introduced and the policies that were followed. Check where the policies of the Labour and Conservative governments converged and diverged. Use the issue boxes and marginal questions as guides.

Answering Structured Writing and Essay Questions on The Age of Consensus, 1964–79

Types of question	Examples of typical questions
Structured questions	1 Describe the difficulties which Edward Heath's government experienced with the trade unions.
	2 What methods did Harold Wilson's governments employ to deal with Britain's economic problems?
	3 In what ways did the oil price rise of 1973 affect Britain's economy?
Questions about *causes*	4 Explain why the 1973 oil price crisis caused major economic and political problems for the Labour governments of 1974–79.
	5 Why did the Labour Party win power in 1964 but lose it in 1970?
	6 Why were the Labour governments of 1974–79 no more successful in dealing with economic problems than the previous Conservative government of 1970–74 had been?
Questions asking for *historical judgement*	7 Examine the validity of the claim that the governments of the period 1964–79 followed policies that were the same in all essentials.
	8 How accurate is it to describe the years 1945–79 as 'the age of consensus'?

Let us consider question 4. This is the type that asks you to analyse the consequences of particular events or trends. Note that the question does *not* ask you to explain why the sudden oil price rise had occurred in 1973, so do not waste valuable time doing so. A brief comment about OPEC's strength and its decision to retaliate against the West would be sufficient. Your task is to describe the consequences for Britain. There are clearly two distinct aspects with which you have to deal. In preparing your answer, therefore, write down two separate lists – economic effects and political effects. Here are some suggestions as to what you might include:

Economic effects
▽ acute inflation (the annual inflation rate rose to 16 per cent)
▽ unemployment doubled to 1.44 million
▽ the balance of payments deficit rose to £1 billion
▽ the value of sterling dropped to $1.57
▽ the interest rate was raised to 15 per cent
▽ a record budget deficit occurred.

The Labour government of 1974–79 felt the brunt of these developments, which forced it to do the following:

▼ negotiate a loan of £4 billion from the IMF, which required that the UK made major cuts in its public expenditure
▼ reduce its spending – by 1979 the Government had reduced its spending programme by £1 billion. This helped stabilise the financial situation but at the cost of increased unemployment.

The political consequence were
▼ the trade unions became embittered and their traditional loyalty to the Labour Party weakened
▼ union troubles grew throughout the period, climaxing with the 'winter of discontent' in 1978–79
▼ such developments discredited Labour, which had come into power with the promise that it would end 'stop-go' and get the economy moving
▼ the opposition to the Labour government grew in the country, thus helping the Conservatives
▼ divisions within the Labour Party grew.

You may wish to alter this list in line with your own views, but such a framework would provide a basis for you to write an informed and balanced answer.

Further Reading

General

Recommended books which cover the whole period are: *The People's Peace, British History 1945–90* by Kenneth Morgan (Oxford University Press, 1999), who is one of the leading authorities in this field, *Hope and Glory: Britain 1900–1990* by Peter Clarke (Penguin, 1996), which is a highly entertaining text, *From Blitz to Blair A New History of Britain Since 1939*, edited by Nick Tiratsoo (Phoenix, 1997), which contains a stimulating set of essays by left-wing writers, and *Post War Britain* by Alan Sked and Chris Cook (Penguin, 1992), which takes a right of centre approach. An important and controversial book explaining Britain's decline is *The Audit of War* by Corelli Barnett (Macmillan, 1986). This could be usefully compared with *Britain's Decline: Problems and Perspectives* by Alan Sked (Blackwell, 1987). The definitive text on the post-45 consensus is *Consensus Politics From Attlee to Major* by Dennis Kavanagh and Peter Morris (Blackwell, 2nd edition 1994). A witty and informative study of the party leaders of the period is *A Question of Leadership: From Gladstone to Thatcher* by Peter Clarke (Penguin, 1992). Among individual biographies which students would enjoy are *Edward Heath: A Biography* by J. Campbell (Cape, 1993) and *Harold Wilson* by Ben Pimlott (HarperCollins, 1992).

FROM THATCHERISM TO NEW LABOUR, 1979–99

POINTS TO CONSIDER

The last 20 years of the century were dominated by two main political developments – Thatcherism and 'New Labour'. Thatcherism broke the consensus that had operated in Britain between 1945 and 1979 and profoundly altered many aspects of economic and political life in Britain. New Labour was a movement that began as an attempt to accommodate itself to the changes that this revolution had brought. This chapter deals with the three elements in this story. The Thatcher Revolution analyses the changes that Mrs Thatcher's government introduced between 1979 and 1990. John Major's Government describes the interlude between Margaret Thatcher and Labour's return to power in 1997. From Old Labour to New Labour analyses the Labour Party's own brand of revolution which had begun during the Thatcher years and was continued under Tony Blair when he became party leader in 1994.

ISSUES:

In what sense was Margaret Thatcher a 'conviction politician'? Was she a revolutionary?

1 The Thatcher Revolution, 1979–90

Margaret Thatcher gave her name to a new form of politics – Thatcherism. She was a striking example of a conviction politician. As early as 1968 she had attacked consensus politics as being devoid of principle.

Source A From a speech to the Conservative Political Centre by Margaret Thatcher in 1968.

There are dangers in consensus: it could be an attempt to satisfy people holding no particular views about anything. It seems more important to have a philosophy and policy which, because they are good, appeal to a sufficient majority.

What were her basic political convictions?

Her Methodist upbringing and the influence of the ideas of Friedrich Von Hayek and Keith Joseph gave her a set of beliefs that motivated her actions. The Thatcher government has been referred to as a revolution. Her 11 years in office ended the consensus politics that had operated since 1945 and which she regarded as a form of creeping socialism. Her belief was not simply that the Labour governments had increased the power and control of the State but that the Conservatives had fallen into the same trap. Conservative governments had encroached upon the free market, subsidised private and public companies, and permitted the undemocratic power of the unions to expand.

As she saw it, the result of all this was inefficiency and low growth, made worse by a welfare system which undermined personal responsibility and created a dependency culture (see page 210). The nation was suffering from a malaise under which the hard-working members of society were subsidising the work-shy. Initiative was being stifled.

Friedrich Von Hayek

was an Austrian economist and a major critic of Keynes. He came to prominence with the publication of his book, *The Road to Serfdom* (1944) in which he attacked the notion of state direction of the economy. 'The more the government plans,' Von Hayek wrote, 'the less can an individual plan, and when the government plans everything the individual can plan nothing.' He argued that the proper role of the State was not to involve itself in the welfare of its citizens but simply to provide the conditions of liberty in which individuals were free to make their own choices. He was a strong supporter of the free market (see page 178), which he believed was the best guarantee of economic and political liberty. He had a particular distrust of trade unions whose power he regarded as a direct cause of unemployment and as a destroyer of democratic freedoms.

Keith Joseph

was the leading Conservative intellectual of his time. Although he held ministerial office, his real importance was as a thinker and as an influence upon Margaret Thatcher. He introduced her to the ideas of Von Hayek and encouraged her to adopt **monetarism** as her government's financial strategy after 1979.

MONETARISM
was particularly associated with the ideas of Milton Friedman. He argued that the basic cause of inflation is increase in money supply, and, therefore, that in order to control inflation governments should restrict the amount of money in circulation and cut public expenditure.

a) Ending the Post-War Consensus

The Conservatives' overall majority of 43 seats was large enough to allow Margaret Thatcher to embark on a policy of radical change.

Margaret Thatcher's intended solution to the problems she inherited was a return to the principle of individual accountability. The State, she believed, should no longer reward the incompetent and the half-hearted. It was false economics and bad social practice. In

ISSUES:
What did Mrs. Thatcher understand by the post-war consensus?
How did she propose to undo it?

Table 35 The 1979 election
result.

The 1979 Election Result	Votes	Seats	% Vote
Conservative	13,697,690	339	43.9
Labour	11,532,148	269	36.9
Liberal	4,313,811	11	13.8
Plaid Cymru	132,544	2	0.4
Scottish Nationalists	504,259	2	1.6
Northern Irish Parties	695,889	12	2.2

her memoirs Margaret Thatcher defined the harm she believed had been done to Britain by a consensus politics that had allowed the State to play too large a part in people's lives.

ACTIVITIES

Questions on Margaret Thatcher's rejection of the post-war consensus.

1. What does she mean by saying, in line 10, that 'the Tory Party merely pitched camp in the long march to the left'?

2. Define the term 'socialist ratchet', as used in line 16.

3. What can be learned from Source A regarding Mrs Thatcher's attitude towards the welfare state?

Source B From *The Downing Street Years* by Margaret Thatcher, 1993.

The Labour Party gloried in planning, regulation, controls and subsidies. It had a vision of the future: Britain as a democratic, socialist society, third way between east European collectivism and American capitalism. And there was a rough consistency between its principles and its policies – both tending towards the expansion of government – even if the pace of that change was not fast enough for its own left.

The Tory Party was more ambivalent. At the level of principle, rhetorically and in Opposition, it opposed these doctrines and preached the gospel of free enterprise with very little qualification. But in the fine print of policy, and especially in government, the Tory Party merely pitched camp in the long march to the left. It never tried seriously to reverse it. The welfare state? We boasted of spending more money than Labour, not of restoring people to independence and self-reliance. The result of this style of accommodationist politics, as my colleague Keith Joseph complained, was that post-war politics became a 'socialist ratchet' – Labour moved Britain towards more statism; the Tories stood pat; and the next Labour Government moved the country a little further left. The Tories loosened the corset of socialism; they never removed it.

After a reforming start, Ted Heath's Government proposed and almost implemented the most radical form of socialism ever contemplated by an elected British government. It offered state control of prices and dividends, and the joint oversight of economic policy by a tripartite body representing the TUC, the CBI and the Government, in return for trade union acquiescent in an incomes policy. We were saved from this abomination by the conservatism and suspicion of the TUC which perhaps could not believe that their 'class enemy' was prepared to surrender without a fight.

MARGARET THATCHER (1925–)

Margaret Thatcher scored two remarkable historical 'firsts' – she was the first woman to become a party leader in Britain and the first woman to become a Prime Minister. Her three election victories in a row – 1979, 1983 and 1987 – meant that she held continuous office for 11 years from 1979 to 1990, the longest unbroken period for any Prime Minister in the twentieth century. Arguably the most controversial Prime Minister since Lloyd George, she was like him in being 'a populist', that is she claimed to have a special understanding of ordinary people that by-passed party politics. One example of this that she often quoted was her experience as a young woman helping to run her father's grocery shop; this, she felt, had given her an insight into the problems of the housewife having to make ends meet every week without getting into debt. She regarded this as appropriate training for running the national economy.

It is not easy to give exact definition to her politics. Some critics dismiss her simply as a right-wing Tory ideologue, but her strong belief in financial probity – the nation paying its way and balancing the books – made her much more a nineteenth-century liberal in the Gladstone tradition. So, too, did her wish to reduce the power of the State and give greater opportunity for people to live their lives without government interference. After Britain's victory over Argentina and the recovery of the Falkland Islands she was likened by some observers to Winston Churchill in her ability to arouse the nation. Others, who believed that she had deliberately provoked the war, found her triumphalism after the British victory in 1982 repellent.

As a staunch anti-Communist, she sided with President Reagan in his condemnation of the Soviet Union as the 'evil empire'. Republicans in the USA suggested that her uncompromising attitude helped to bring about the end of the Cold War. Interestingly, for many people in Eastern Europe she became a symbol of freedom. In Poland, for example, chapels and shrines were dedicated to her. This was in gratitude for her support of 'Solidarity', the Polish anti-Communist trade union movement. There was a bitter irony in this for those in Britain who believed she had trampled on the rights of trade unionists at home.

One of Margaret Thatcher's most controversial statements was 'There is no such thing as society'. Her critics seized upon this as evidence of her lack of compassion and her willingness to ignore the consequences of unbridled individualism. She defended herself by quoting the statement that followed that sentence: 'There are individual men and women, and there are families. And no government can do anything except through people, and people must look to themselves first. It's our duty to look after ourselves and then to look after our neighbour.' She claimed that her purpose had in fact been to emphasise the individual's responsibility towards society.

-Profile-

1925	born the daughter of a shopkeeper in Grantham, Lincolnshire;
1943 –47	read Chemistry and Law at Oxford;
1947 –50	trained as a lawyer;
1950 –51	stood unsuccessfully as Conservative candidate;
1950	married Denis Thatcher, a millionaire businessman;
1959	elected Conservative MP for Finchley;
1964	became Opposition spokeswoman on pensions;
1970 –74	Secretary of State for Education and Science under Heath;
1975 –90	Leader of the Conservative Party;
1979	became Prime Minister after election victory;
1982	her declining popularity was reversed by the Falklands victory;
1983	won second election victory;
1987	won third election victory;
1990	resigned as PM and party leader;
1992	became Lady Thatcher of Kesteven.

KEY EVENTS AND DEVELOPMENTS, 1979–90

1979 the Thatcher government came to power;
1980 monetarism introduced;
1981 riots in Bristol, London, Liverpool and Manchester; serious slump occurred;
1982 the Falklands War; unemployment topped three million;
1983 Margaret Thatcher's second election victory;
1984 the miners' strike;
–85
1984 IRA bombed Brighton hotel in which Thatcher was staying during the Conservative Party conference; Sino-British Joint Declaration on Hong Kong;
1985 further riots in major cities; the Anglo-Irish Agreement;
1986 the Westland affair; supply-side economics adopted; deregulation programme widened; the Single European Act;
1987 Margaret Thatcher's government won its third election;
1987 'Black Monday' collapse of stock market;
1988 Thatcher's Bruges speech;
1989 the leadership challenge of Anthony Meyer defeated;
1990 the poll tax crisis; UK joined ERM; Mrs Thatcher resigned.

b) Key Features of Thatcherism

Thatcherism is best understood as the set of aims which Margaret Thatcher sought to achieve during her 11 years as Prime Minister.

▽ Keynesianism to be abandoned and the free market allowed to operate.

▽ Monetarism would end wasteful government spending.

▽ The undemocratic power of the trade unions to be broken and unions leaders to be made fully responsible to their members.

▽ Companies and the public utilities to be removed from government control and **privatisation** to be introduced.

▽ Government subsidies for unprofitable industries to end and the competitive spirit to be promoted.

▽ Income tax and corporation tax to be reduced so that individuals and companies could keep more of their own money.

▽ Public institutions and bodies, in particular local government, to be made truly accountable to the public they existed to serve.

▽ Welfare dependency to be discouraged by targeting benefit on those who genuinely needed it rather than by providing it indiscriminately.

▽ The maintenance of law and order to be given priority in order to provide greater protection to ordinary citizens.

▽ British independence and sovereignty to be enhanced by resisting EEC encroachments.

▽ Britain would promote the cause of world freedom by promoting international justice in the face of Communist oppression.

▽ The rights of the individual and the family would take precedence over abstract notions of social good.

These aims were complemented by a policy of privatisation. Of the 50 enterprises sold off during the Thatcher years the largest were British Airways, British Steel, British Coal, Cable and Wireless, British Telecom, and the regional electricity and water boards. Table 36 shows how much was raised by this policy.

Table 36 Government revenue derived from privatisation.

1979–80	1985–86	1988–89
£377 million	£2,600 million	£7 billion

ACTIVITY

As you work through this chapter use the 'key features' as a check list to how see many of her objectives Margaret Thatcher was able to achieve.

Privatisation

is the selling of nationalised (government-owned) concerns fully or in part to private buyers and investors. As well as providing the Treasury with large additional funds, the policy aimed at increasing 'popular capitalism' by giving far more ordinary people the chance to become shareholders. Between 1979 and 1990 the number of shareholders rose from 3 to 9 million.

c) The Falkands War, 1982

In 1982 Britain went to war with Argentina. Arguably, it was Margaret Thatcher's handling of this crisis that helped her to stay in office until 1990. Her tough monetarist measures after 1979 had not increased her popularity and there were fears among some Conservatives that the economic recession that began in 1981 might well scupper the government's chances at the next election. Britain's success in the Falklands War reversed the position. Margaret Thatcher enjoyed a popularity (sometimes referred to as 'the Falklands factor') that enabled her to win the elections of 1983 and 1987.

The legal ownership of the islands had long been disputed between Argentina and Britain. The historical arguments over **sovereignty** were complicated. Britain's position was that the Falklands had legally been a British Dependency since 1833. What was not in dispute in 1982 was that 98 per cent of the population of some 2,000 islanders wished to remain under the British flag. This was the point constantly emphasised by Margaret Thatcher. It gave her the justification for insisting that 'sovereignty is not negotiable'. On 2 April 1982 General Galtieri, the Argentine dictator, eager to make his regime acceptable to the nation, ordered the seizure of the Falklands. A force of 4,000 troops invaded the islands and quickly overcame the resistance of the garrison of 80 Royal Marines.

This act of aggression was condemned by all parties in Britain, but whereas the Labour opposition wanted British reaction to be channelled through the United Nations, which formally condemned Argentina's action, Mrs Thatcher was adamant that it was entirely a matter for Britain to resolve. Its sovereignty had been affronted and its people in the Falklands put under occupation. It was, therefore, entitled to take action. She immediately ordered the retaking of the Falklands. Between 5 and 8 April a British Task Force was rapidly put together and sailed from Portsmouth and Southampton. On 25 April South Georgia, which Argentina had also seized, was recaptured. Air strikes began on 1 May against the occupying Argentine forces on the Falklands.

On 2 May, having placed a 200-mile exclusion zone around the islands, Britain began its naval campaign. In an action that caused controversy in Britain, the Argentine cruiser *Belgrano* was sunk by a British submarine. Two days later HMS *Sheffield* was destroyed by an Argentine Exocet missile. In subsequent engagements two British frigates were also sunk and others damaged in air attacks. However, the Royal Navy had prepared the way effectively for British troops landings to begin on 21 May. By the end of the month the two key areas of San Carlos and Goose Green had been recaptured. The climax came with the liberation of Port Stanley on 14 June. Argentina then surrendered.

ISSUE:

How responsible was Margaret Thatcher for the Falklands conflict?

Why did Britain go to war over the Falkands in 1982?

SOVEREIGNTY

Mrs Thatcher's government had originally been willing to negotiate a compromise with Argentina. Nicholas Ridley, a Foreign Office Minister, had proposed 'a leaseback' agreement by which Britain, while maintaining ultimate sovereign rights over the Falklands, would allow Argentina to administer the region as its own. However, any chance of a settlement on these terms was destroyed by Galtieri's decision to take the islands by force.

THE BELGRANO

Opponents of the war asserted that Mrs Thatcher had ordered the *Belgrano* to be torpedoed even though it was sailing out of the exclusion zone at the time it was struck. The accusation was that she had done this deliberately to wreck the efforts of the UN Secretary General to bring about a negotiated settlement of the conflict. Mrs Thatcher's defence was that, regardless of its position and heading, the *Belgrano* in a war situation remained a real threat to British personnel – ships can always turn round.

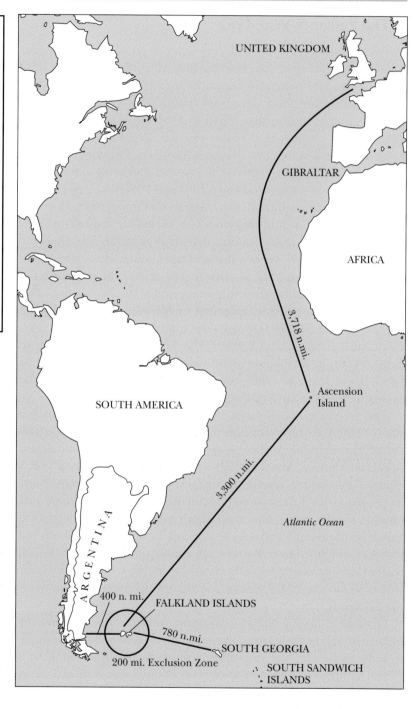

Figure 29 Map of the South Atlantic showing the Falkland Islands.

The conflict had claimed the lives of 255 British and 665 Argentine servicemen. Though some found it tastelessly jingoistic, Mrs Thatcher's cry of 'rejoice, rejoice' at the news of the Task Force's victory found an echo with the population at large who read the tabloid press.

Having regained the Falklands through battle, Mrs Thatcher let it be known she had no intention of now negotiating them away. A large permanent British garrison was to be established on the islands to guarantee their security.

The political gains that Mrs Thatcher derived from her leadership during the Falklands crisis were summarised by a modern historian, Bernard Porter:

> It came at an ideal time for the government, when its fortunes were at their lowest. It may have saved Thatcher's political bacon. It certainly revived her reputation and saw her through a difficult patch. All this, it should be emphasised, was because of the way she responded to the crisis; another leader could quite easily have been destroyed by it. Thatcher rode her luck courageously and cleverly. The political gain she reaped from it was, in this sense, merited.

Source C From *Britannia's Burden: The Political Evolution of Modern Britain 1851–1990* by Bernard Porter, 1994.

THE RESOURCEFUL LOVER
LATIN TROUBADOUR *(serenading the fair Maggie):* "IF SHE WON'T LISTEN TO MY LOVE-SONGS, I'LL TRY HER WITH A BRICK!"

Q What benefits did Margaret Thatcher gain from the Falklands War?

ACTIVITY

Having read section 1c, how would you respond to the suggestion that Mrs Thatcher used the Falklands crisis to promote her own interests rather than Britain's? Jot down the pro and anti arguments as a series of headings.

Figure 30 Cartoon, depicting Galtieri's decision to end negotiation and take the Falklands by force.

ISSUE:
Was the confrontation deliberately provoked?

d) The Miners' Strike, 1984–85

Margaret Thatcher's insistence on the nation's paying its way meant that subsidies would not normally be used to shore up ailing industries, a practice for which she had sharply criticised Edward Heath. Her argument was that, while sympathy might lead one to assist enterprises that were in difficulties, it had always to be remembered that public subsidies by definition came from the public purse. This meant that some other area would be deprived of resources to pay for the failing ones. Robbing Peter to pay Paul made no sense economically if Peter was productive and Paul unproductive. This merely rewarded the inefficient at the expense of the efficient.

What factors explain the outbreak of the miners' strike in 1984?

It was such arguments that lay at the heart of the government's dispute with the miners which came to a head in 1984. It was part of a long story that went back to the General Strike of 1926 (see page 65). Throughout the century British coal had become increasingly costly and difficult to mine. Nationalisation in 1948 had not altered this. Indeed, there was a case for saying that lack of government investment since that date had added to the problem. For some time Britain had been importing coal from abroad. With the exception of a few pits producing particular types of coal, British mines by the 1970s were running at a loss. The Thatcher government declared its unwillingness to put further public money into an industry which had little real chance of being able to recover its place in a competitive market. Its argument was that not to take hard measures when necessary simply delayed the inevitable. Better to face the situation now and lessen the consequences of closure by generous redundancy settlements than pretend things could get better.

However, there was a strong counter argument advanced by the miners' unions and other analysts. They suggested that, with a proper investment programme backed by a genuine government commitment to coal as a long-term power source, large parts of the British coal industry still had a profitable future. Nor, they argued, was it only a matter of economics. The social consequences of widespread pit closures would be catastrophic. In areas such as south Wales, Yorkshire and Durham, coal was not simply an industry; it was a way of life. Whole communities were dependent upon it. If the local mine closed, the local community would cease to exist.

How much did personalities matter in the dispute?

These opposing viewpoints became personalised in the leading protagonists in the coal strike of 1984–85. The National Coal Board (NCB) had recently appointed as its Chairman Ian McGregor, an unsentimental Canadian manager, whose remit was to cut out the non-profitable parts of the coal industry. He was faced by the equally uncompromising Arthur Scargill, the Marxist president of the NUM, who was totally opposed to any pit closures. Although the government claimed to be a neutral in the dispute and concerned only with upholding law and order, it fully backed McGregor and the NCB. It is arguable that the government deliberately encouraged a showdown with the miners as part of its campaign for bringing the trade unions to heel. Anticipating a prolonged strike, the government had made careful plans. Its strong man, Norman Tebbit, the Employment Minister, had already steered through an **Employment Act** which lessened the unions' effectiveness. Coal and coke were stockpiled at the fuel stations and emergency plans were drawn up for importing further stocks should the need arise.

The strike which began in 1984 lasted a year and saw violent clashes between striking miners and the police. But the NUM never had any real hope of success. Arthur Scargill's refusal to call a national ballot suggested that he knew he would not win majority support for the strike from the union members. This weakened his moral case and gave justification to the breakaway miners who remained at work. A critical handicap to the strikers was the refusal of key unions, such as the power workers, to join the struggle.

The strike petered out early in 1985, leaving a legacy of bitterness and recrimination. The miners' defeat marked a major success for the government's anti-union campaign and emboldened other employers to begin resisting union demands. Union power was on the decline. This was clearly evident in 1986 in the failure of the print workers, despite prolonged and desperate efforts, to prevent Rupert Murdoch, the proprietor of the Times Newspaper group, from obliging them to accept new technology and modern work practices.

EMPLOYMENT ACTS

Separate Acts had been introduced in 1980 and 1982 as the first steps towards destroying union power. The measures forbade mass picketing, outlawed the 'closed shop' – the requirement that all workers in a particular plant or factory had to be union members – and declared that industrial action was illegal unless the members had voted for a strike in a formal union ballot.

ACTIVITY

It would be an interesting exercise to debate the rights and wrongs of the miners' strike of 1984–85. Try to put both sides of the argument.

▼ How strong do you find the purely economic considerations?
▼ Did coal have a future?
▼ What weight should be given to the social consequences of pit closures?
▼ Was the issue a matter of principle or was it essentially a clash between powerful and conflicting personalities?
▼ Did the government provoke the strike as a pretext for further weakening the unions?

ISSUE:
How far was Mrs
Thatcher the cause of
her own downfall?

e) The Fall of Margaret Thatcher – the Poll Tax

Two particular issues help to explain why Margaret Thatcher's long period in office came to an end in 1990. These were the European question (see pages 247–9) and the Poll Tax. It is important to put this second issue in the context of Mrs Thatcher's attempt to bring local government into line with her ideas of public accountability.

The Poll Tax (Community Charge)

The Community Charge was intended to replace the existing system of local rates, based on property values, with a flat-rate charge for services, set by each local authority. The charge was to be paid by all the adults resident in the local area. Its opponents scathingly called it the poll tax after the similar levy that had led to the Peasants' Revolt in 1379. The poll tax was introduced into Scotland in 1989 and a year later into England and Wales. It was withdrawn in 1991, and substituted by a new council tax, based on a sliding scale of property values.

What were the origins of the poll tax?

**THE ADAM SMITH
INSTITUTE (ASI)**
was a Conservative 'think-tank', which had a strong influence on Margaret Thatcher's policies. It opposed as inefficient and wasteful the idea that the State should redistribute resources by taxing the rich and providing for the poor. The ASI believed that the free play of market forces was the best way of fulfilling people's needs.

There was no doubt that the existing rates system was unfair. For example, a single pensioner living alone might well be charged the same rates as a household of four wage-earners living in a property of equal value. The idea of a poll tax in place of the rates came originally from the **Adam Smith Institute (ASI)**, which suggested that since there would be 38 million poll-tax payers, compared with only 14 million ratepayers, the charges for local services would be much more evenly and justly spread. Moreover, if everybody had to pay for local services then everybody would become much more conscious of the quality of the services provided.

This very much fitted in with Margaret Thatcher's campaign to make public institutions, in this case local government, accountable to the people. She knew that many local authorities were unpopular. Only a minority of people (sometimes under 25 per cent) voted in local elections. This had allowed extreme socialist groups to dominate areas such as the London boroughs and the city councils in Liverpool and Manchester. These were among the high-spending 'loony left' Labour authorities that she had successfully attacked by breaking up the metropolitan councils and abolishing the Greater London Council (GLC) in 1983. The community charge would help make local authorities answerable to their 'customers', who would be the people now paying for the services. Her hope was that in local elections the poll-tax payers would throw out high-spending Labour councils and vote in responsible Conservative ones. Not all in her party were happy with Mrs Thatcher's thinking on this. The '**one-nation Conservatives**' had serious doubts.

The prelude to the poll tax was Mrs Thatcher's third consecutive electoral victory. Although the 1987 results showed some recovery by the Labour Party from its disastrous showing in the 1983 election (see page 192), the government maintained its share of the popular vote and despite losing 22 seats still had an overall majority in the Commons of 100.

Mrs Thatcher interpreted this as a mandate for pressing on with her reforming policies. The path to the poll tax was cleared by a series of changes in local government finance that were introduced in 1988. A system of Standard Spending Assessments (SSAs) enabled the central government to control local authority spending levels. Councils were also required to adopt 'compulsory competitive tendering' (CCT), that is, to contract out their services to the companies that could provide the best service at the lowest price. The government's expectation was that these changes would be welcomed by the general public who would then be attracted to the poll tax since it would continue the process of creating 'more gainers than losers'.

But the government had misjudged the situation. The financial merits that the poll tax might have had meant little to a public who saw it was a new regressive tax imposed by a grasping government intent on trapping everybody in the same net. The government did, in fact, list a large number of exemptions from payment for the less well off, but these concessions were lost sight of in the furore that the poll tax aroused. Opposition to the charge when it was introduced into Scotland in 1989 and England and Wales in 1990, was immediate and organised. Millions of people refused or avoided payment.

More disturbing for Mrs Thatcher was the reaction of many in her own party. She had had a forewarning of this in 1988 when several Conservative backbench rebellions against the poll tax had occurred,

THE 'ONE-NATION CONSERVATIVES'

The term refers to those in the party, Edward Heath and Michael Heseltine being among the most prominent, who argued that the government should use redistributive taxation to help the disadvantaged members of society. For these liberal Conservatives the poll tax's main disadvantage was that it was a regressive tax, i.e., as a flat rate levy it bore hardest on the poorest. They believed that the riots that had occurred in various English cities in the 1980s held a message. Although the disturbances had complex causes they could be interpreted at least in part as an expression of the disaffection of many people, particularly the young unemployed, from Thatcherite Britain.

Why did the poll tax arouse fierce opposition?

The 1987 Election Result			
	Votes	**Seats**	**% Vote**
Conservative	13,763,747	375	42.2
Labour	10,029,270	229	30.8
Liberal/SDP	7,341,275	22	22.6
Plaid Cymru	123,589	3	0.3
Scottish Nationalists	416,873	3	1.4
Northern Irish Parties	730,152	17	2.3
Others	151,517	1	0.4

Table 37 The 1987 election result.

the most worrying arising from an amendment to modify the proposed tax in the interests of 'fairness'. When the charge came into force in England in March 1990, it was on average double the original estimate. At this, even the respectable middle classes, previously Margaret Thatcher's staunchest allies, began to protest. The most serious disturbance came with a violent anti-poll tax demonstration in London's Trafalgar Square on 31 March.

A further irony was that, owing to the resistance it aroused, the poll tax cost two and a half times more to collect than the rates had. In an effort to keep down poll tax levels, the government 'charge-capped' a number of authorities (mostly Labour, but also some Conservative). This involved compelling them to reduce their budgets even if it meant cutting services. This seemed to stand on its head the original notion of improving local government services in the interest of the 'customer'. Critics had strong grounds for asserting that the whole exercise had been aimed not at encouraging greater local democracy but at imposing the will of the central government on the local authorities.

Q How did the battle over the poll tax affect Mrs Thatcher's position?

Given the anger and disappointment aroused by the government's inept handling of the poll tax, it was no surprise that the Conservatives lost all four by-elections held in 1989 and 1990. In April 1990 opinion polls showed that Labour had gained a 20-point lead over the Conservatives. The polls also revealed that Margaret Thatcher's personal popularity rating was lower than at any other time in her 11 years at the helm. Such developments led a growing number of her party to question whether they could win the next general election if she remained leader. These doubts were intensified by the disagreements within the Cabinet over Europe (see page 249). It was in this atmosphere that Michael Heseltine decided in November to mount an open challenge for the leadership. Although Margaret Thatcher won the first ballot by 52 votes she regarded the narrowness of the margin as evidence that she had lost the confidence of two out of five of the Conservative MPs. So, she withdrew from the second ballot which was won not by Heseltine but by John Major, her choice as successor. The party had decided that after 11 years of Margaret Thatcher they wanted a safer, even if a much duller, leader.

ACTIVITY

Having read section 1e write down a list of reasons explaining: a) why the poll tax was introduced, and b) why it proved so unpopular.

f) The Legacy of Thatcherism

Mrs Thatcher's emphasis on accountability left an enduring mark on British attitudes. It was a new form of **utilitarianism**. Indeed, there was about her much more of the Victorian Liberal than the modern Conservative. She often expressed admiration for what she called 'Victorian virtues'. The wish to restrict the power of the State and to prevent the wasteful spending of public funds were key aspects of her approach. This largely explained her unpopularity in intellectual circles. Institutions, including higher education, were subjected to the same demands of accountability as other areas of public life that were receiving government funds. On the grounds that her policies were undermining education, Oxford University in 1983 in a controversial gesture voted to deny her the honorary degree that had traditionally been conferred on prime ministers.

Margaret Thatcher proved to be one of the most remarkable politicians of modern times. Her strength of character and purpose has been likened to that possessed by other notable female leaders in British history, such as Boudicca and Elizabeth I. However, some of her strongest critics were women, who complained that she showed an unwillingness to support female causes. Revealingly, she appointed only one woman to her Cabinet. It has been suggested that this was because as the lone woman she was able to exploit her femininity among her male colleagues and did not wish for competition from other females. A weightier charge is that in 11 years of government she made no effort to introduce structural changes to advance the role of women in politics and society.

Against that, it might be said that in the end what really mattered historically about Margaret Thatcher was not what she did but what she was. For a woman to lead a political party for 15 years, to be Prime Minister for 11, and during that time to be acknowledged internationally as a stateswoman were extraordinary achievements.

ISSUE:
What were the main changes that Margaret Thatcher brought about?

UTILITARIANISM
was an influential attitude in the early Victorian period. It emphasised that public institutions and government bodies should be judged by how effectively they operated. It was false sentiment to keep them in being and spend pubic money on them once they had lost their 'utility' and become wasteful and expensive.

Q
How significant was Margaret Thatcher's role as a woman in politics?

ACTIVITY

Having read this section, how would you respond to the following propositions?

▼ Margaret Thatcher was a destructive not a constructive force in British politics.

▼ What really mattered about Margaret Thatcher was not what she did but what she was.

ISSUE:
Did John Major simply
continue his predeces-
sor's policies?

2 John Major's Government, 1990–97

Capable of arousing both intense admiration and deep dislike, Margaret Thatcher had been the dominant political figure of her time. John Major was not in the same mould. For some, this was his attraction. He did not have the abrasive, combative character of his predecessor. Yet personally likeable though he was, he was not an inspiring figure. Despite being given key ministries by Margaret Thatcher he had not held them long enough to create a lasting impression. The satirical television puppet show, 'Spitting Image', portrayed him as a literally grey figure, boringly consumed with the unimportant details of life. The caricature accorded with the picture many people had of him. John Keegan described the Major government as 'one of the dreariest administrations of the century'. Major's problem was that he really had no distinctive strategy other than to continue in office. It is true that he presented a less combative image of Conservatism than his predecessor had done and he spoke of wishing to see Britain become a 'classless society'. But Major made no attempt to modify the changes that Thatcherism had introduced. The exception was Europe. His enthusiasm for the European Union was in marked contrast to Margaret Thatcher's vociferous scepticism (see page 249).

KEY POSTS HELD BY JOHN MAJOR
Minister of Health, 1985–87
Foreign Secretary, 1989
Chancellor of the Exchequer, 1989–90
Leader of the Conservative Party and Prime Minister, 1990–97

The surprise was that Major won the election of 1992. Until the week before polling day it was generally assumed that after 13 years in power the Conservatives would lose. However, the Labour Party led by Neil Kinnock conducted an ill-judged campaign. Having in the early part of the campaign successfully promoted itself as the caring party, it assumed from the opinion polls that it was going to win. This was evident in an embarrassingly triumphalist rally in Sheffield in the week before the election. The party also got itself into a tangle by pre-

The 1992 Election Result			
	Votes	**Seats**	**% Vote**
Conservative	14,092,891	336	42.0
Labour	11,559,735	271	34.2
Liberal-Democrats	5,999,384	20	17.9
Plaid Cymru	154,439	4	0.5
Scottish Nationalists	629,552	3	1.9
Northern Irish Parties	740,485	17	2.2
Others	436,207	0	1.3

Table 38 The 1992 election result.

senting a shadow budget that seemed to promise large increases in taxation. John Major exploited this by literally getting on his soap-box and suggesting in a homely way that only the Conservatives could be trusted to run the economy. *The Sun* newspaper was sufficiently convinced to switch its support from Labour to Conservative.

This victory proved a mixed blessing for Major. Although his new government ran its full term it faced mounting problems within the Conservative Party itself. The European issue proved the most disturbing. The growth of a strong Euro-sceptic group, deeply disturbed by the implications of the ERM and the Maastricht Treaty which Major had signed in 1992 (see page 250), threatened to cause a permanent split in the party. His troubles were highlighted by the fact that his party lost every by-election held during his period of office.

One result of this was the whittling down of his government's majority in the Commons, which made him rely increasingly on the support of the Ulster Unionists. He survived an open challenge to his authority by winning a party election in 1995 but sniping against him continued within the Cabinet. In an unguarded moment, he was heard referring to his critics within the government as 'those bastards'. By the time of the 1997 General Election, Major's position had been gravely weakened by a press campaign determined to expose leading Conservatives as being guilty of corruption or 'sleaze'. The term covered such activities as 'cash for questions', the practice whereby, in return for payment, MPs asked questions in the Commons to promote the interests of particular commercial companies.

What factors weakened John Major's position?

Major himself was blameless, but this did not prevent his administration from suffering the heaviest defeat that any government had undergone in the twentieth century. The Conservatives had clearly outstayed their time. It should also be said that 1997 was in a sense a delayed reaction against Thatcherism. Although it was seven years since she had been Prime Minister, the shattering defeat of the Conservatives in 1997 was a rejection not just of Major's government but of 18 years of Thatcherite Conservatism.

The 1997 Election Result			
	Votes	**Seats**	**% Vote**
Conservative	9,600,940	165	30.7
Labour	13,517,911	418	43.2
Liberal-Democrat	5,243,440	46	16.8
Scottish Nationalists	622,260	22	2.0
Plaid Cymru	161,030	4	0.5
Others	2,142,621	29	6.8

Table 39 The 1997 election result.

ISSUE:
Why was the Labour Party unable to mount an effective challenge to Thatcherism in these years?

LEADERS OF THE LABOUR PARTY SINCE 1945

1945–55	Clement Attlee
1955–63	Hugh Gaitskell
1963–76	Harold Wilson
1976–80	James Callaghan
1980–83	Michael Foot
1983–92	Neil Kinnock
1992–94	John Smith
1994–	Anthony Blair

3 From Old Labour to New Labour, 1979–99

a) Labour Under Foot and Kinnock, 1980–92

If Margaret Thatcher had a profound effect on her own party, her impact on the Labour Party was hardly less significant. She obliged the Labour Party to redesign itself. Despairing of gaining electoral support if it kept to its old ways, it set about recreating itself. This naturally led to dissension within the party. The 1980s and 1990s saw the old guard resist the modernising thrust.

The 1980s were a disastrous decade for the Labour Party. Between 1979 and 1992 it lost four elections in a row. The last year of James Callaghan's administration in 1978/79 witnessed the 'winter of discontent', a series of damaging strikes by public service workers. The Labour Party's strong links with the unions was seen by the voters as a contributing factor to the industrial strife, and to Labour's inability to govern. This view held for the next 13 years. The electorate no longer seemed to regard Labour as a party of government. In many respects Labour was its own worst enemy in this period. It presented an image of a divided party more concerned with its own internal wrangles than with preparing itself for government. A major problem was the split between the left and right of the party. Callaghan had been a moderate but he was followed as leader in 1980 by Michael Foot, whose election marked a success for the left-wing backbench MPs.

Apart from Foot himself, the outstanding spokesman of the left was Tony Benn. He interpreted Labour's 1979 defeat as proving the need for it to embrace fully socialist polices. As a step towards achieving this, he led a campaign to change the party's constitution. At Labour's 1981 conference the left forced through a resolution that required all MPs to seek reselection by their constituencies. The aim was to give greater power to left-wing activists who, although being a minority in the party overall, were disproportionately stronger in the constituencies. Benn hailed this as a victory for party democracy, but for Labour moderates it signalled the takover of the party by extremists. One significant consequence was the decision of a number of Labour MPs to leave the party in 1981 and form the **SDP**.

Tony Benn

proved to be one of the most interesting figures in Labour Party history. He was born Anthony Wedgwood Benn, the heir to Lord Stansgate. However, having adopted socialist principles he successfully campaigned to have the law changed so that he could renounce his peerage and remain a commoner and a member of the House of Commons. He was a minister under both Wilson and Callaghan but despite gaining a loyal following on the left of the party was never able to convert his popularity into a successful bid for the leadership. Moderates regarded him with suspicion and the tabloid newspapers portrayed him as a dangerous representative of the 'loony left'. From the 1960s he was a consistent opponent of Britain's membership of EEC and the EU, regarding these bodies as the enemies of democracy.

Throughout the 1980s Benn led the left-wing campaign that urged the party to adopt genuinely socialist policies. Although he remained a Labour MP during the transformation of the party into New Labour, there was little doubt that he regarded the process as the abandonment of true socialism. Perhaps the last of the great parliamentary orators, he continued throughout the 1990s to speak out trenchantly on the major issues of the day.

THE SDP (SOCIAL DEMOCRATIC PARTY)

Believing that the party had fallen into the hands of extremists, a number of Labour MPs broke away to form a new Social Democratic Party which would be radical but not socialist. The most prominent among these were Shirley Williams, David Owen, William Rodgers and Roy Jenkins, known as the 'gang of four'. Their hope was that the SDP would attract disaffected members from both the Labour and Conservative parties. In alliance with the Liberals the SDP gained a quarter of the popular vote in the 1983 election. But, despite such early success, it was never able to establish itself as a credible alternative to the major parties. By the early 1990s the SDP had formally merged with the Liberal Party to form the Liberal-Democrats.

Weakened by internal disputes and uninspiringly led by Michael Foot, the Labour Party suffered a humiliatingly heavy defeat in the 1983 election. Its ill-thought out manifesto was largely a concession to its left wing and in particular to **CND**. Among its vote-losing pledges was the promise to abandon Britain's independent nuclear deterrent and reintroduce nationalisation. The Labour MP, Gerald Kaufman, wittily if despairingly described the manifesto as 'the longest suicide note in history'.

Michael Foot was replaced as party leader in 1983 by Neil Kinnock. This was to prove a turning point in Labour's fortunes. Although Kinnock had earlier been on the left of the party he was realistic enough to appreciate that the hard left path was unlikely to lead Labour back to power. He began a wide-ranging policy review which rejected many of the programmes, such as unilateralism, which the

Table 40 The 1983 election result.

The 1983 Election Result			
	Votes	**Seats**	**% Vote**
Conservative	13,012,315	397	42.4
Labour	8,456,934	209	27.6
Liberal/SDP	7,780,949	23	25.4
Plaid Cymru	125,309	2	0.4
Scottish Nationalists	331,975	2	1.1
Northern Irish Parties	764,925	17	2.6
Others	232,054	0	0.5

THE CAMPAIGN FOR NUCLEAR DISARMAMENT (CND)

had been founded in 1958. It reached the peak of its membership and influence in the early 1980s, when Cruise missiles were deployed in Britain. CND demanded the renunciation of nuclear weapons by Britain as a step towards universal nuclear disarmament. Strongly anti-American and pro-Soviet, CND also urged Britain to leave NATO. Labour adopted unilateralism as part of its defence policy for the 1983 election, but had abandoned it by 1987.

Q How did Neil Kinnock try to reform the Labour Party?

ISSUE:

In what sense was New Labour new?

PUBLIC OWNERSHIP

Since 1919, Clause IV of the Labour Party's constitution had committed it to nationalisation, which was defined as 'the common ownership of the means of production, distribution and exchange'.

party had saddled itself with under Foot. A key moment came in 1985 at the annual conference when Kinnock denounced the 'loony left' Labour councillors, such as those in Liverpool and Manchester, whose extreme activities had earned the contempt of the electorate. He told the party that it had to drop its 'rigid dogmas' and adapt to the real world.

Neil Kinnock's efforts undoubtedly laid the base for the modernisation of the Labour Party, but during his nine years as leader he was unable to persuade the electorate to trust him sufficiently and lost to Margaret Thatcher in the 1987 and 1992 General Elections. He stood down after the second defeat. His successor, John Smith, was very popular in the party but had little time to build on this before his premature death in 1994. Smith was succeeded as leader by Tony Blair.

b) New Labour, 1994–99

Despite its defeat in the 1992 General Election, there were clear signs that the Labour Party's move away from the left had begun to find favour with the electorate. Tony Blair picked up on this and continued the process by which the party distanced itself from dated policies that had deterred rather than encouraged support from the general public. The chief features of this were:

▼ The abandonment of **public ownership** as a central objective.

▼ The instructing of Labour MPs and candidates to avoid using the term 'socialist' in their public statements.

▼ The City and the business world were to be wooed by the promise that capitalism was safe in Labour hands.

▼ The legal restrictions on trade unions were to be maintained.

▼ Labour would not present its policies in terms of class struggle – it accepted that class-based politics were no longer relevant in Britain.

This new line of approach naturally upset the socialist wing of the party. They characterised it as a sell-out by the Labour Party to the forces of expediency. They were concerned that New Labour lacked a distinct, radical ideology. Instead, it presented itself to the electorate as wanting to do the same things as the Conservatives, only more efficiently. The response of the supporters of New Labour within the party was to point out that the world had changed. Loyalty to old Labour values and refusal to modify policy had simply made the party unelectable for 18 years. The argument was convincingly vindicated in the sweeping victory of New Labour in 1997.

Blair's great asset was his youthful air and appearance. He looked younger than his years and his buoyant personality was greatly to his advantage when contrasted with the greyness of John Major. In the 1997 election, he skilfully played upon the tired character of the Conservative government that had been too long in government and

What were the distinctive features of Blair's style of government?

Tony Blair

came from a Scottish background. He was educated at public school and at Oxford. A lawyer by training, he entered politics, became an MP in 1983 and a shadow Cabinet member in 1988. After the sudden death of John Smith in 1994, he was elected Labour Party leader. He continued the process that had begun in the 1980s under Neil Kinnock of modernising the party. This meant weakening its links with the trade unions, abandoning Clause IV, and avoiding the taint of socialism.

Figure 31 Photo of Tony Blair at the age of 31 campaigning in the run-up to the 1983 election. As a young politician he was a member of CND and tended to take a left-wing position on most issues.

SPIN DOCTORS

The term was borrowed from the USA in the late 1990s to describe the special advisers employed by politicians to present their policies in the best light possible. Spin was essentially a form of public relations. Tony Blair relied on a team of advisers to handle the media and help him judge the public mood, so that he could adjust his approach accordingly. The practice was not new. Margaret Thatcher, for example, had employed a well-organised press team, led by Bernard Ingham. What was new about the spin doctors was the large degree of influence they appeared to have not simply on the presentation but on the shaping of government policy.

that had become associated with corruption and scandal. By April 2000, after three years in office, he was riding high in the opinion polls. His own and his government's popularity rating was 20 points ahead of William Hague and the Conservatives.

Sceptics suggested that his popularity had been earned too easily, that he was liked for his style rather than the content of his policies, and that he relied too greatly on **spin doctors**, who tried to make him appear to be all things to all men. Blair watchers noted that his style and even his accent changed to match the particular audience he was facing. He declared on one television chat-show that he wanted to be thought of 'as a regular sorta guy'. It was not an expression that one could imagine Clement Attlee or Harold Macmillan ever using but its colloquial style seemed perfectly fitted to its time. Style and presentation mattered. That was what was meant by saying that politics had become presidential in style. There was no denying that he was in tune with his times. A sign of this was that his popularity rating was at its highest among young voters who were attracted by what they saw as New Labour's progressive stance.

New Labour's Progressive Stance

New Labour's approach was in part defined by a number of slogans or 'buzz words' with which the young could identify. Among these were:
- ▼ 'inclusiveness' – referring to a society where nobody was left out, where there would be no 'social exclusion'. It was similar to John Major's idea of a classless society.
- ▼ 'stake-holder society' – meaning in a practical sense ordinary people having State-protected investments and pensions, and in an abstract sense people feeling that they belonged collectively to society.
- ▼ 'forces of conservatism' – a blanket term, first used by Tony Blair in 1999, to condemn everything that held back his idea of progress.

 What were New Labour's domestic policies?

New Labour's first three years went well. The economy appeared healthy and Gordon Brown proved a major success as Chancellor of the Exchequer. His prudent budgets swelled Britain's reserve funds while at the same time keeping inflation down. But there were difficulties. The Blair government's commitment to devolution, which it honoured by the creation of a Scottish parliament and a Welsh assembly, raised the question of whether full independence was intended. Traditionally Labour had its strongest electoral support in Scotland and Wales, and it would seriously, perhaps even permanently, weaken its position if they were to be allowed full independence.

Similarly, the reform of the House of Lords raised problems for the government. Ending the right of unelected hereditary peers to sit in the upper house may have been sincerely intended to strike a blow for democracy. But the problem was what form the new chamber would take and what powers it would have. By 2000 Blair had created more life peers in his three years of government than the Conservatives had in their 18. Critics complained that it was part of his scheme for consolidating New Labour's authority by packing the House of Lords with his own appointees so that it would cease to be obstructive. Even some of his own side were unhappy at this. Tony Benn described the process as going back 700 years to the time when monarchs got their way by surrounding themselves with placemen.

What was particularly observable about Tony Blair's government was that though it was very different in style and tone from the Thatcher-Major Conservatism that it replaced, it made no substantial effort to undo what had been done in the previous 18 years. Margaret Thatcher's legacy proved a powerful one. She had weakened the trade unions, reintroduced the principle of accountability into the public services, and made the nation acknowledge that in economic matters nothing was for nothing. Although she was attacked for it in her time, the effectiveness of what she had done convinced those who came after her that they had to follow much the same path. As the contemporary historian, Peter Clarke, put it:

> The fruits of her reforms were accepted by many long-standing opponents. Though their hearts might have bled for the miners, they did not propose to put the unions back in the saddle; although they might have been scornful of privatisation, they did not propose to go back to a regime of nationalised industries and council houses. The post-Thatcher Labour Party bore a closer resemblance to the SDP of ten years previously than partisans of either cared to acknowledge.

Q Was there a continuity between Thatcherism and New Labour?

Source D From *Hope and Glory: Britain 1900–1990* by Peter Clarke, 1996.

This continuity between Thatcherism and New Labour was a point emphasised by John Keegan:

> Britain is still living in the fourth period of its post-1914 history that Margaret Thatcher inaugurated. It is her financial and industrial regime that prevails, and her mode of government also – centralist at home, Atlanticist in strategic affairs, cautiously co-operative in its relations with the European Community. These positions, the centralising tendency perhaps apart, seem to suit the electorate.

Source E From *The British Century* by John Keegan, 1999.

Q What problems did New Labour face on the foreign front?

Blair had certainly made a strong impression abroad. EU ministers and officials had warmed to him (see page 250), and the Clinton administration in the USA was impressed. Indeed Bill Clinton had personal reason to be grateful to Tony Blair for offering his moral support in 1999 when impeachment proceedings were instituted against the President over alleged sexual misdemeanours. But at the close of the century the new government faced two particularly difficult problems in foreign affairs – i) war in the former Yugloslavia, and ii) Iraq. Soon after becoming Foreign Secretary in Tony Blair's government Robin Cook had declared that New Labour would pursue an 'ethical foreign policy'. The dilemma that this created was evident in the way the government handled these issues.

i) The Balkan Question

In the complex civil war in the former Yugoslavia, the government gave its full support to the NATO air strikes against the Serbian forces in 1999. Blair's justification was that the Serbs had been engaging in the genocide of the Albanian people of Kosovo. However, there were critics who argued that the NATO action had led the Serbs to intensify their mistreatment of the Kosovars. There were also voices raised against the manner in which NATO bombing raids, carried out principally by the USAF and the RAF, had been conducted. To minimise the chance of casualties amongst themselves the bomber crews had flown above 15,000 feet; this meant that, even with the sophisticated guidance systems available, bombs might well strike wrongly identified non-military targets. The Serbs produced evidence to show that this, indeed, had happened.

ii) Iraq

The accusation of indiscriminate bombing was also at the centre of the dispute in another area – Iraq. As part of a programme to make Saddam Hussein, the Iraqi leader, comply with UN resolutions requiring him to open up his country to weapons inspection, Blair's government joined with the USA in imposing sanctions. Observers reported that the effect of sanctions was not to hurt the Saddam regime but to deprive ordinary Iraqis of vital supplies such as medicines. It was also charged that the frequent nightly bombing raids that the Allies carried out against military installations had in fact caused the death of many innocent civilians.

ACTIVITY

Having read section 3, say how convincing you find the argument that there was a clear line of continuity between Thatcherism and New Labour.

Points to consider:
▼ What were the main features of Thatcherism?
▼ In what respects did New Labour policies match or differ from these?
▼ How important were the personalities of the different leaders?

▽ Working on From Thatcherism to New Labour, 1979–99

The approach in this chapter has been to view Thatcherism as a break from the consensus that had characterised politics in Britain since 1945. Whether this was a revolution is open for you to debate, but it will certainly provide a basis from which to analyse Margaret Thatcher's policies and their effects. At the time this book was completed Tony Blair's government had just completed three full years in office. Any judgement on his record is, therefore, interim and partial. But this should not prevent you from seeing the points of difference from, and continuity with, his Conservative predecessors. It would also be appropriate to view the last Labour government of the century in the context of the party's growth across 100 years.

Answering Essay Questions on From Thatcherism to New Labour, 1979–99

One of the demands in some specifications is that students should be able to present answers that cover material over a 100-year time span. An appropriate example, based on this chapter, might be:
▽ How far did the Labour Party move from its original principles in its development between 1900 and 1999?

Some pointers to help your analysis:
You will notice this requires you to combine historical judgement and knowledge over a wide period. When preparing an answer to a time-span question, make sure you do not get bogged down in detail. You are being asked to survey a broad pattern. In this case it

is the development of the Labour Party from its beginnings through to its transformation into New Labour. You will obviously need to check back to Chapters 1, 3, 5 and 6 to provide the continuity over the century. The question gives you a very strong push in a particular direction. It suggests that the Labour Party began with a set of principles in 1900 and then asks you how closely it kept to these during the next 100 years. To assemble your material, list the key phases in Labour's history. Obviously you cannot include everything; you have to be selective. Do not worry about leaving things out. Concentrate on what you regard as the vital points. Your list might end up like this:

1900	various political and industrial organisation came together to form the LRC;
1906	the Labour Party formally created to represent working-class interests;
1906–14	co-operated with the Liberals in the Lib-Lab pact;
1914–18	after initial misgivings supported the war effort;
1919–31	took over from the Liberals as the second largest party;
1924 and 1929–31	Labour in government;
1931	Ramsay MacDonald's 'betrayal';
1940–45	joined Churchill's Coalition government;
1945–51	Labour's greatest period – established the welfare state and introduced nationalisation;
1951–64	weakened by internal left/right rowing;
1964–70	Wilson's government disappointed the left;
1974–79	Wilson/Callaghan governments weakened by conflict with the unions;
1979–94	in the Thatcherite wilderness but under Kinnock/Smith after 1983, the party began to modernise itself;
1994–99	this process carried forward into New Labour under Tony Blair – broke its links with the unions, abandoned Clause 4, dropped class politics; accepted the essential of the Thatcherite revolution.

Having compiled your material, your essential starting point is to define what you understand the principles to have been when the LRC came into being. The various influences should be mentioned, e.g., Fabianism, the co-operative movement, the trade unions, etc. Ask yourself, did the LRC define its principles or did it simply declare its aims, namely to establish a separate party to represent working-class interests? Was it truly socialist, i.e., did it want radical social change or merely the improvement of working-class conditions? It is worth recalling that the Labour Party did not formally adopt a constitution until after the First World War. Is the constitution, therefore, the definition of Labour principles? If so, were they to be considered fixed and unchangeable? Ramsay MacDonald was a vital figure. He opted to make the party moderate and, therefore, electable. But in doing so did he weaken the party's socialist principles? That charge has weight only if socialism is considered an essential part of Labour's programme.

But if you think that the party was never committed to a rigid dogmatic position then there is no question of its being untrue to its principles at any stage. Its only consistent concern was to protect working-class interests. Since these interests altered with the changing character of the working class over the century then the party's main task was to adapt its policies to these changes. Labour's high point came under Attlee in 1945–51. But even though the welfare state was an extraordinary achievement it was very much the fulfilment of a liberal programme. Moreover Labour's nationalisation programme was a very muted and limited affair. All the Labour governments of the century accepted capitalism and struggled to defend it, hence the many financial crises from the dole cuts in 1931 to devaluation in 1967. As the arguments in the party showed, the left continually claimed that on the big issues in domestic and foreign affairs the party was not taking genuinely socialist steps. But Herbert Morrison once shrewdly defined socialism as 'what Labour governments do', in other words a form of pragmatism. New Labour could be seen as taking that notion to its logical conclusion. Rather than being a betrayal of principle New Labour's approach was a shrewd piece of applied realism. The old world of old socialist Labour had disappeared. Heavy industry had gone and the large mass unions, the party's traditional strength, had gone with it. Like it or not, Thatcherism had redrafted the political agenda. The only realistic response for Labour was to become a 'new' party modified in such a way that it could meet the aspirations of an electorate which was very different in composition and outlook from the one in 1900.

By all means find fault with the points that have just been made. Their purpose is to help stimulate your own ideas by suggesting the type of approach you might adopt.

Answering Source-Based Questions on From Thatcherism to New Labour, 1979–99

Study the following source material and then answer the questions which follow.

Source F From 'The Legacy of Thatcherism', a prize-winning entry in the United States Inter-Collegiate Studies Institute Essay Competition, 1998.

> The Thatcherite conception of freedom holds that in human affairs – in politics and society – weight must always be laid upon duty and responsibility as much as upon rights. Rights indeed have no moral base unless they are attached to responsibilities. Thatcher's conception of liberty is thus very much in the tradition of nineteenth-century liberalism, which is to say that the State exists primarily to create the conditions in which the individual may exercise his or her individual rights. The State is never a substitute for personal moral action. The antipathy of Thatcherism towards socialism may thus be said to spring from an impulse which many Americans understand: the right to pursue one's own legitimate (and by implication, moral) interests without interference from officialdom and bureaucracy.

Source G From *The Thatcher Revolution* by Stuart Hall and Martin Jacques, 1983.

> Thatcherism is a novel and exceptional political force. Its novelty lies, in part, in the success with which this 'populist' appeal was then orchestrated with the imposition of authority and order. It managed to marry the gospel of free market liberalism with organic patriotic Toryism. 'Free market, strong state, iron times': an authoritarian populism.

Source H From *Marxism Today*, 1980.

> The state is to be rolled back in some areas and rolled forward in others. The real innovation of Thatcherism is the way it has linked traditional Conservative concern with the basis of authority in social institutions and the importance of internal order and external security, with a new emphasis upon free market exchange and the principles of the market order.

▼ QUESTIONS ON SOURCES

1. Use Source F and your own knowledge. Explain and comment on the writer's suggestion that 'Thatcher's conception of liberty is thus very much in the tradition of nineteenth-century liberalism.' **(8 marks)**

2. Use Source G. How do the writers arrive at their conclusion that Thatcherism is 'an authoritarian populism'? **(10 marks)**

3. Do Sources F, G, and H complement or contradict each other in their view of Thatcherism? **(12 marks)**

Points to note about the questions:

Question 1 calls for comprehension and cross-referencing.
Question 2 calls for comprehension, cross-referencing and evaluation.
Question 3 calls for comprehension, cross-referencing, evaluation and synthesis.

Do note the varying allocation of marks for each question.

Points to assist you

Question 1 In the first part of the extract the writer clearly defines both the Thatcherite concept of freedom and the nineteenth-century liberal tradition and draws a close connection between the two. Your main task, therefore, under 'explain' is to show that you understand his definitions: the Thatcherite concept – 'weight must always be laid upon duty ... as much as upon rights'; and the liberal tradition – 'the State exists primarily to create the conditions in which the individual may exercise his or her individual rights'. Do not quote the pieces at length but put them into your own words. The other half of the question, 'and comment on', asks you to evaluate the appropriateness of his description of Thatcherism and liberalism. This is where your own understanding of those movements comes into play. Do not be reluctant to challenge or qualify his definitions. Equally, if you find them appropriate, draw on your own knowledge in saying why you do.

Question 2 Source G is by no means an easy analysis. That is why it carries high marks. You have to follow the writers' argument through from its assertion that 'Thatcherism is a novel and exceptional political force' to the conclusion that it is 'an authoritarian populism'. This means that along the way you have to explain Thatcherism's novelty, its populist appeal, its relationship to authority and to the gospel of free market capitalism and organic patriotic Toryism. Fortunately for you it offers a neat summary of the argument in the quotation – 'Free market, strong state, iron times'. If you explained each of those three terms by reference to what the writers have said earlier you would have met the demands of the question. Remember to use your own words in defining the terms.

Question 3 The demand on you is to explore the three sources for the points where they coincide or differ. Look for implied similarities and differences as well as direct ones. G and H are much closer in their approach since they are both concerned with the central issue of authority. They are also interested in exploring the relationship of Thatcherism with Toryism and Conservatism, whereas F's emphasis is on its connection to old liberalism. Does this suggest a contradiction or simply an emphasis on different aspects? There is a strong implication in F that the writer approves of Thatcherism because of its affinity with American values. Does this distance it, therefore, from the Marxist viewpoint in H. Be careful on this point. Although H comes clearly from a Marxist source, if you read it carefully it is descriptive; nowhere in the extract is there criticism of Thatcherism. Similar care should be taken with G. Although words like 'orchestrated,' 'imposition' and 'patriotic Toryism' might be interpreted as denoting disapproval of Thatcherism, the extract, like H, is essentially descriptive. However, if you know from your own reading that Hall and Jacques are left-wing writers, you would be entitled to point this out.

Further Reading

Recommended books covering the Thatcher years are: *Britannia's Burden: The Political Evolution of Modern Britain 1851–1990* by Bernard Porter (Edward Arnold, 1994), which regards Thatcherism as having succeeded in almost all its aims, *Hope and Glory: Britain 1900–1990* by Peter Clarke (Penguin, 1996), which is strongly critical of Thatcherism but also acknowledges its high degree of success, and *From Blitz to Blair A New History of Britain Since 1939,* edited by Nick Tiratsoo (Phoenix, 1997), which takes a critical left-wing view of Thatcherism. *British Political History 1867–1995: Democracy and Decline* by Malcolm Pearce and Geoffrey Stewart (Routledge, 1996) provides a very informative set of primary sources from the Thatcher period, as does *Britain Under Thatcher* by Anthony Seldon and Daniel Collings (Longman, 2000). An interesting analysis of Thatcherism from a Conservative angle is *The Conservative Party from Peel to Major* by Robert Blake (Fontana, 1994), while the emergence of New Labour is described in *Tony Blair, The Moderniser* by J. Sopel (Michael Joseph, 1995). A very readable study of the man whom some regard as the Labour Party's conscience is *Tony Benn A Biography* by Jad Adams (Macmillan, 1992). *The Downing Street Years* by Margaret Thatcher (HarperCollins, 1993), the author's reflections on the movement that bore her name, is well worth consulting. This should be contrasted with the critical and entertaining *One of Us: A Biography of Margaret Thatcher* by Hugo Young (Pan, 1993) and *Margaret Thatcher* vol 1 by John Campbell (Cape, 2000), which offers an interesting psychological analysis of its subject.

SOCIAL POLICY IN BRITAIN AFTER 1945

The twentieth century was a time of extraordinary social change in Britain. The outstanding feature of this was the rise in the standard of living of the population. Why this occurred is a matter of considerable controversy but two factors seem indisputable. One was the growth of a consumer economy which had the effect of bringing essential goods within the reach of even the poorest. The other was the acceptance by successive Labour and Conservative governments of the need to provide a national system of welfare, financed with funds raised by taxation. This chapter surveys the stages by which central government became increasingly involved in the creation and development of the welfare state. The chapter begins with the Beveridge Report, the outstanding social policy document on which so much of the welfare state was based. The contentious issue of whether Beveridge's plans were subsequently distorted to produce a dependency culture is then examined. The concluding sections deal with immigration and with the changing status of women in the second half of the twentieth century.

1 The Beveridge Report, 1942

> **ISSUE:**
> In what sense was the Beveridge Report a revolutionary document?

The wartime Coalition under Churchill gave considerable thought to post-war reconstruction. This had been badly handled after 1918 and there was a general determination not to allow it to happen a second time. By the end of 1940, despite the terror of the Blitz, the danger of an invasion of Britain had largely passed. Morale had risen and made planning for peacetime seem not wholly unrealistic. The presence in the government of a number of Labour Party leaders was a guarantee that social issues would be kept to the fore. Planning was not a matter of political dispute at this stage; all the parties accepted the need to extend social welfare in the post-war world.

It was against this background that late in 1940 Arthur Greenwood, who had been a Health minister in the Labour government of 1929–31, was instructed by Churchill to take the preliminary steps towards post-war re-organisation. In June 1941, Greenwood set up an Interdepartmental Committee to study the existing schemes of social insurance and make recommendations for their improvement. Sir William Beveridge was appointed Chairman of this Committee of senior civil servants. His long experience of social security provision extended back to the pre-1914 Liberal era. Taking his remit very seriously, Beveridge immersed himself totally in his work. His role in the drafting of the Report was so central that it was considered appropriate that he alone should sign the document which bore his name and which was presented to the House of Commons in November 1942. The Report is regarded as the most significant social policy document of the century. The following is a key passage:

> The plan is based on a diagnosis of want; it starts from facts. The scheme proposed here is in some ways a revolution, but in more important ways it is a natural development from the past. It is a British revolution. Now, when the war is abolishing landmarks of every kind, is the opportunity for using experience in a clear field. A revolutionary moment in the world's history is a time for revolutions, not for patching.
>
> This is first and foremost a plan of insurance – of giving, in return for contributions, benefits up to a subsistence level, as of right and without means test, so that individuals may build freely upon it. Organisation of social insurance should be treated as one part only of a comprehensive policy of social progress. Social insurance fully developed may provide income security; it is an attack upon Want. But Want is only one of five giants on the road of reconstruction, and in some ways the easiest to attack. The others are Disease, Ignorance, Squalor and Idleness.
>
> The place for direct expenditure and organisation by the State is in maintaining employment of the labour and other productive resources of the country, and in preventing and combating disease, not in patching an incomplete system of insurance. The plan is not for giving to everybody something for nothing, or something that will free the recipients for ever thereafter from personal responsibilities. It leaves room and encouragement to all individuals to win for themselves something above the national minimum, to satisfy higher needs than bare physical needs.
>
> Freedom from want cannot be forced on or given to a democracy. It must be won by them. Winning it needs courage and faith and national unity; courage to face facts and difficulties and overcome them; faith in our future and in the ideals of fair play and freedom for which century after century our forefathers were prepared to die; a sense of national unity overriding the interests of any class or section. The Plan for Social Security is submitted by one who believes that in this supreme crisis the British people will not be found wanting, of courage and faith and national unity, of material and spiritual power.

Source A From the Report of the Interdepartmental Committee on Social Insurance and Allied Services under the Chairmanship of Sir William Beveridge, 1942.

GOVERNMENT SOCIAL INSURANCE PLAN

Guaranteed New Laid

BEVERIDGE

ZERO HOUR FOR THE CURATE

Figure 32 A 1944 *Daily Herald* cartoon, welcoming the Beveridge plan, but suggesting that, like the proverbial curate's egg, it might be good only in parts.

Beveridge aimed at the abolition of material want. He believed that it was possible to establish a national minimum level of welfare without recourse to extreme methods. He proposed a universal scheme of insurance which would provide protection against the distress that invariably accompanied sickness, injury and unemployment. Additionally, there would be grants to ease the financial hardships that came with maternity, parenthood and bereavement. The term 'protection from the cradle to the grave', although not Beveridge's own, was an appropriate description of the envisaged scale of welfare provision. The Plan was to replace the current unsystematic pattern of welfare with a centrally funded and regulated system. Since it would be based on insurance, it would avoid being associated with the hated means test or the Poor Law.

Insurance was to form the base with welfare organisations providing the superstructure. Beveridge's **'five giants'** to be defeated on the road to reconstruction, were a figurative representation of the major ills afflicting society. Beveridge's scheme pointed towards the welfare state, a term which pre-dated the Report by some ten years but which began to be widely used during the war years. Hardly any of Beveridge's proposals were new. What made them significant in 1942 was their integration into a comprehensive scheme. Beveridge had laid the theoretical foundations for all subsequent developments in the field of social-welfare provision.

Q

Why was the Beveridge Report such a significant social document?

THE FIVE GIANTS

'Want' – to be ended by national insurance;
'Disease' – to be ended by a comprehensive health service;
'Ignorance' – to be ended by an effective education system;
'Squalor' – to be ended by slum clearance and re-housing;
'Idleness' – to be ended by guaranteed employment.

Figure 33 'The Five Giants' , a cartoon showing the size of the problems facing Beveridge.

Although Beveridge spoke of the Report as a 'revolution', he emphasised that it was one of the British variety, which was to say that it did not challenge the past but grew from it. He proposed to take the best aspects of the existing welfare systems and integrate them into a universal plan. It was no mere coincidence that as a younger man Beveridge had been directly involved in the introduction of the social service programme of the pre-1914 Liberal governments.

In his proposals Beveridge, true to his Liberal background, insisted on the principle of insurance. He specifically denied that his plan aimed at 'giving everybody something for nothing'. Freedom from want could not be 'forced on or given to a democracy'; it had to be desired by the people. Beveridge stressed that a good society depended not on the State but on the individual. He spoke of the retention of 'personal responsibilities'. Individuals would be encouraged to save as private citizens. These ideas were very much in the Liberal tradition, as was his belief that his proposals would not involve an increase in government expenditure.

Q What were the Report's basic social principles?

ACTIVITY

Having studied the extract from the Report and the accompanying analysis, show that you understand the principles behind it by explaining in your own words why Beveridge reckoned that state welfare could be introduced without undermining the responsibility of the individual.

2 The Growth of a Dependency Culture

Those, such as Aneurin Bevan, who first created the welfare state (see page 131) believed that not only would it solve the nation's major social problems, but that it would also pay for itself. A healthy society would mean far fewer workers being absent. Efficiency and wages would rise. Higher wages would produce higher tax yields. From that increased revenue the State would be able to finance its welfare provision. But in the event the opposite occurred. The demand for medical treatment and benefit payment did not decline; it grew. Moreover, it grew at such a pace that it outstripped resources. A spokesman for the Department of Social Services commented in 1990: 'We're in this giant oil tanker, and all we can do is slow down the speed with which it is accelerating.'

> **ISSUES:**
> **Why did the welfare state not develop the way its originators had hoped?**
> **Did State welfare produce a 'dependency culture'?**

By the 1990s

▽ The cost of welfare provision had risen to a level where it made up 33 per cent of total government expenditure.

▽ The number of persons receiving old age pensions doubled between 1950 and 1995 from five million to ten million.

▽ Fifty per cent of households in Britain had at least one member receiving State benefit.

The health and social security budget:
▽ in 1949 = £597 million (4.7 per cent of GDP)
▽ in 1990 = £91 billion (14 per cent of GDP)
▽ in 1994 = £95 billion (15 per cent of GDP)

---

i) The Population Factor

One critical development that increased the demand for welfare services was simply that people were living longer. There were twice as many old age pensioners in 1999 as there had been 50 years earlier. As people grew older they needed a greater amount of medical treatment, yet, because they were no longer working, they contributed a relatively smaller amount of revenue. They had, of course, contributed during their working life time, but, given inflation and the ever-rising cost of medical technology, their original payments were inadequate to pay for their current needs.

> **Q** Why had the demand for State welfare risen to such proportions?

ii) Unemployment

A second major cause of spiralling welfare costs was the rise in unemployment. By the last decade of the century, unemployment benefit payments amounted to £10 billion.

	1901		1931		1961		2001 (estimate)	
	M	**F**	**M**	**F**	**M**	**F**	**M**	**F**
At birth	45.5	49.0	58.4	62.5	67.9	73.8	74.5	79.9
At age 1	53.6	55.8	62.1	65.1	68.6	74.2	74.0	79.3
At age 10	50.4	52.7	55.6	58.6	60.0	65.6	65.2	70.5
At age 20	41.7	44.1	46.7	49.6	50.4	55.7	55.4	60.6
At age 40	26.1	28.3	29.5	32.4	31.5	36.5	36.2	41.0
At age 60	13.3	14.6	14.4	16.4	15.0	19.0	18.7	22.7
At age 80	4.9	5.3	4.9	5.4	5.2	6.3	7.0	8.8

Table 41 Life expectancy for males and females (in years).

iii) Changes in Benefit Assessment

Of equal importance was the highly significant change in the way benefits were assessed. Down to the early 1960s benefit levels had been determined by the cost of living, that is, the price of essential goods. However, in the 1960s and 1970s Labour and the Conservatives decided that those on benefit were entitled to share in Britain's growing prosperity. These, remember, were the 'never had it so good' years (see page 143). In order to achieve this, the size of benefit payments was brought into line not with prices but with incomes. Since incomes in this period invariably stayed ahead of prices, the result was a rapid rise in the real value of benefits. From the beginning there were critics of this change who argued that the productive tax payer was now having to subsidise the non-productive benefit receiver beyond subsistence level. This was a fundamental divergence from the intention of the original Beveridge plan.

iv) Changes in National Insurance

A further notable change was the decision in 1961 by Harold Macmillan's government to alter the national insurance scheme. This had started in 1948 with flat-rate contributions paid by workers who then drew flat-rate benefits when in need. The new method required that the higher the worker's wages or salary the higher his insurance contributions were to be. Yet benefits were paid according to need rather than in proportion to the amount contributed. Again this aroused sharp controversy. One view was that it was socially just since the richer were helping the poorer by a redistribution of resources. Against that it was argued that the new scheme undermined the basic notion of insurance which had always tied the size of benefits to the amount previously contributed. Whereas Beveridge had thought in terms of contributory benefits, the amended scheme allowed a wide range of non-contributory payments. Entitlement to these would be calculated by means testing. The income of an individual or a family claiming benefit would be added up; if the total income fell below a certain level then the claimants were qualified to receive payment.

Major State-Paid Non-Contributory Benefits

▼ *Income Support* paid to those of working age who are unable to work, or to those who have inadequate pensions. It has been called 'the safety net of the welfare state'. In the late 1990s income support was costing over £13 billion annually.

▼ *Invalidity Benefit* paid to those medically certified as being physically or mentally unable to work. Between 1982 and 1998 the number of recipients trebled from 0.6 to 1.8 million, at a cost of £5.2 billion per year.

▼ *Housing Benefit* rent and rate rebates for those on inadequate incomes.

▼ *Child Benefit* (previously called family allowance), a weekly amount paid to parents (usually the mother) for each child. This was a universal payment, i.e., there was no means testing. By 1998 this was costing £6 billion per year.

▼ *Family Income Supplement* provided a cash benefit for poorer families with children.

Government Expenditure	Amount	%
Social Security	£65.0 billion	26.66
Environment	£38.9 billion	15.9
Health	£29.9 billion	12.2
Local Government	£24.2 billion	9.9
Defence	£23.5 billion	9.64
Scotland	£13.9 billion	5.6
Education	£9.5 billion	3.9
Northern Ireland	£8.4 billion	3.5
Wales	£7.2 billion	3.0
Foreign and Overseas	£6.5 billion	2.7
Transport	£6.4 billion	2.6
Home Office	£6.1 billion	2.5
Employment	£3.7 billion	1.5
Trade and Industry	£2.6 billion	1.06
Agriculture	£2.6 billion	1.06

Table 42 Government expenditure in the year 1993–94, showing the amounts and the percentages spent. Notice the huge cost of social security.

Q What were some of the major anxieties about the direction the welfare state had taken?

DEPENDENCY CULTURE

is the notion that State benefit payments destroy the incentive to work, thus creating a society in which the long-term unemployed come to expect permanent State support. The result is that large segments of the population in areas of persistent unemployment lose their sense of independence and social worth.

THE POVERTY TRAP

refers to the situation in which the low paid find themselves in an impossible position. If they continue working they are penalised by being taxed, which may well reduce their net income to a level little higher than if they were drawing unemployment benefit. In such a position it is extremely difficult for them to gain genuine control over their living standards.

A growing concern for many in the second half of the twentieth century was that the welfare state had gone beyond Beveridge's dream of a society freed from poverty to the creation of a **dependency culture**. The benefits system, rather than acting as a means of helping people through temporary difficulties, had created a **poverty trap** and had encouraged fraudulent claims on a wide scale. The pessimistic view had been powerfully put forward in 1976 by two social analysts, R. Bacon and W. Eltis, who claimed that the welfare state had both weakened Britain economically and done great social harm.

The case against the welfare state may be summarised as follows:
a) In practice, it has channelled resources away from wealth-creating industries;
b) By subsidising strikes (and indirectly trade unions) it undermines the economy;
c) Its maintenance requires high taxation which destroys incentive and causes inflation;
d) The payment of social security benefits acts as a disincentive to the unemployed to seek work, thus decreasing their dependency on the State;
e) In undermining the work ethic, the welfare state creates a hostility to productivity and industrial efficiency, thereby making economic growth harder to achieve.

Source B From *Britain's Economic Problem: Too Few Producers* by R. Bacon and W. Eltis, 1976.

Not surprisingly, Mrs Thatcher's own perception when she entered office in 1979 accorded with this view.

Welfare benefits, distributed with little or no consideration of their effects on behaviour, encouraged illegitimacy, facilitated the breakdown of families, and replaced incentives favouring work and self-reliance with perverse encouragement for idleness and cheating.

Source C From *The Downing Street Years* by Margaret Thatcher, 1993.

It might be thought that such convictions would have made her government eager to reform the welfare state. It is true that certain steps were taken. To tackle what Mrs Thatcher called the 'Why Work?' problem, her reference to the poverty gap, the government introduced a measure taxing short-term income relief. It also imposed a five per cent cut in unemployment, sickness, injury, maternity and invalidity benefits. But the government's public-spending cuts were largely restricted to her first administration in the early

1980s. This was because unemployment remained so high during her 11 years in office that it necessitated not a decrease but a major increase in unemployment payments. The remarkable fact is that Margaret Thatcher's governments spent more on welfare and social security than any previous administration. Between 1977 and 1994 government expenditure on the NHS rose by 60 per cent in real terms.

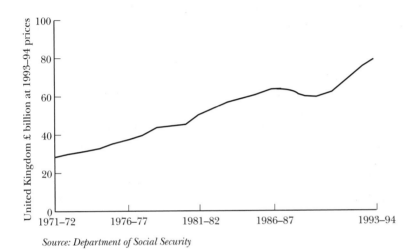

Source: *Department of Social Security*

Figure 34 Graph showing the real growth in social security benefit expenditure.

As might be expected, there are many analysts who did not accept that the welfare state has been socially and economically harmful. The following sources illustrate the spirited defence of the welfare state that the attack by Bacon and Eltis aroused.

a) The welfare state, far from being disruptive, is a force for social reconciliation in that it fulfils a vital role in maintaining the existing politico-economic system.
b) The ameliorative effects of the social services lessen individual and group discontents.
c) Since statistically only a small proportion of workers receive social security benefit while on strike (less than five per cent between 1955 and 1980, and less than ten per cent during the miners' strikes of the 70s and 80s), it is difficult to accept the notion of the welfare state as a direct incentive to industrial disruption.
d) Studies of work practices suggest that taxation levels are not a major consideration determining willingness or otherwise towards taking up employment.

Source D From a Report by the Organisation for Economic Co-operation and Development, 1988.

(i) the proportion of the unemployed who actually get more money in benefit than in work is very small. They are mainly men in the early months of unemployment for which higher benefits have been deliberately designed and when the disincentive effects seem small anyway; or men on supplementary benefit with low earnings potential and large families;

(ii) this latter group are among the poorest on supplementary benefit and many of them are in poor health and have other personal problems;

(iii) financial benefits cannot be considered in isolation, and in many cases may not be the major determinant of whether someone works. Of far more importance in present circumstances is whether jobs are available.

Source E From The Report of the Supplementary Benefits Commission, 1978.

It is quite possible that by taking care of the old, the very young, the sick and others, public services replace the old-fashioned enlarged family and make the adults more available for employment, particularly the women who were traditionally responsible for household work and bringing up children. It is likely that by providing minimum standards of living, social services reduce public apathy and dejection and thus maintain the will to work.

Source F From *The Impact of Social Policy* by V. George and P. Wilding, 1984.

Yet in the 1990s it was clear that debate over the welfare state was far from settled. In 1995, a cross-party group of MPs, led by Frank Field, Labour spokesman on welfare, produced a report which concluded:

Designed originally as a short-term resting place for those of working age, income support now helps create the very long-term welfare dependency which the government says it is out to destroy. Those who work lose benefit, savings are confiscated and honesty is taxed. Hence many people remain on benefit rather than take work opportunities. It has also encouraged fraud and in some cases large-scale criminal activity.

Source G From the Report of the Dahrendorf Commission, July 1995.

ACTIVITIES

1 Having read section 2, say whether you think Beveridge would have been pleased or displeased with the way the welfare state had developed by the end of the century. List the reasons for your conclusion.

2 Does your reading of Sources C to G lead you to accept or reject the notion that the welfare state in Britain had deteriorated by the end of the twentieth century into a dependency culture?

3 Living Standards

Despite periods of serious hardship for some of the population in Britain the broad picture was one of a continuous rise in living standards. This is strikingly illustrated in Table 41 showing the increase in life expectancy during the century. The various financial problems that confronted the nation did not prevent the great majority of the population from gaining in material prosperity. This is an area where figures speak loudest. Wages rose ahead of prices and credit became widely available, enabling consumers to buy an unprecedented range of manufactured goods. In the period 1945–60 the sales of private cars nearly quadrupled from one and a half million in 1945 to 5.5 million by 1960. Perhaps the most impressive feature of the consumer boom was the growth in house buying (see Tables 43 and 44). Encouraged by the government, banks and building societies advanced the necessary capital in the form of mortgages that allowed increasing numbers to own their own homes thus forming what became known as the '**property-owning democracy**'. It was such developments that Harold Macmillan had in mind when he declared in 1957: 'Let's be frank about it: most of our people have never had it so good' (see page 143).

ISSUE:
Was poverty eradicated in Britain during the second half of the twentieth century?

PROPERTY-OWNING DEMOCRACY
a term first used by the Conservatives in the 1950s to describe their aim of providing the economic conditions that would encourage as many people as possible to become homeowners. It relates to the notion that the ownership of property is an example of practical democracy that gives citizens a genuine stake in society.

	Local Authority	Private	Total
1919–24	176,914	221,543	398,457
1945–49	432,098	126,317	558,415
1965–69	761,224	994,361	1,755,585
1986–90	155,500	903,600	1,059,100

Table 43 Houses built in England and Wales.

	Owner Occupiers	Council Tenants	Private Tenants	Others
1914	10.0	1.0	80.0	9.0
1939	31.1	14.0	46.0	9.0
1966	46.7	25.7	22.5	5.1
1977	54.0	32.0	9.0	5.0
1985	61.9	27.3	8.3	2.5
1990	67.0	24.0	7.0	2.0

Table 44 Housing tenure, England and Wales (%).

Table 45 Households in Britain with consumer durables (%).

	1972	1981	1991	1993
colour television	48	74	95	96
black & white television only	45	23	4	3
telephone	42	75	88	90
washing machine	66	78	87	88
video recorder	–	–	68	73
microwave	–	–	55	62
tumble drier	–	23	48	49
CD player	–	–	27	39
dishwasher	–	4	14	16

By the end of the century all the evidence was that material poverty had been largely eradicated. The standard of living had risen for the whole population. Income stayed ahead of prices. Even for the poorest, the range and quality of their resources improved so much so that the notion of poverty itself had to be reassessed. How poverty is to be defined continues to be a matter of lively debate among economists and social historians. One simple measurement is to take average national income and then say that anyone below half that average is poor. But by that definition there will always be poverty and the term will not necessarily describe serious material deprivation. If the general standard of living improves the poor will be become less poor in real terms even though their income declines in relation to the top earners in society. This indeed was one of the most remarkable social features of the second half of the twentieth century in the Western world. In that period, Western countries experienced an unprecedented rise in the standard of living of their populations.

Of course, the rise was not evenly spread. Some people did better than others and there were always pockets of the population which did relatively badly. Yet even allowing for these, the overall standards rose. By 2000, Britain was enjoying a level of health that would have been inconceivable a century earlier. Life expectancy, educational opportunity and access to leisure were in advance of anything thought possible in 1900. That is why many analysts felt it necessary to reformulate their definitions. The threshold at which poverty was judged had to be continually lowered. Terms such as 'relative poverty' and 'social poverty' were introduced in order to suggest that it was no longer helpful to think of poverty simply as a matter of material deprivation. University students, for example, are technically classed as poor even though the majority of them within a few years of graduation join the ranks of those earning well above the national average.

Q

In what ways did concepts of poverty change?

ACTIVITIES

▼ Having read section 3, list the main reasons why Britain experienced a sustained rise in its standard of living.

▼ Explain what you understand by the term 'relative poverty'.

4 Immigration

One of the most notable features of Britain in the second half of the twentieth century was its development as a multi-racial society. The story may be said to have begun in 1948 with the sailing of a converted troopship, *Empire Windrush*, from Kingston to Britain. The ship carried hundreds of Jamaican workers; the majority were young males but there were also a number of older men and families. They were coming to find work. The official welcome they received was a warm one. Cinema newsreels enthusiastically recorded the event and assured the newcomers that they would soon find homes and jobs. Under existing law, the newcomers had full rights of British citizenship. This encouraged further emigration from the West Indies. The government encouraged this with organised appeals for Caribbean workers to fill the vacancies, principally in the hospital and transport services, that Britain's acute post-war labour shortage had left. By the mid-1950s employers in Britain had extended their recruitment to the Indian sub-continent. Textile firms in London and the north of England eagerly took on workers from India and Pakistan.

Decade	Outflow	Inflow
1900–09	4,404,000	2,287,000
1910–19	3,526,000	2,224,000
1920–29	3,960,000	2,590,000
1930–39	2,273,000	2,361,000
1940–49	590,000	240,000
1950–59	1,327,000	676,000
1960–69	1,916,000	1,243,000
1970–79	2,554,000	1,900,000
1980–89	1,824,000	1,848,000

Table 46 Migration to and from the UK (to nearest 100,000).

However, by the late 1950s, disturbing reactions had begun to occur among some of the white host population. 'No coloured' notices appeared in boarding house windows and on factory gates. Mutterings were heard to the effect that the newcomers were attracted to Britain as much by the generous welfare benefits as by the prospect of work. The actual number of white residents who believed such slanders may have been small, but troublemakers were able to exploit the housing shortage, which was a major problem in the poorer areas, by suggesting that it was all the fault of the immigrants.

Race relations problems have never been simply about numbers. Extremists who spoke of Britain being 'swamped' by 'waves of immi-

Table 47 Commonwealth immigrants living in the UK.

	Old Commonwealth	New Commonwealth	Total
1961	307,697	289,058	596,755
1971	528,810	765,095	1,293,905
1981	350,382	915,768	1,266,150
1991	905,960	1,729,451	2,635,411

New Commonwealth – largely West Indians, Indians, Pakistanis and Bangladeshis

Old Commonwealth – largely Australians, New Zealanders, Canadians, and South Africans.

grants' were talking nonsense. The proportion of people of non-European origins has never been more than six per cent of the overall population of Britain. Moreover, as Table 46 shows, in every decade of the century net emigration exceeded net immigration. The main difficulties arose over accommodation. Immigrants tended, quite naturally given their limited resources when they first arrived in Britain, to live in the poorer areas of cities and urban areas. This was where cheaper properties for buying or renting were. But since Britain suffered from a severe shortage of reasonably priced housing there was bound to be competition between residents and newcomers.

Figure 35 Map showing numbers and concentration of ethnic minorities in London in 1991.

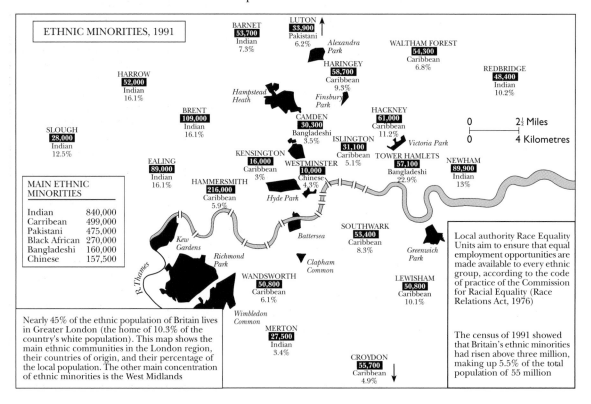

The tension that this caused was evident in the rioting that broke out in 1958 in Nottingham and Notting Hill in London. Long prison sentences were imposed on the white ringleaders of the disturbances but the authorities interpreted the disorder as indicating the need to control the number of new Commonwealth entrants. A **Commonwealth Immigrants Act** was introduced in 1962. This was highly controversial and condemned in many quarters as being racist since it placed restrictions on would-be entrants according to their ethnic origin. The Labour Party stoutly opposed the measure, but in office itself it introduced a second Commonwealth Immigrants Act in 1968. Both major parties had concluded that limitations on entry into Britain was necessary in the interests of good race relations; hence the Labour governments introduced **Race Relations Acts** in 1965 and 1968.

One consequence of the first Immigration Act was a rush of entrants into Britain in the period before its terms came into force. Between 1960 and 1962, over 230,000 New Commonwealth citizens entered. This in fact marked an immigration peak but it was such numbers that fuelled the anxieties of those who called for a complete block on entry. Voice was given to these concerns by Enoch Powell, but, significantly, he remained the only politician of note who took an openly anti-immigration stance.

The immigration and race relations measures were undeniably well intentioned but they had limited success in improving racial harmony. Again the economic situation contributed largely to this. It was one thing to introduce laws against discrimination, it was another to enforce them. The inflation that followed the oil price crisis of the early 1970s appeared to have the worst effects in immigrant areas where there were disproportionately higher numbers of unemployed than in the population at large. The frustration of the immigrant

---

Enoch Powell (1912–98)

was an able but maverick Conservative politician, who was Minister of Health from 1960 to 1963. Ironically, during that time he had actively encouraged the recruitment of Commonwealth immigrants as nurses and hospital workers. An intense nationalist, he came to regard unlimited immigration as a threat to the character of the UK. In a notorious speech in 1968, he gave his nightmare vision of a future Britain torn by racial conflict. Quoting Virgil's *Aeneid*, he prophesied: 'As I look ahead, I am filled with foreboding. Like the Roman, I seem to see "the River Tiber foaming with much blood".' The speech was condemned from all political sides and Edward Heath felt obliged to dismiss him from the shadow Cabinet.

The Commonwealth Immigrants Acts, 1962 and 1968
- ▽ attempted to limit immigration by creating a voucher scheme which restricted the right of entry to those who actually had jobs to go to.

British Nationality Act, 1981
- ▽ restricted citizenship to those born in the UK or whose parents or grandparents had been.

Race Relations Act, 1965
- ▽ prohibited racial discrimination in public places;
- ▽ made incitement to racial hatred an offence;
- ▽ set up a Race Relations Board with the power to investigate complaints of racial discrimination.

Race Relations Act, 1968
- ▽ outlawed racial discrimination in areas such as employment and housing;
- ▽ widened the scope and powers of the Race Relations Board and set up the Community Relations Commission to promote inter-racial understanding.

Race Relations Act, 1976
- ▽ outlawed racial discrimination in employment, education and training, and in the provision of goods and services;
- ▽ made it an offence to provoke racial hatred;
- ▽ combined the Race Relations Board and the Community Relations Commission in a new Commission for Racial Equality.

How effective were the Race Relations Acts?

community, particularly of second- and third-generation West Indians, who had been born and brought up in Britain, was expressed in serious riots in 1981 in Brixton, Birmingham, Bristol and Liverpool and tragically in 1985 when a policeman was killed during the Tottenham Broadwater Farm riot.

The feeling among the black community that they were subject to unwarranted harassment by the police was a continuous grievance. The killing in South London of Stephen Lawrence, a black teenager, by a gang of white youths, who went unconvicted, led eventually to a commission of enquiry which in 1999 accused the Metropolitan Police of being 'institutionally racist'. This did not seem to augur well for the future of race relations in the new millennium. Yet it would be wrong to understate what had been achieved. In 2000 Trevor Philips, a black writer born in Britain of Guyanan parents, wrote enthusiastically of what had happened in his own city of London.

ACTIVITY

Having read section 4, list the main consequences for Britain of large-scale immigration from the New Commonwealth. Say how effectively you think Britain adapted to these developments.

Things have changed from the days when Caribbean immigrants were warned by their landladies to leave home early and return late so the neighbours could not see them. Surveys show that the number of 'white' Londoners who object to having Black or Asian neighbours has fallen steadily for decades; intermarriage is on a scale that would make Americans' eyes pop. London is not a melting pot. The loss of identity is not an option for young Londoners ... But that does not mean a retreat to the ghetto. Young Londoners have found ways of sharing their heritage with their friends that my generation never managed. One colleague told me a few years ago that he had to change his frame of reference when walking behind a group of teenagers; so mixed were their styles, ways of walking and talking, he had to get in front of them to discover who was white and who black.

London is on the verge of doing what every great world city has tried in vain – to welcome all comers and embrace them with ease and comfort.

Source H From 'Londoners' by Trevor Philips in the *Observer*, 23 April 2000.

ISSUES:
Why did an influential feminist movement develop in the UK from the 1960s onwards?
What successes did it achieve?

5 The Status of Women

Another key development in British social life was the changing status of women. Measuring social change is not always easy, but in this case a convenient guide is provided by the reform measures introduced by government and parliament. Female advance in the twentieth century has been described as 'playing catch up', that is women gaining constitutional and legal rights as citizens on the same terms as men. Already by the middle of the century specific reforms had made a major breakthrough. Among these were:

▼ Sex Disqualification (Removal) Act, 1919 – opened all the professions (except holy orders) and the universities (though not all individual colleges) to female entry.

▼ Matrimonial Causes Act, 1923 – gave the wife the right to divorce the husband on the grounds of his adultery.

▼ New English Law of Property, 1926 – entitled married and single women to hold and dispose of their property on the same terms as a man.

▼ Representation of the People Act, 1928 – gave women over 21 the right to vote in parliamentary and local elections.

▼ British Nationality of Women Act, 1948 – gave British women the right to retain British nationality on marriage to a foreigner.

Subsequent legislation covered a wide range of matters and could be said to have laid the formal and legal basis of women's equality. Among key measures introduced during the second half of the century were:

▼ Equal Pay Act, 1970 – women were to receive the same rates of pay as men for doing work of equal value.

▼ Finance Act, 1971 – allowed husband's and wife's earnings to be taxed separately if they so applied.

▼ Employment Protection Act, 1975 – denied employers the right to dismiss pregnant employees and required them to offer paid maternity leave.

▼ Sex Discrimination Act, 1975 – outlawed discrimination on grounds of sex in regard to employment, education and training, housing, provision of services, banking, insurance and credit. It also set up the Equal Opportunities Commission to monitor the working of the Act.

▼ Social Security Act, 1975 – provided a special maternity allowance fund.

▼ Social Security Pensions Act, 1975 – required pension schemes to be open equally to women engaged in the same work as men.

▼ Equal Pay (Amendment) Act, 1984 – brought British law in line with European law on equal pay.

▼ Sex Discrimination Act, 1986 – brought the 1975 Sex Discrimination Act into line with European directives, and also removed some restrictions on hours of work for women.

▼ Finance Act, 1988 – introduced separate taxation for husbands and wives.

▼ Employment Act, 1989 – removed further restrictions on women's conditions of employment.

▼ Trade Union Reform and Employment Rights Act, 1993 – introduced much stronger employment protection for pregnant women in line with European directives.

▼ Child Support Agency, 1993 – was established to enforce separated husbands to continue paying maintenance to their wives for their joint children.

Table 48 Women as a percentage of those in higher education in the UK.

	%
1929	28
1959	25
1989	40
1999	48

Table 49 A 1984 poll, showing the distribution of domestic duties in the UK.

9 out of 10 women did the washing and ironing
7 out of 10 women did the household cleaning
5 out of 10 women did the shopping
1 out of 16 women did the household repairs

Table 50 Children born to
unmarried mothers in the UK.

3% of all births in 1914
10% of all births in 1970
25% of all births in 1988
34% of all births in 1996

Table 51 Divorce rates in the
UK.

pre-1939	1 for every 100 marriages
1960	1 for every 10 marriages
1980	1 for every 3 marriages

Source 1 From An Economic &
Social History of Western Europe
since 1945 by Anthony Sutcliffe,
1997.

Table 52 Women as a percentage of the workforce in the UK.

	%
1911	33
1951	31
1970	35
1990	43

THE 'PILL'

The female contraceptive pill
became widely available in
the 1960s; for the first time
in history women had gen-
uine control over their own
fertility.

▼ Minister for Women, 1997 – appointed with responsibility for monitor-
ing women's affairs in general.

These later reforms did not come out of the blue. They were in
large part a response to the feminist movement in Britain. It is hard
to give a precise date to the start of this movement but what was certainly significant was the growth in the formal education of women at
secondary and higher level.

A particularly striking aspect of feminism is that it illustrates the
trend that developed in the 1960s for particular interest groups to
pursue their aims individually rather than as part of a broad reforming movement for the change of society. This suggested that people
were losing faith in the traditional parties as forces of social change.
Anthony Sutcliffe, a social historian, puts it in these terms:

> In Britain, feminism partially replaced the New Left position of the
> 1960s, which had united a large part of the young socialist intelli-
> gentsia but which had sought general change ... What this meant
> was that until the 1970s, advocates of social change and people's
> rights pursued their aims via the reform of society as a whole. From
> the 1970s, increasingly a fragmentation occurred. The old structures
> of social class, convention and national character were in decline,
> while associations linked to age, status and leisure interests were
> growing up.

Although there is a natural emphasis on the success of feminism
in bringing about legal change, equally important was the feminists'
insistence that there were many social injustices afflicting women
which were beyond the scope of legislation since they belonged to
the world of ingrained prejudice among women as well as men. What
was needed was a fundamental change of attitude in society at large.
This is why feminism in turn has to be understood as part of a broad
movement of thought that became particularly influential in the
1960s. This was made up of many strands but essentially what motivated it was the wish to remove traditional social and moral restraints.

Where this tied in with feminism was in its approach to sexual
questions. The 1960s saw changes that merited the term 'sexual revolution'. Four critical developments can be identified: the use of 'the
pill', the Lady Chatterley Case, the Abortion Act, and the Sexual
Offences Act. Not all these related to women's rights but they helped
to create an atmosphere in which the old taboos were broken down.
Much of the 'swinging sixties' and the 'youth rebellion' was media
hype, but there was enough reality behind the image-making to suggest that a significant change had occurred in British social attitudes.
Women were among the main beneficiaries.

The Lady Chatterley Case, 1960

In 1960 Penguin Books were prosecuted for publishing an obscene book, D.H. Lawrence's 1928 novel, *Lady Chatterley's Lover*, which contained four-letter words and explicit descriptions of sexual high-jinks. The trial became a test case. The not-guilty verdict can be interpreted as the beginning of the permissive age for the arts.

The Abortion Act, 1967

permitted the legal termination of pregnancy where two doctors certified there was a serious risk to the physical or mental health of the mother, or a strong possibility that the child would be born with serious abnormalities. It was a highly controversial measure. Some moralists saw it as the State's sanctioning of the murder of the innocent, but most feminists hailed it as a major step in the liberation of women since it gave them 'the right to choose'.

The Sexual Offences Act, 1967

was based on the recommendations of the Wolfenden Report of 1958. It permitted male homosexual acts in private between 'consenting adults'. Female homosexuality was not mentioned in the Act, since this had never been illegal.

Table 53 Legal abortions in England and Wales.

1968	22,332
1975	106,648
1980	128,600
1985	141,000
1990	173,900

(By 1999 over four million abortions had taken place since the 1967 Act)

ACTIVITY

How far do Tables 49 to 53 support the notion that women's liberation had genuinely occurred in the second half of the twentieth century?

▼ Working on Social Policy in Britain after 1945

In regard to government social policy, the Beveridge Report and Labour's post-war creation of the welfare state should be taken in chronological sequence. This will help you see the development of welfare policy over time. Here is where the various issues boxes come into their own. Select what you think are the most important dates and then put beside them the accompanying issues with your own accompanying questions and answers. The same approach should be taken in regard to immigration. The controversial questions of the dependency culture, living standards, and the social revolution in the 1960s standards are best studied as separate topics. The time-line on page 219 could be used as a base for studying the changing status of women.

Answering Structured Writing and Essay Questions on Social Policy in Britain after 1945

Types of question	Examples of typical questions
Structured	1 Describe how the Beveridge Report proposed to improve the workings of social welfare. 2 In what ways did the introduction of the NHS in 1948 change the provision of health care in Britain? 3 In what ways did the legal status of women advance in the second half of the twentieth century?
Causes	4 Why was there a significant increase in the number of Commonwealth immigrants coming into Britain in the 1950s and 1960s? 5 Explain why the standard of living rose in Britain in the second half of the twentieth century. 6 Account for the heavy financial cost of maintaining the welfare state at the end of the twentieth century.
Historical judgement	7 'Since 1945 the Conservative and Labour governments have been equally determined to make a success of the welfare state.' How far do you agree with this view? 8 Examine the validity of the claim that the welfare state in Britain failed to achieve its original objectives. 9 How far do you agree that it was the sexual revolution of the 1960s which enabled British women to achieve full emancipation?

Let us consider question 8, the type that asks you to make a historical judgement. Remember as always to marshal your material before thinking about how you are going to answer the question. Here the key material might be listed under three headings:

▼ the Beveridge report
▼ main features of the welfare state as created by 1951
▼ subsequent developments and adjustment.

Possible line of argument:
Degrees of success are best judged by comparing them with original aims. In this case clearly Beveridge's landmark Report spelled out the aims. So a good part of your answer should describe what Beveridge's intentions were. Build your description around his proposal that his welfare programme should be integrated, universal, compulsory, contributory and should encourage and reward responsibility. His 'five giants' – Want, Disease, Ignorance, Squalor and Idleness will also serve as a very useful guide. After all, the destruction of those was his driving purpose. With that established, you are then in a posi-

tion to test all the subsequent measures against this set of standards and aims. Take the measures of 1945 to 1951 and the various modifications of these in the 1960s and 1970s and apply Beveridge's yardsticks to them. Did they defeat the giants and did they keep to the principles of the integrated, universal, compulsory and contributory plan? National Insurance obviously demands considerable attention on your part since it was the linchpin of Beveridge's proposed system.

The arguments and disagreements over the 'dependency culture' should figure in your response, as these highlight the question of personal responsibility by which Beveridge put such store. If you accept that a dependency culture did develop in the last part of the century, then you have grounds for agreeing that the welfare state failed to achieve its original aims. But you could also argue that success can also be partial. Moreover, is there not a case for saying that the giants were all defeated and that the dependency culture was a price worth paying if it meant the end of poverty and deprivation.

Answering Source-Based Questions on Social Policy in Britain after 1945

Re-read Source A in this chapter and section 1c in Chapter 6 (pp.132–36), and then attempt the following questions:
1. In what ways does Source A reveal William Beveridge's social reform principles? **(5 marks)**
2. How do you account for the readiness with which the Labour Party adopted the Beveridge Report? **(10 marks)**
3. By what means did the Labour government put the Beveridge Report into effect? **(15 marks)**

Further Reading

Key texts on the theme of social change are *Britain in the Century of Total War: War, Peace and Social Change* (Penguin, 1968), *British Society since 1945* (Penguin, 1982), *Culture in Britain since 1945* (Penguin, 1991) and *A History of the Modern British Isles 1914–99* (Blackwell, 2000), all by Arthur Marwick. Highly recommended books that have been specially written for students are *Twentieth-Century Britain* by Paul Johnson and *An Economic & Social History of Western Europe since 1945* by Anthony Sutcliffe (Longman, 1997). Useful facts and figures on social developments in Britain are to be found in *Atlas of British Social and Economic History since c.1700* by Rex Pope (Routledge, 1989). Two provocative studies that students would enjoy are *The Rise of Consumer Society in Britain, 1880–1980* by John Benson (Longman, 1994) and *Britain's Decline: Problems and Perspectives* by Alan Sked (Blackwell, 1987).

10

BRITAIN'S ROLE IN THE POST-WAR WORLD

POINTS TO CONSIDER

The question that confronted Britain after 1945 was what role it should play in the post-war international order. Britain's attempt to answer that question determined the character of its foreign policy for the next half century. Four major themes dominated the story and provide the substance of this chapter: 1 Britain and the Cold War, 2 Britain's retreat from empire, 3 Britain's relations with Europe, and 4 Britain's relations with Ireland. Although it is possible to study each of these separately, the themes impinge on each other so directly that, if your aim is to gain a clear understanding of British foreign policy in this period, you would be well advised to study the whole picture.

THE UNITED NATIONS ORGANISATION (UNO)

was formed in 1945 to replace the League of Nations. Its two main bodies were the General Assembly, to which all member states belonged, and the Security Council, which had the direct responsibility for maintaining peace and resolving international crises. From the beginning the UN was dominated by the USA. This was because its operations depended on American money and because the majority of member states were pro-American. The UN had high ideals but its effectiveness was greatly weakened by the Cold War tensions between East and West.

In the aftermath of war Britain made two momentous decisions. It became one of '**the big five**' members of the Security Council of the **United Nations** and it chose to become a nuclear power. These decisions indicated that Britain, led by a Labour government, had opted to remain a world power. This was in keeping with historical tradition; Britain had regarded itself as a major player on the world stage since the early-nineteenth century. It had had the economic strength to back up its claims and had been at the head of a worldwide empire. However, by the late 1940s this was no longer the case. Its defence commitments were a huge drain on its material and financial resources and the cost of its nuclear development programme was crippling. By taking on such heavy burdens Britain, at a time when it was beginning to abandon its imperial possessions, subjected itself to severe and chronic economic strain. Its record overseas during the next half century showed how great that strain proved to be.

The Big Five

was the term to describe the major victor nations – the USA, the USSR, Britain, France and China – which became permanent members of the Security Council of UNO. Outnumbered by four to one, the USSR sought to defend its interests by using its veto in Council to block what it regarded as anti-Soviet proposals put forward by the USA and its allies. It was certainly true that Britain invariably supported the USA at the UN.

1 Britain and the Cold War

ISSUES:
Why did Britain side with the USA against the Soviet Union throughout the Cold War?
Was Britain still a world power after 1945?

A useful way into gaining an understanding of Britain's role in the Cold War issues is to study the following extracts:

> We hope that the Government will so review and recast its conduct of International Affairs as to afford the utmost encouragement to, and collaboration with, all Nations striving to secure full Socialist planning and control of the world's resources and thus provide a democratic and constructive Socialist attitude to an otherwise inevitable conflict between American Capitalism and Soviet Communism. We get the impression that not only is there a complete and exclusive Anglo-American tie-up, but a tie-up between the two front benches.

Source A From a speech by Richard Crossman in the House of Commons, 18 November 1946.

> Not very much will be found to distinguish the policy of pre-Revolution Russia and that of post-Revolution Russia. I am not saying whether they are right or wrong, but I am saying that these things are dictated by the geographical position in which a nation finds itself.

Source B From a speech by Clement Attlee in the House of Commons, 18 November 1946.

The immediate occasion of the statements by Crossman and Attlee was an Amendment to the King's Speech put forward by a group of some 60 backbench Labour MPs representing the left of the Party. Moved by Richard Crossman, one of the Party's young intellectuals, the Amendment criticised Attlee and his Cabinet for their pro-American foreign policy and called upon them to foster relations with the socialist countries of the world. Suggesting that a clash was inevitable between the Soviet Union and the USA unless the truly socialist nations came together, the Amendment appealed to the government to take the initiative in creating this third force in world affairs.

Crossman developed his complaint to suggest that the 'Anglo-American tie-up' represented not merely government policy but was a feature of the whole political establishment in Britain. Attlee's reply to the charge was to point out that the government was not anti-Soviet and pro-American through prejudice. The reality was that Stalin's Russia was now as threatening to British interests as Tsarist Russia had earlier been; Attlee contended that the present situation was a continuation of Russia's traditional hostility to Britain. Interestingly, a similar argument had been made earlier by Churchill, the leader of the Opposition, in his **iron curtain** speech.

THE IRON CURTAIN

In a speech in March 1946 at Fulton in the USA, Churchill spoke of the Soviet occupation of large areas of eastern Europe as having created an 'iron curtain' running from the Baltic to the Adriatic. To the west of that line lay the democracies; to the east lay the Soviet-dominated countries – Poland, East Germany, Czechoslovakia, Hungary, Romania, Yugoslavia, Albania and Bulgaria. He warned that while the USSR did not want war they did desire 'the fruits of war and the indefinite expansion of their power and doctrines'. It was, therefore, the duty of the Western world, led by the United States, to unite to prevent further Soviet expansion. Although Attlee pointedly declined to comment on Churchill's Fulton speech, there is little doubt that it coincided in its key points with the pro-American, anti-Soviet attitude that the Labour government had adopted.

THE LABOUR LEFT

A significant number of Labour MPs, some of whom were committed Marxists, were sympathetic towards Stalin's Soviet Union, and distrustful of the USA, the home of capitalism. At this stage, the full horrors of Stalin's regime had yet to be revealed, so it was still possible to believe that it was truly the workers' state it claimed to be.

Q Why was the Labour Party divided over its attitude towards the USA?

NATO (NORTH ATLANTIC TREATY ORGANISATION)

was a defensive alliance formed in 1949 by Britain, France and the Benelux counties as a safeguard against Soviet expansion into Western Europe. The USA, which had declared its attitude two years earlier in the Truman Doctrine, eagerly accepted the invitation to join. Its great industrial strength and nuclear power made it the dominant force in the alliance. Throughout the Cold War NATO remained the West's first line of defence. After the removal of the Soviet threat with the collapse of Communism in the early 1990s it continued to exist but became very uncertain of its role.

Behind the disagreement between Attlee and **the Labour Left** lay a fundamental and lasting difference of opinion as to the real character and purpose of the Labour Party. It was as British statesmen rather than international socialists that Attlee and Ernest Bevin, his Foreign Secretary, approached the problem of Britain's policies in the post-war world. Their intention was to protect British interests in the face of Soviet expansionism. Bevin often said that his natural desire was not to be anti-Soviet, but the stubborn and unco-operative attitude of the Kremlin obliged him to be so in reality.

The left took this bitterly. They had hoped that with a Labour government in power, Anglo-Soviet relations would naturally improve; 'left would understand left'. The rapid development of the Cold War shattered this hope. On all major points, Britain found herself siding with the United States against the Soviet Union. The left argued that in accepting the Truman Doctrine and leaning so heavily on the USA for financial aid, the British government was destroying the chance of genuine British independence in international affairs. The Marshall Plan (see page 137) and **NATO** were the results of this fawning pro-Americanism. Bevin's angry reaction was to accuse the left of a lack of political realism. In the world as it was, and not how the left would like it to be, the Soviet Union was a threat and without American dollars and military assistance, Britain and Europe could not be sustained. Weight was given to Bevin's argument in 1949 when the USSR successfully tested its first atomic bomb. East now matched West in its power of destruction.

The Truman Doctrine, 1947

In 1947, an exhausted Britain announced that it intended to withdraw its forces from Greece and Turkey. Fearful that this would leave those countries prey to Soviet takeover, as had occurred throughout the Balkans, President Truman pledged the USA 'to support free peoples who are resisting attempted subjugation by armed minorities or by outside pressure'. Although he did not mention the Soviet Union by name he clearly had it in mind as the aggressor. The Truman Doctrine gave definition to the Cold War. It committed the USA and by implication its allies to active resistance to Communist expansion. This was soon put into practice in the Berlin Airlift (1948–49) and the Korean War (1950–53).

a) The Berlin Airlift, 1948–49

At the end of the war the four allied powers divided defeated Germany into four separately occupied zones. The eastern zone, under Soviet control, included Berlin which itself was divided into four sectors. The descent of the Iron Curtain left West Berlin in a very vulnerable position. A hundred miles within East Germany it was accessible from the West only by the most limited routes. When the Western powers in June 1948 introduced the new German currency, already operative in West Germany, into West Berlin, the Soviet Union retaliated by imposing a blockade. This amounted to cutting off all electricity and fuel supplies to West Berlin and closing all road links to West Germany. The Soviets' aim was to oblige the Western allies to abandon their plans for a separate German state.

The USA and Britain decided to break the siege by a massive airlift of essential supplies, using the narrow air corridors; if the Soviet Union dared to interfere with the planes, it would be an act of war. In a period of 318 days the Western allies maintained the two and a half million population of West Berlin with one and a quarter million tons of food and fuel by an average of over 600 flights per day. The prodigious effort was successful. In May 1949, the Soviet Union ordered the siege to be abandoned.

	Number of Flights	Supplies in Tons
USAF	131,918	1,101,405
RAF	49,733	255,526
British Charter	13,897	79,470

Table 54 The Berlin Airlift, 1948–49.

b) The Korean War, 1950–53

This was the first open military conflict of the Cold War. In 1945 Korea, after being liberated from Japanese occupation, was divided between a Communist-dominated north and an American-dominated south. In 1950 northern troops, strongly supported by Chinese Communist forces, invaded the south. (Mao Zedong had led his Communist People's Liberation Army to power in China in 1949.) South Korea appealed to the UN Security Council for assistance. The USA immediately proposed that a UN force be sent to aid the South Koreans. By a twist of fate the Soviet Union had temporarily withdrawn from the Security Council in protest against its refusal to recognise Mao Zedong's Red China. This enabled the American resolution to be pushed through without the USSR being present to exercise its usual veto. Large numbers of American troops under the UN flag were dispatched to Korea where bitter fighting causing heavy casualties, particularly on the Chinese side, ensued before a stalemate truce ended the war in 1953. From the first Britain gave the USA substantial diplomatic and military support. British casualties were 686 servicemen killed, 2,498 wounded and 1,102 reported missing.

c) The significance of the Attlee Governments' Foreign Policy

Interesting though such ideas as Richard Crossman's were, in the event they had little impact on the shaping of Labour policy. The importance of Bevin as Foreign Secretary at this critical period was that he established the tradition of post-war British foreign policy, pro-American and anti-Soviet, that prevailed throughout the Cold War from the 1940s to the 1990s, regardless of which party held office. Bevin's policies were a triumph for the centre and right of the Labour Party. As with economics, so with foreign policy, Attlee and Bevin were traditionalists at heart. Given this, a dispute with the left of the party was bound to be a feature of internal Labour politics. What is to be stressed is that although internal wrangles often embarrassed Labour, the left had no success in determining party policy on major issues. In office, the Labour Party always governed from the moderate centre. An interesting example of this was its attitude towards the development and retention of Britain's independent nuclear deterrent.

> If you carry this resolution [to ban the bomb] you'll send the British Foreign Secretary whoever he was naked into the Conference Chamber.

Source C From a speech by Aneurin Bevan at the Labour Party Conference, 3 October 1957.

What did the Berlin airlift and the Korean War reveal about Britain's foreign policy?

Britain's Independent Nuclear Deterrent

Attlee's Labour government decided that Britain should maintain its status as a world power by constructing its own independent nuclear weapon. In January 1947 Attlee told a secret Cabinet sub-committee that Britain could not allow the United States to have a nuclear monopoly. The research programme was begun in 1947, although this information was not revealed to parliament or people. Britain's first atomic bomb was detonated in 1952 and its hydrogen bomb in 1957. The issue of whether the possession of an independent nuclear deterrent was morally defensible or strategically necessary caused deep dissension in the Labour Party for generations. Anti-nuclear resolutions were passed at party conferences, but in government Labour remained committed to the retention and development of the British deterrent. Aneurin Bevan, a traditional left-winger, disappointed those in the party who had hoped that he would champion the anti-nuclear cause by declaring that Britain's international standing required that the bomb be kept. He accused those who wanted Britain to abandon it of being guilty of 'an emotional spasm'.

These crises confirmed Britain's commitment to a pro-American, pro-nuclear, anti-Communist foreign policy. Except for one extraordinary episode, the Suez Affair of 1956 (see page 230), Britain and the USA were to be found in agreement on all the major issues in the

Cold War. This rarely involved fighting together as allies, but in all other respects the Anglo-American alliance was sustained. The two countries invariably gave each other diplomatic support in the UN and in the international disputes of the period. What this co-operation could not hide was that without American support Britain was not strong enough to act independently in international affairs. Two critical episodes revealed Britain's weakness and indicated that it would have to adjust its position in the post-war world. The first was Britain's involvement in the Palestine issue, the second was the Suez affair.

d) Britain and Palestine

Since accepting the League of Nations mandate for Palestine, Britain had had enormous difficulties trying to keep the balance between Arabs and Jews in the region (see page 86). It was in a cleft stick; whatever it did would anger one or other of the parties. In the hope of achieving a compromise, the British government announced in 1939 that Jewish immigration would be brought to an end after a final number had been allowed in. But Britain's resolve was undermined by developments in occupied Europe during the Second World War. When the full horrors of the Holocaust were revealed at the end of the war, international sympathy for the Jews increased dramatically. Pressure on Britain, especially from America, to increase the immigration quotas became intense. At the same time, Jewish terrorism increased. Fearful for their own survival, the Palestinian Arabs retaliated in kind. A bitter civil war ensued with Britain again caught in the crossfire. The assassination of the British minister, Lord Moyne, the murder of the UN representative, Count Bernadotte, and the bombing of the King David Hotel in Jerusalem were merely the more outstanding examples of the atrocities committed.

On becoming Foreign Secretary in 1945, Ernest Bevin promised that he would solve the Palestinian problem. Three years of frustration, during which he was accused both at home and abroad of being anti-Semitic, disillusioned him. Despite Britain's efforts to control Jewish entry after 1945, immigration, illegal as well as legitimate, increased unstoppably. The grim truth dawned on Bevin that, short of the total destruction of one or other of the sides, there was no way of resolving the Arab-Israeli conflict. In 1948 he announced that Britain was handing its mandate back to the UN and withdrawing from Palestine. Within a few months of this, the triumphant Jewish population was able to declare the creation of the sovereign state of Israel. This led to a mass 'exodus' of Arabs from Palestine, nearly three-quarters of the Arab population leaving the region. Arab propaganda described them as having been driven out. Jewish propaganda spoke of their having chosen to leave. What was certain was

> **Q** What was the lesson for Britain of its withdrawal from Palestine?

that a problem had been left that was to curse Middle-Eastern politics from that time onwards. Statehood for Israel had created as many international problems as it had solved. The critical lesson for Britain was how powerless it had been in the face of determined Zionism. The abandonment of its mandate showed the limitation of its ability to police international affairs. That lesson was to be brought home even more strongly by the outcome of the Suez venture.

ACTIVITY

Re-read section 1d and refer back to page 86 in Chapter 4. Explain briefly (a list of headings would be adequate) how Britain came to be involved in Palestine and why it eventually withdrew under Bevin.

How did Britain become embroiled in the Suez affair?

e) The Suez Affair, 1956

Colonel Nasser, who had become President of the new Egyptian republic in 1952, had at first been on good terms with the West. He had been promised American and British loans for the construction of the Aswan Dam, a project on which he had staked his own and his country's future. However, when the USA learned that he had also approached the Soviet bloc for aid, it withdrew its original offer. In desperation Nasser announced the nationalisation of the Suez Canal as a means of raising the necessary finance. Foreign ships would have to pay to pass through what was now an Egyptian waterway.

The British Prime Minister, Anthony Eden, who had come to regard Nasser as an Arab Hitler, declared that such a man could not be allowed 'to leave his thumb on Britain's windpipe', a reference to the threat to the essential oil supplies that came to Britain from the Middle East. He began to plot Nasser's downfall. France, which had long resented Egyptian support for the Arab nationalists in French Algeria, was very willing to join the British against Egypt. Eden also believed that the Americans would give at least diplomatic backing to any Anglo-French attempt to free the Canal. The Americans did, indeed, join Britain and France in trying to apply pressure on Egypt by the creation of a Canal Users' Association. But Nasser refused to budge. Britain and France then referred the issue to the Security Council. However this proved fruitless, since the Soviet Union vetoed the UN proposals condemning Egypt.

All this confirmed Eden in his belief that only force could shift Nasser. He began secret discussions with the French and the Israelis, who were eager to launch a major strike against Egypt, the chief source of Arab terrorism against them. Plans for a combined military invasion of Egypt were prepared. The strategy, finalised in mid-October, was that the Israelis would attack Egypt across the Sinai

How did Britain attempt to resolve the Suez problem?

peninsula. Britain and France, after allowing sufficient time for the Israelis to reach the Canal, would then mount a joint assault on the Canal region from the North, under the pretence of forcing Egypt and Israel to observe a cease-fire. The plan was accepted by Eden's Cabinet. On 29 October, the Israelis duly attacked across the Gaza Strip; on 30 October the Anglo-French ultimatum was delivered and on the following day the two European allies began their invasion of Egypt. The United Nations entered into an emergency debate in which the Americans, infuriated by Eden's having totally ignored them, led the condemnation of Israel and her two allies. Britain for the first time used its veto to defeat a resolution demanding an immediate cease-fire. Besides anger, what moved the Americans was their determination not to allow the Soviet Union to seize the initiative.

However, by a remarkable coincidence the USSR was at this very time wrestling with the Hungarian crisis and so its reaction was delayed. When it did enter the dispute it delivered a diplomatic **Note** to Britain condemning Anglo-French actions and threatening to use rockets against the aggressors if their forces did not withdrawn from Egypt. The day after the receipt of the Note, Britain began to obey the UN demand for a disengagement. But this was not simply a response to the Soviet threat. What led Eden to withdraw from Egypt was the deep division of opinion at home, as evident in impassioned parliamentary opposition, the fury of the Americans and, above all, a run on sterling, which threatened Britain with economic collapse with no prospect of US aid being available.

The Hungarian Crisis, 1956

After Stalin's death in 1953, the Soviet Union appeared to allow greater freedom to its satellites. However, when Hungary pushed too hard for independence Moscow reacted firmly. Khrushchev, the new Soviet leader ordered an invasion of the country. In October 1956, Soviet tanks entered Budapest to crush Hungary's liberal experiment. Desperate appeals for Western assistance were made by the Hungarians. But while the West expressed outrage at the Soviet behaviour no interference was seriously contemplated. While it is unlikely that the West would have intervened even had the Suez affair not coincided with the Hungarian rising, the Anglo-French-Israeli attack on Egypt made it difficult for the West to adopt the moral high ground over matters of invasion.

THE SOVIET NOTE

The Soviet government considers it necessary to draw your attention to the aggressive war being waged by Britain and France against Egypt, which has the most dangerous consequences for the cause of peace. In what position would Britain have found herself if she herself had been attacked by more powerful States possessing every kind of modern destructive weapon? And there are countries now which need not have sent a navy or air force to the coasts of Britain, but could have used other means, such as rockets … We are fully determined to crush the aggressors and restore peace in the Middle East through the use of force. We hope at this critical moment you will display due prudence and draw the corresponding conclusions from this.

Source D From the Official Note of the Soviet Government to the British Government, 5 November 1956.

Britain's withdrawal from Suez at the point when its forces were on the verge of military success showed how exposed it felt diplomatically. Historians, reflecting on the Suez crisis, have seen it as a landmark in British foreign policy. In attacking Egypt, Britain had

Q Why did Britain eventually withdraw from the Suez venture?

attempted to act independently of NATO and the United States, without consulting the Commonwealth, and in disregard of the UN. The international and domestic protests that the Suez venture aroused meant that it was the last occasion Britain would attempt such unilateral action. Imperialism had made its last throw.

ACTIVITY

Having studied Britain's involvement in the Suez venture, write down a set of headings which show that you understand a) why/how Britain became involved, and b) what it revealed about Britain's limitations as an international power after 1945.

---

f) Major British Military Engagements, 1945–99

The burdens and costs which Britain's international role imposed on it in the second half of the twentieth century can be gauged from the following list. What is particularly notable is that, with the exception of the Korean War, British forces were not actively engaged in any Cold War conflict.

i) The Malayan Emergency, 1948–66

The Malay peninsula, rich in tin and rubber and strategically important, contained nine independent states under British protection and three British settlements including Singapore. On 1 February 1948, these states formally came together as the Federation of Malaya. Although the area was multi-racial, the two largest groups were native Malays and expatriate Chinese. Backed by Mao Zedong's People's Republic of China, the Malay Chinese began a Communist guerilla insurrection against the Federation. Responding to an appeal from the Malay government Britain sent forces to the area, declared an emergency, and began a series of determined anti-Communist campaigns, involving troops from a range of Commonwealth countries. After six years of fierce fighting the Communist guerillas finally withdrew from Malaya in 1954. Britain signed a defence and mutual assistance pact with Malaysia in 1957. This was put to the test in 1963 when President Sukarno of neighbouring Indonesia declared the Federation of Malaysia 'neo-colonialist' and ordered Indonesian raids on the area. In defending Malaysia, British and Commonwealth forces suffered over 300 casualties before a peace settlement was signed in Bangkok in June 1966.

ii) The Cyprus Emergency, 1952–59

Since the late nineteenth century Britain had maintained a presence in the strategically important island of Cyprus in the eastern-Mediterranean. Eighty per cent of the island's population were of

Greek origin; the other 20 per cent were Turkish. The Greek majority demanded the union of Cyprus with Greece (*enosis*). When Britain declined to grant this, EOKA, the militant wing of the *enosis* movement, turned to terrorism against British forces and the Turkish minority. A complex and bloody civil war followed before a cease-fire was agreed in March 1959, followed a year later by the creation of the Independent Republic of Cyprus. However, the bitterness between Greeks and Turks remained and an uneasy truce was kept only by partitioning the island.

iii) The Kenyan Emergency, 1952–60

In an effort to preserve stability in the east African colonies of Tanganyika, Uganda and Kenya, Britain proposed that these areas be joined in an East African Federation. The official line was that the Federation would pursue multi-racial, equal shares, policies. However, in Kenya where white settlers dominated the government and owned the best land it was unlikely that genuine social or political equality would follow. The Kikuyu, Kenya's largest native tribe, began to organise resistance. This took its most violent form in the shape of the Mau Mau secret society. Between 1952 and 1959 thousands of British troops were deployed in Kenya. A grim cycle of Mau Mau outrages and British coercion occurred before the state of emergency was ended in 1960. Around 100 Europeans and 13,000 native Kenyans lost their lives in the violence.

Figure 36 Map showing the main military engagements in which Britain was involved in the second half of the twentieth century.

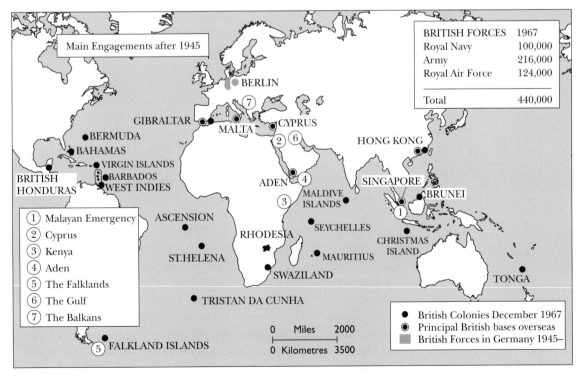

iv) Aden, 1963–67

Aden, a key strategic port at the southern end of the Red Sea, had been a British protectorate since the early-nineteenth century. In the post-war world, Arab nationalists began to demand independence for Aden. In 1963 Britain found itself facing internal unrest and cross-border attacks from Yemen. Following a four-year conflict during which 50 British troops were killed and 650 wounded Britain withdrew after recognising Aden's independence within the People's Republic of South Yemen.

v) The Falkands War, 1982
(See page 179.)

vi) The Gulf War, 1991

Following the occupation in 1990 of Kuwait by its Arab neighbour, Iraq, the United Nations condemned the invasion as an unwarranted act of aggression. The USA and Britain, concerned for their oil supplies, joined a number of Arab states to form a military alliance, which called upon Saddam Hussein, the Iraqi leader, to withdraw his troops. When he refused Britain joined the USA in dispatching land and naval forces to the Gulf region. After months of preparation an attack was finally launched by the allies. This proved successful in its immediate aim; Kuwait was liberated and Iraq was required to dismantle much of its weaponry. Saddam Hussein, however, remained in power in Iraq. His refusal to co-operate with UN inspection teams and his acts of genocide against the Kurds within Iraq led the UN to impose economic sanctions which caused considerable distress to ordinary Iraqis but which by 2000 had still not dislodged Saddam Hussein from power.

vii) The Balkans War
(See page 196.)

The Vietnam War, 1963–75

In pursuit of its containment principle, the notion that Communism should not be allowed to spread, the USA became involved in what proved to be a long drawn out struggle in Indo-China. The Americans decided to give direct support to the South Vietnamese governments in their resistance to invasion by Communist North Vietnam. However, the ensuing war in Vietnam was never a simple conflict between good and evil. The various regimes that came to power in South Vietnam may have been anti-Communist but they were seldom genuinely democratic. The US government met growing opposition at home to a war that became increasingly difficult to justify on strategic or moral grounds. Eventually the USA withdrew all its forces from Vietnam in 1975 leaving the Communists under Ho Chi Minh victorious. Britain did not become directly involved in Vietnam, but throughout the struggle the Labour and the Conservative governments gave their diplomatic backing to the USA.

Interestingly, British forces took no part in the Vietnam War, the longest military struggle of the Cold War years. Britain did, however, give consistent moral support to the USA. For many on the left this was further evidence of Britain's subservience to the United States in foreign affairs. This charge has particular resonance during the Thatcher years when Britain's **special relationship** became personalised in the friendship between the Prime Minister and Ronald Reagan, President from 1981 to 1989. A modern British historian, Peter Clarke, expressed it in these terms:

> Nowhere was Thatcher more warmly received than in the USA. An idealised USA was held up by Thatcherites as a model of society based on the free market, minimal government, anti-Communism, the mighty dollar and Almighty God. After Ronald Reagan was elected President in 1980, Thatcher found a real ally, with her trenchant expositions of their common outlook complemented by his benignly bemused concurrence. This was indeed a special relationship which helped to inflate Thatcher's international standing.

Source E From *Hope and Glory: Britain 1900–1990* by Peter Clarke, 1996.

THE SPECIAL RELATIONSHIP
The term refers to the notion of a natural understanding and sympathy between Britain and the USA resulting from their common language and shared democratic and cultural values, cemented by their alliance in the two world wars.

The collapse of Communism in the USSR and Eastern Europe between 1989 and 1991 was due primarily to domestic problems in

Figure 37 Photo of a dinner at 10 Downing Street, held in honour of President Reagan in July 1988. It shows Reagan, Thatcher and George Shultz, the US Secretary of State. At the bottom of the picture Reagan wrote: 'Dear Margaret – As you can see, I agree with every word you are saying. I always do. Warmest Friendship. Sincerely Ron.' Opponents of Thatcher and Reagan found such sentiments either comic or nauseating.

ACTIVITY

Having studied section 1, take each conflict separately and say why and with what consequences Britain became involved.

ISSUES:
Why was Britain prepared to give up its empire?
What were the effects on Britain of its loss of empire?

THE STATUTE OF WESTMINSTER, 1931

came to be regarded as the charter of the New Commonwealth. It made the equality of the dominions a basic legal principle. It recognised the autonomy of the white dominions – Canada, New Zealand, South Africa and Australia – in their relations with Britain and their right to adopt any status they chose.

What influence did the Second World War have on Anglo-Indian relations?

those areas. But there is a case for saying that the resolute anti-Communism of the West, associated with Reagan and Thatcher, increased Soviet instability by giving heart to the disruptive opposition forces within the Communist systems. Margaret Thatcher made a number of visits to the Eastern bloc, including Poland, Hungary and the USSR itself. It is significant that she was feted by the anti-Communists in those countries as a beacon of liberty.

2 Britain's Retreat from Empire

An outstanding feature of British history after 1945 was the retreat from empire. 'All the empires of the past were founded on the idea of assimilation. But the British Empire does not stand for assimilation but for the richer and fuller life of the individual nations within it.' These words, spoken by Jan Smuts of South Africa at a meeting of dominion prime ministers in 1917, defined the Commonwealth as an association of free and independent nations. This principle was formally recognised in **the Statute of Westminster** of 1931.

However, the Statute referred only to Britain and the dominions. It did not touch on the question of whether the UK's non-white colonies would subsequently be granted the same degree of freedom as the white dominions. Nationalists in the colonies and their supporters in Britain claimed that the Statute of Westminster clearly implied eventual equality and independence for all. The test case would be India. For generations India had been at the heart of the empire, 'the jewel in the Crown'. Possession of India was still a powerful symbol of Britain's world status. Three-quarters of the population of the entire empire were to be found in the sub-continent. If India were granted independence, there would be no reason for keeping any other part of the empire. Opinion in Britain was sharply divided over this. Some protested that if India were given up Britain's international status would be diminished. Others urged that the democratic spirit of the times and the principle of self-determination for which the Allies had fought in 1914–18 made it unacceptable to keep colonies if their peoples wanted independence.

Such feelings were strengthened by the Second World War. The early defeats suffered by British forces at the hands of the Japanese revealed Britain's weakness east of Suez. Seizing the moment, the Indian nationalists re-doubled their attacks; in 1942, the worse year of the war for the British, **M.K. Gandhi** inaugurated the 'Quit India' movement. Violence and reprisals followed, with the misery made worse by a famine in Bengal. The native police and army remained largely loyal and British control was unbroken, but at the cost of many lives and more political repression.

At the close of the Japanese war in 1945 it was clear that to retain India against the wish of her peoples would stretch British resources beyond breaking point. Moreover, the will to do so had largely gone. The Labour Party came into power in 1945 fully determined to grant self-government to India. The problem was how this could be best arranged in view of the religious divisions in India. The Muslim League, led by M. Jinnah, was increasingly suspicious of the Hindus, represented by the Congress Party and its leader Pandit Nehru. A sizeable Sikh minority was equally apprehensive of being swamped in an independent India. When the Labour government's representative, Stafford Cripps, proposed a federation within a single sovereign state of India, it was rejected by all the parties.

If federation was unacceptable, the only solution was partition. To gain agreement on this, the British government appointed Earl Mountbatten as special envoy with authority to negotiate Britain's final withdrawal from India. After much haggling, the Hindu Congress and the Muslim League agreed to the Mountbatten proposals. The sub-continent was to be divided into two distinct states: India, overwhelmingly Hindu; Pakistan and East Pakistan, predominantly Muslim. The question of the status of Kashmir, a strongly Sikh region, was left unresolved. The date for the formal end of British rule was brought forward from 1948 to 1947.

The Religious Divisions in India

The three great faiths of the people of India – Hinduism, Islam and Sikhism – were a source of profound social and political division and prevented a peaceful transition to independence. For many decades after 1947, India was disfigured by bloody conflict between the rival groups. In 2000 the enmity between India and Pakistan was still one of the major problems in international affairs.

What steps led to the independence of India?

M.K. GANDHI

Mohandas Gandhi was the single most important influence in the growth of Indian nationalism. As a young lawyer in South Africa he had organised passive resistance to the race laws there. On returning to India he set about employing the same techniques as a means of undermining the British hold on India. A devout Hindu, Gandhi nonetheless sought mutual respect and tolerance between all religions and castes. His simple, even saintly, lifestyle endeared him to the great mass of the Indian peasantry.

What was the significance for the British empire of the achievement of Indian independence?

The gaining of Indian independence opened the way for the dismantling of the whole British empire. The broad political consensus in Britain was that the age of imperialism had passed. There was a general acceptance that decolonisation was essential in an age of democracy and representative government. Harold Macmillan put this memorably in 1960 when addressing the South African parliament; he spoke of the need to recognise 'the wind of change' blowing through Africa. He meant that in the face of the growing national consciousness of the African peoples the only politically realistic and morally acceptable policy was to grant independence to those peoples who wanted it. Between 1957 and 1968 Britain gave independence to all its remaining colonies in Africa and the majority of those elsewhere. For

Figure 38 Clement Attlee with the scimitar of partition ponders how to divide India (represented by a two-headed elephant) in such a way that it satisfies both Nehru's Congress and Jinnah's Muslim League.

JUDGMENT OF SOLOMON?
22nd May, 1947. Mr. Attlee is trying to find a solution to the Indian Problem.

the most part, this proved a remarkably smooth and bloodless process. Britain did not experience the bitter colonial wars that France underwent in trying to cling on to its empire. Where there were problems in the British retreat, they arose not over whether independence was

The Rhodesian Unilateral Declaration of Independence (UDI), 1965–80

The white settler community which held political power in Rhodesia refused to accept the principles of 'majority rule' and 'one person, one vote'. They claimed that majority rule in Rhodesia would give authority to the backward black Africans, who were incapable of exercising it responsibly. Having failed to reach agreement with successive British governments, Ian Smith, the Prime Minister and leader of the white Rhodesian Front Party, declared UDI in 1965. For the next 15 years Rhodesia defied international condemnation. But eventually a combination of economic sanctions and a dispiriting civil war forced Smith to the conference table. Talks with Margaret Thatcher's Conservative government produced a new settlement which accepted majority rule. Free elections in 1980 saw a victory for Robert Mugabe, who had been a black guerilla fighter against UDI. The new nation adopted the name Zimbabwe. The main problem that remained after independence was how long the majority black Zimbabweans would continue to tolerate the possession of the nation's best land by the minority white farmers. Tension over this issue was growing ominously at the beginning of the twenty-first century.

to be granted but when. One big exception was the struggle over UDI in Southern Rhodesia.

An idea of both the extraordinary size of the British empire and the equally extraordinary speed with which it was dismantled can be gained from the timeline opposite.

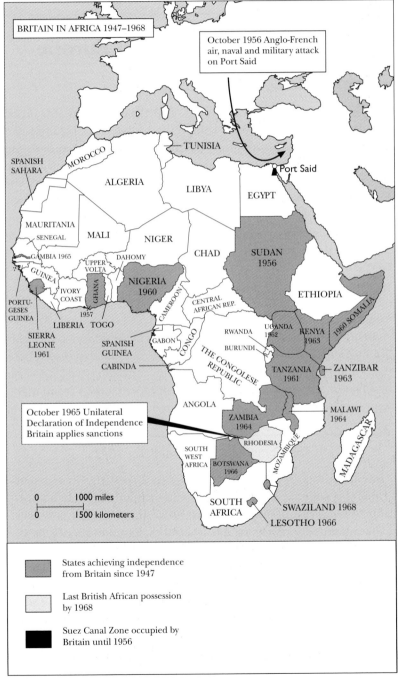

BRITAIN IN AFRICA 1947–1968

October 1956 Anglo-French air, naval and military attack on Port Said

October 1965 Unilateral Declaration of Independence Britain applies sanctions

States achieving independence from Britain since 1947

Last British African possession by 1968

Suez Canal Zone occupied by Britain until 1956

COLONIES GAINING INDEPENDENCE
(NEW NAME IN BRACKETS)

1947 India, Pakistan;
1948 Burma;
1956 Sudan;
1957 Gold Coast (Ghana), Malaya;
1960 Nigeria, Somalia, Cyprus;
1961 Sierra Leone, Tanganyika and Zanzibar (Tanzania), Kuwait;
1962 Uganda, Jamaica, Trinidad and Tobago;
1963 Kenya, Seychelles; Malaya, Singapore, North Borneo and Sarawak formed Malaysia;
1964 Northern Rhodesia (Zambia), Nyasaland (Malawi), Malta;
1965 Singapore, Gambia, Maldives;
1966 Basutoland (Lesotho), Bechuanaland (Botswana), Barbados, British Guiana (Guyana);
1968 Swaziland, Mauritius;
1970 Fiji, Tonga;
1971 Bahrain, Qatar, Trucial Oman (United Arab Emirates);
1972 Ceylon (Sri Lanka);
1973 Bahamas;
1974 Grenada;
1978 Dominica, Ellice Island (Tuvalu);
1979 Gilbert Islands (Kiribati), St Lucia, St Vincent and the Grenadines;
1980 Southern Rhodesia (Zimbabwe), New Hebrides (Vanatu);
1981 British Honduras (Belize);
1983 Brunei, St Christopher and Nevis;
1997 Hong Kong.

Figure 39 Map of Africa, 1947–68 indicating the dates when independence was gained by the British colonies.

ACTIVITY

In the light of what you have read in section 2, explain why Britain was willing to give up its empire in the second half of the twentieth century. Explain also why the transition from empire to colonial independence occurred relatively smoothly and peacefully.

ISSUES:

What principles underlay the formation of the EEC?

Why was Britain slow to join the movement for European union after 1945?

3 Britain's Relations with Europe

a) Britain's detachment, 1945–63

The motives that underlay Western Europe's progress towards union in the post-war period were an interesting mixture of idealism and national self-interest. One powerful impulse was the deep desire to prevent European war ever breaking out again. In 1957 a major step was taken towards permanent union with the creation of the **European Economic Community** (**EEC**). This defined itself formally as an economic organisation, but from the first the EEC was driven by political considerations. Its aim was to create a **federation** of European states. Its origins lay in a post-war pact between France and Germany. In return for Germany's financing the reduction of French agriculture and expansion of French industry, France had agreed to open itself to German manufactures. (This became the basis of the **Common Agricultural Policy**.)

Behind this economic agreement was Germany's desire to re-establish itself as a respectable and acceptable nation that had wholly thrown off its Nazi past. For its part, France was motivated primarily by a fear of a resurgent Germany. As Jean Monnet, the French minister whose work for European union earned him the title of 'the father

THE EUROPEAN ECONOMIC COMMUNITY

was formed in 1957 when 'the Six' – France, Germany, Italy and the Benelux Countries (Belgium, the Netherlands and Luxembourg) – signed the Treaty of Rome. The Treaty created a common market and a customs union to regulate all aspects of trade between the member states, which were required to operate a protectionist policy against all non-member nations.

FEDERATION

The essence of a federation, as opposed to the much looser grouping of an association or a confederation, is that member states forego a significant degree of individual sovereignty. This is necessary if the federal union of states is to have effective executive power.

The Common Agricultural Policy (CAP)

was based on the notion of ending rural poverty by a system whereby 'poor areas' in the Community were subsidised by a transfer of money from the 'rich areas'. Critics attacked it as a system that rewarded inefficiency and as a bribe offered to French farmers to persuade them to accept the reduction of the agricultural sector. The subsidy system, which provided the farmers with guaranteed prices for their produce regardless of actual demand or cost, meant high prices for the consumer. This deliberate and sustained dear food policy undermined the free-trade principles of Monnet and Schuman and became one of the most controversial aspects of the operation of the EEC.

of Europe', acknowledged, what led him to promote a Franco-German union was his conviction that despite its defeat in war Germany still had the potential to out-produce and to dominate France. Far better, therefore, to control Germany within a formal organisation to which they both belonged than try to compete separately against it. As for the other four members, the Benelux countries and Italy, they judged that the post-war years offered them an opportunity to extract as many economic concessions as possible from Germany – their more powerful but guilt-ridden neighbour. This, they judged, could best be achieved within a formal European union.

Significantly, Britain had not experienced occupation by a hostile power in wartime. It was not, therefore, convinced in the way that the Six were of the need for immediate formal European union. When pressed to join the **Schuman Plan** in 1950, Attlee rejected it unequivocally.

> We are not prepared to accept the principle that the most vital economic forces of this country should be handed over to an authority that is utterly undemocratic and is responsible to nobody.

Source F From a speech by Clement Attlee in the House of Commons, June 1950.

Interestingly, the Conservatives at this time shared exactly the same view towards Europe as the Labour government. Harold Macmillan, a British observer at **the Council of Europe** in Strasbourg, declared as directly as Attlee had that Britain was not prepared to take risks with the British economy by subjecting it to the control of a foreign organisation.

> We will allow no supra-national authority to put large masses of our people out of work in Durham, in the Midlands, in South Wales and in Scotland.

Source G From a speech by Harold Macmillan in the House of Commons, August 1950.

Britain's ability to remain aloof from the movement for European co-operation rested on the conviction, first voiced by Winston Churchill, that its economic future lay not in Europe but in its continued relationship with the United States and the Commonwealth.

> He never for one moment during or after the war contemplated Britain submerging her sovereignty in that of a United States of Europe or losing her national identity. In January 1941 he went so far

---

THE SCHUMAN PLAN

Robert Schuman, who became premier and foreign minister in post-war France, believed that peace could best be achieved in Europe by the French and Germans taking the lead in the formation of a federation. He declared 'Europe must be organised on a federal basis. A Franco-German union is an essential element in it.' He devised a plan for France and Germany to pool their most productive resources – coal and steel – in a European Coal and Steel Community (ECSC). His scheme became the model on which the economic foundations of EEC were laid.

THE COUNCIL OF EUROPE

was established in 1949 with the aim of encouraging co-operation between the states of Europe. Since it claimed no executive powers over member states, Britain was willing to be one of the Council's founders.

What led Britain to consider joining the EEC?

as to say that there must be a United States of Europe and that it should be built by the English: if the Russians built it there would be Communism and squalor; if the Germans built it there would be tyranny and brute force. On the other hand, I knew he felt that while Britain might be the builder and Britain might live in the house, she would always preserve her liberty of choice and would be the natural, undisputed link with the Americas and the Commonwealth.

Source H From the memoirs of Jock Colville, Private Secretary to Winston Churchill.

ISSUES:
Why did Britain finally decide to apply for membership of the EEC?
Why was there such a long gap between the UK's first application and its eventual membership?

THE EUROPEAN FREE TRADE ASSOCIATION (EFTA)

Britain was a founder member of this organisation which was set up in 1959 as a free-trade counter-balance to the protectionist EEC. The other members were Norway, Sweden, Austria, Portugal, Switzerland and Denmark. EFTA was never able to match the influence of the EEC and by 1972 most of its members had joined the EEC.

b) Britain Moves Towards European Membership, 1963–75

In the 1950s and 1960s the poor performance of the British economy compared to that of the EEC countries (see page 154) threw serious doubt on whether Britain could continue to remain detached. Equally disturbing for Britain was the failure of the **European Free Trade Association** to match the economic success of the EEC.

There was a vital political aspect to all this. The Suez affair of 1956 (see page 230) put a question mark against Britain's status as an independent world power and raised doubts about the Anglo-American special relationship. Added to this, was Britain's difficulty in remaining a truly independent nuclear force. To maintain its strike power Britain had become increasingly reliant on US Polaris submarines. Such developments obliged British politicians to adjust their thinking. Equally significant was the decline within the Conservative Party of the traditionally influential agricultural lobby and its replacement by the younger, City-orientated, managerial element, who were becoming increasingly pro-European in their sympathies. It was against this background that Macmillan appointed Edward Heath as minister with special responsibility for negotiations with the Six. In announcing this new departure in 1961, Harold Macmillan insisted that the existing privileges and interests of EFTA and the Commonwealth must be preserved.

The maintenance of unrestricted and duty-free entry of New Zealand's products into the United Kingdom was absolutely vital. The possible damage that might be inflicted on British agriculture and Commonwealth trade was a question of vital importance. Much would therefore depend upon the issue of any negotiations. We must persuade the Six of the value of the Commonwealth to the Free World, and the meeting of Commonwealth leaders concurred in the belief that neither the Commonwealth countries nor British public opinion would accept that Commonwealth interests should only be safeguarded during the transitional period.

Source I From *Memoirs* by Harold Macmillan, 1970.

Macmillan's concern for the rights of the Commonwealth and EFTA made Britain's readiness to negotiate appear grudging. It suggested that Britain wanted to have its cake and eat it. It was for this reason that President De Gaulle used the French veto to block Britain's formal application to join the EEC in 1963.

> How far is it possible for Great Britain at the present time to accept a truly common tariff, as the Continent does, for this would involve giving up all Commonwealth preferences, renouncing all claims for privileges for her agriculture, and treating as null and void obligations entered into with countries forming part of the Free Trade Area?

Source J From a speech by Charles De Gaulle, 14 January 1963.

There was a powerful logic to De Gaulle's doubts concerning British sincerity. His rhetorical question in reaction to Macmillan's claim that 'we must persuade the Six of the value of the Commonwealth to the Free World' made sound sense. How, indeed, could Britain assert such sentiments and then genuinely undertake the removal of all the preferential claims and privileges currently enjoyed by EFTA and the Commonwealth? Strong grounds for De Gaulle's scepticism had been provided in 1962 when the independent Commonwealth countries of Africa, fearing a compromising of their newly won freedom, had rejected a specially negotiated offer to become associate members of the EEC.

Q Why was France unwilling to admit Britain into the EEC?

De Gaulle's reservations did not end with economics. More important to him were the political implications of British entry. These were spelled out by the French Agricultural Minister.

> It is very simple. At present, in the Six there are five hens and one cock. If you join, with other countries, there will be perhaps seven or eight hens. But there will be two cocks. I am afraid that is not acceptable to us.

Source K From a letter of the French Minister of Agriculture to the British Ambassador in France, January 1963.

De Gaulle's opposition to British entry has to be seen in historical perspective. As a committed patriot, De Gaulle had been appalled at the humiliation of France in 1940. Conscious that its liberation and his return in 1944 had depended not on French arms but on those of the USA and Britain, De Gaulle believed passionately that France should atone for its failings by re-asserting itself in the post-war world. It should make itself pre-eminent in a Europe that was independent of Britain and America. When he returned to lead his country in the late 1950s, he saw in the EEC a way of achieving this objective, an objective that would be threatened if Britain was permitted to join.

Q

What was the Labour Party's attitude towards the EEC?

DISADVANTAGES TO BRITAIN OF ITS MEMBERSHIP OF THE EEC

▼ It was no longer able to buy cheap food from the Commonwealth.

▼ As victims of the Common Agricultural Policy British consumers found themselves paying inflated food prices.

▼ The Common Fisheries Policy, (CFP) severely restricted Britain's right to fish in its customary grounds and led to the virtual destruction of the UK's fishing industry.

▼ It had to make higher contributions to the EEC budget than it received in grants from Europe. By the early 1980s Britain was paying 20 per cent of the revenue raised by the EEC but was receiving only 8 per cent of the expenditure.

A personal meeting between De Gaulle and Macmillan in December 1962 had done nothing to ease these fears. Indeed, the failure to reach an Anglo-French understanding on joint nuclear-arms development, followed only days later by an Anglo-American agreement in which the USA agreed to supply Britain with Polaris missiles, served to confirm De Gaulle's suspicions that Britain was the thin edge of a large American wedge about to be thrust into Europe.

Four years after the French veto, Harold Wilson's Labour government made Britain's second application, this despite the Labour Party's continuing uncertainty on the issue. Hugh Gaitskell, Wilson's predecessor as leader, had told the Labour Party Conference in 1962 that if Britain joined the EEC it would mean 'the end of Britain as an independent European state … the end of a thousand years of history'. Wilson's decision to re-apply was prompted by economic fears. Discussions took place against the background of a serious sterling crisis which led to devaluation and raised serious questions regarding Britain's economic capacity. Again, on the same grounds as in 1963, De Gaulle vetoed Britain's application. On this occasion the annoyance of the other five members of the EEC with the French became quite open. However, following De Gaulle's retirement in 1969, tension relaxed within the Community and the way became clear for Britain to enter. It was in fact invited to re-apply, which it duly did during Edward Heath's premiership (1970–74). In 1972, Britain signed the treaty of accession and became a full member of the EEC on New Year's Day, 1973.

The matter did not end there. The left wing of the Labour Party, which was returned to power under Wilson in 1974, remained deeply suspicious of the Common Market. They regarded it as a capitalist club, necessarily hostile to socialism. 'The Durham miners don't like it', was the essence of their argument. To quieten the left and to give the electorate a chance to vote on the question of Britain's EEC membership, Wilson renegotiated the terms of Britain's membership, an exercise that was largely a gesture since it produced no major changes. He then called a national referendum in 1975. In the words of the modern historian, Martin Pugh, the electorate voted 'more out of fear of the consequences of leaving than out of enthusiasm for remaining in'. It was no great surprise when the referendum results showed a large majority for Britain's staying in the Community. Opponents of the 'yes' vote claimed that the whole affair had been a betrayal of democracy. They argued that the referendum should have preceded Britain's entry, not followed it; Britain was voting on a *fait accompli*, not making a free choice. They also pointed out that twice as much had been spent on the 'yes' campaign as on the 'no', proportions which exactly matched the vote distribution.

	Total Votes	'Yes' Vote	'No' Vote	Turnout
England	21,772,222	68.7%	31.3%	64.6%
Wales	1,345,545	64.8%	35.2%	66.7%
Scotland	2,286,676	58.4%	41.6%	61.7%
Northern Ireland	498,751	52.1%	47.9%	47.4%
UK total	29,453,194	64.5%	35.5%	64.5%

Table 55 Results of the UK referendum on EEC membership, 1975.

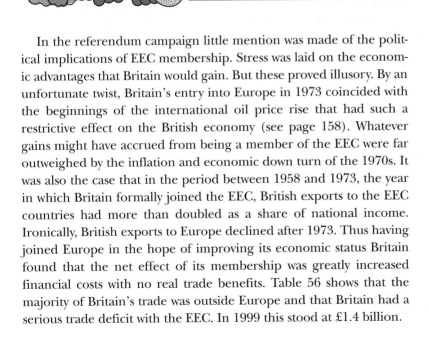

Figure 40 The food supplies destroyed under CAP policy.

THE WASTE

Fruit and vegetables destroyed for which EU withdrawal compensation was paid

All weight in tons	1991/92	1992/93
Apples	26,088	968,619
Pears	652	55,079
Cauliflowers	40,480	126,727
Tomatoes	44,179	32,850
Apricots	937	19,503
Nectarines	36,387	164,690
Peaches	337,120	720,262
Lemons	13,448	80,941
Aubergines	553	148
Grapes	291	3,222
Satsumas	0	3,587
Mandarins	2,723	2,492
Clementines	1,655	43,856
Oranges	154,877	504,794

In the referendum campaign little mention was made of the political implications of EEC membership. Stress was laid on the economic advantages that Britain would gain. But these proved illusory. By an unfortunate twist, Britain's entry into Europe in 1973 coincided with the beginnings of the international oil price rise that had such a restrictive effect on the British economy (see page 158). Whatever gains might have accrued from being a member of the EEC were far outweighed by the inflation and economic down turn of the 1970s. It was also the case that in the period between 1958 and 1973, the year in which Britain formally joined the EEC, British exports to the EEC countries had more than doubled as a share of national income. Ironically, British exports to Europe declined after 1973. Thus having joined Europe in the hope of improving its economic status Britain found that the net effect of its membership was greatly increased financial costs with no real trade benefits. Table 56 shows that the majority of Britain's trade was outside Europe and that Britain had a serious trade deficit with the EEC. In 1999 this stood at £1.4 billion.

Summary of the Pros and Cons of Britain's Membership of the EEC

The Case For

Security – no war in Western Europe since 1945.

Common Market – provided free trade among member states.

Free movement – European citizens able to live and work where they chose.

Employment – increased number and range of job prospects.

Common currency – created ease of exchange and lowered prices.

Resources – were properly assessed and reallocated within the union.

Markets – became larger and more accessible.

Federalism – stimulated unity and understanding.

The Case Against

Undemocratic – decisions made in Brussels by unelected officials.

Corrupt – large bureaucracy encouraged fraud.

Protectionist – union out of date in a world of global markets.

Expensive – EC budgeting meant Britain had to make higher contributions.

Wasteful – CAP and CFP harmed British agriculture and fishing.

Unstable – divergent growth rates between members created instability.

Federalism – created rivalry between members.

Table 56 Distribution of British trade in 1989 (value in billions of £).

	Exports to	Imports from
Germany	11.1	20.1
France	9.5	19.8
Italy	4.6	6.7
Holland	6.5	9.6
Belgium	4.8	5.7
Japan	2.3	7.1
Sweden	2.3	3.7
Switzerland	2.2	4.1
USA	12.1	12.8
Saudi Arabia	2.4	0.5
Ireland	4.7	4.3
Spain	3.1	2.8
Total	**65.6**	**97.2**

ACTIVITIES

Study Table 56.

▼ Identify the EEC countries. By how much was Britain in a trade surplus or deficit with them?

▼ Do the figures support or challenge the notion that by 1989 Britain needed Europe more than Europe needed Britain?

c) Mrs Thatcher and Europe

When Margaret Thatcher came into office in 1979 she was confronted by the record of Britain's poor economic performance in the 1970s, caused at least in part by the difficult adjustments that had had to be made on entering the EEC. Mrs Thatcher claimed later that she had not been initially anti-EEC but when she realised how much waste and inefficiency the Brussels bureaucracy was responsible for she felt compelled to speak out. She was also disturbed at a deeper level by the threat that European federalism held for Britain. She was conscious of how young the European institutions were; none of them pre-dated 1945 whereas Britain's governmental system had evolved over centuries. She felt that Europe could easily become the prey of creeping socialism and bureaucracy because in the final analysis the EEC was not subject to genuine democratic control.

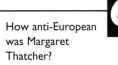

How anti-European was Margaret Thatcher?

These fears were not new. They had shaped the attitude of both Labour and Conservative parties as early as the 1940s when the first moves were taken towards European union. What made Margaret Thatcher appear particularly hostile was her combative manner. She carried over into her discussion with European ministers the adversarial style of debate which she had learned in British politics. But this was out of place in a European context. Direct confrontation was rare between European ministers and officials. They tended to get things done by compromise and concession. Such techniques irritated Mrs Thatcher and she was not reluctant to show it. The ground on which she chose to defend the British position most strongly was the issue of Britain's disproportionately high payments to the EEC budget. She defined her position in these terms:

> Britain's unique trading pattern made her a very large net contributor to the EC budget – so large that the situation was indeed unacceptable. We traditionally imported far more from non-EC countries than did other Community members, particularly of foodstuffs. This meant that we paid more into the Community budget in the form of tariffs than they did. By contrast, the Community budget itself is heavily biased towards supporting farmers through the Common Agricultural Policy … The British economy is less dependent on agriculture than that of most other Community countries; consequently we receive less in subsidy than they do.

Source L From *The Downing Street Years* by Margaret Thatcher, 1993.

Her battling did achieve some results, the EEC reluctantly authorising a reduction in Britain's budget payments. But Mrs Thatcher's dislike of the centralising process within Europe remained. She was at her most forthright in attacking the federalist notions of Jacques Delors (EU President from 1985 to 1995), whom she regarded as typical of the unelected and unaccountable bureaucrats who were making the rules for Europe. In a landmark speech at Bruges in 1988 she decided 'to strike out against the erosion of democracy by centralisation and bureaucracy'.

Source M From a speech by Margaret Thatcher at Bruges, 20 September 1988.

It is ironic that just when those countries, such as the Soviet Union, which have tried to run everything from the centre, are learning that success depends on dispersing power and decisions away from the centre, some in the Community seem to want to move in the opposite direction. We have not successfully rolled back the frontiers of the state in Britain only to see them reimposed at a European level, with a Brussels super-state exercising a new dominance from Brussels ... Willing and active co-operation between independent sovereign states is the best way to build a successful European Community ... Let us have a Europe which plays its full part in the wider world, which looks outward not inward.

Figure 41 Map showing the main features of Britain's relations with Europe, 1957–93.

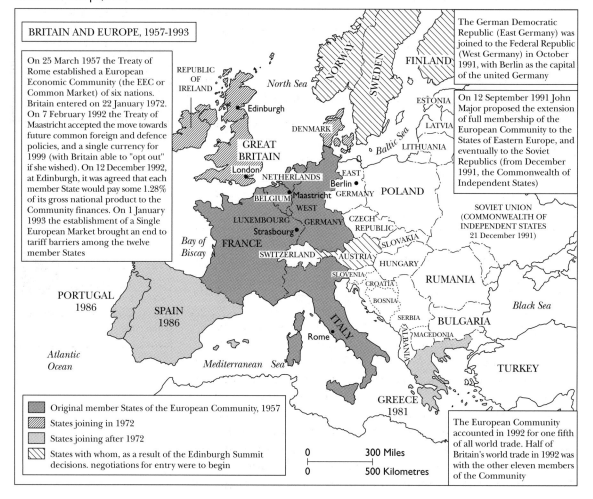

BRITAIN AND EUROPE, 1957-1993

On 25 March 1957 the Treaty of Rome established a European Economic Community (the EEC or Common Market) of six nations. Britain entered on 22 January 1972. On 7 February 1992 the Treaty of Maastricht accepted the move towards future common foreign and defence policies, and a single currency for 1999 (with Britain able to "opt out" if she wished). On 12 December 1992, at Edinburgh, it was agreed that each member State would pay some 1.28% of its gross national product to the Community finances. On 1 January 1993 the establishment of a Single European Market brought an end to tariff barriers among the twelve member States

The German Democratic Republic (East Germany) was joined to the Federal Republic (West Germany) in October 1991, with Berlin as the capital of the united Germany

On 12 September 1991 John Major proposed the extension of full membership of the European Community to the States of Eastern Europe, and eventually to the Soviet Republics (from December 1991, the Commonwealth of Independent States)

SOVIET UNION (COMMONWEALTH OF INDEPENDENT STATES 21 December 1991)

The European Community accounted in 1992 for one fifth of all world trade. Half of Britain's world trade in 1992 was with the other eleven members of the Community

Original member States of the European Community, 1957

States joining in 1972

States joining after 1972

States with whom, as a result of the Edinburgh Summit decisions. negotiations for entry were to begin

0   300 Miles

0   500 Kilometres

Her speech was widely regarded as a rallying cry to all those who wished to prevent the absorption of national identities into a centralising Europe. It was a piece of populism; she was trying to appeal over the heads of Europe's bureaucrats to the ordinary people in France and Germany as well as to the British. Yet the great paradox was that despite her fighting words it was Mrs Thatcher who presided over the process by which Britain was drawn ever closer into Europe. It was she who in 1986 accepted the Single European Act, which marked the biggest step towards a centralised Europe that had yet been taken. She was also in office when Britain agreed to enter the **Exchange Rate Mechanism** (ERM). Margaret Thatcher claimed later that she had been misled into accepting this by her Chancellor of the Exchequer, Nigel Lawson, and her Foreign Secretary, Geoffrey Howe. When she became aware of the implications of ERM she obliged Lawson to resign and demoted Howe. It was Howe who in his resignation speech in 1990 revealed the serious divisions within the Conservative Party over Europe. His attack upon Margaret Thatcher for her obstructive attitude towards European development was the prelude to the leadership struggle that led to her own resignation in November 1990 (see page 186).

Main Terms of the Single European Act, 1986

▼ The signatory countries committed themselves to closer monetary and political union.

▼ The principle of supra-nationality (the subordination of individual member states to the EU) was established.

▼ The right of individual member states to veto majority decisions was abolished.

> **THE EXCHANGE RATE MECHANISM** was a system whose main aim was to reduce inflation. This was to be done by creating parity between the various European currencies by pegging them to the value of the Deutschmark (DM), Europe's strongest currency, rather than let them find their market value. When Britain joined the ERM in 1990 the exchange value of the pound sterling was DM2.95. This was unrealistically high and caused British exports to become overpriced. It proved impossible to sustain the value of the pound in the international markets. The result was a serious stock-market collapse in September 1992. Britain promptly withdrew from the ERM.

Without openly rejecting Margaret Thatcher's approach her successor John Major wished to show that he was a good European. He took a momentous step by signing Britain up to **the Maastricht Treaty** in February 1992. However, the concern of his own party, and of a significant number of Opposition MPs, over the loss of sovereignty entailed by this deeper integration into Europe was shown by the House of Commons' refusal to ratify the Treaty. Having committed his government to Maastricht, Major was not prepared to accept the verdict of the Commons. In a hurried move he re-introduced the proposal to accept the Maastricht Treaty and made it part of a formal vote of confidence in the government. In this way the proposal was forced through. But the desperate means he had used gave strength to the growing number of Euro-sceptics within and outside parliament who claimed that Britain was being railroaded into European integration.

> **Q** How did John Major differ from Margaret Thatcher in his approach to Europe?

THE MAASTRICHT TREATY, 1992

Member states agreed to work towards:

▼ full European integration

▼ a common European foreign policy

▼ a common European defence policy

▼ a single European currency, 'the Euro', to be adopted by 1999 (Britain obtained an opt-out clause, which it exercised in 1999).

SUBSIDIARITY

is the principle that in matters of special concern to a particular member state, that state should have the right to by-pass EU decisions.

How had the Labour Party changed its attitude on the European question?

Calls for a national referendum, such as those held in Ireland, Denmark and France, were rejected by the government on the grounds that a referendum was 'unconstitutional'. Major's success later in 1992 in obtaining the EC's agreement to the principle of **subsidiarity** did little to lessen Euro-sceptic fears. By the end of his administration in 1997 the adverse reaction to the Maastricht Treaty, the growth of scepticism within his party, and the enforced withdrawal from ERM had undermined whatever credit he had gained from his willingness to co-operate with Britain's European partners.

As we noted earlier, down to the 1970s the Labour Party had been far from pro-European and it was not until 1983 that it officially dropped its commitment to withdraw Britain from the EEC. Thereafter, as part of its reformation as New Labour, the party began to warm towards Europe. In part this was opportunistic. Labour was swift to exploit Mrs Thatcher's ambiguous European attitude and it made the most of John Major's embarrassments over Maastricht and the ERM. But there was a more positive aspect to it. The party's earlier fears that Europe was essentially a club for capitalists had diminished. Labour could see, for example, the gains that workers could now derive from the generous European employment laws. The party declared its commitment to the European ideal. Tony Blair strove to impress the other European leaders with his sincerity.

The question that confronted him and his government at the beginning of the new century was how far they should lead Britain down the path of European integration. The critical test would be whether the government would abandon the pound sterling and enter fully into the single currency system, a step which all the other EU members, apart from Denmark, had taken by 1999. Labour's interim answer was that it would prepare the ground for entry but would make a final commitment only if and when it could be established that entry was in Britain's economic interests. Its decision would then be put to a referendum of the people.

ACTIVITY

Having read section 3, trace the changing attitude of British governments towards Europe between 1945 and 1999. Make your analysis chronological and look at it from two particular angles – the attitude of the Conservatives and the attitude of the Labour Party.

4 Britain's Relations with Ireland, 1969–99

ISSUES:
Why did an Anglo-Irish question re-emerge in the late 1960s?
How near to a genuine settlement of the Northern-Irish issue had the parties come by the end of the twentieth century?

Britain's formal links with southern Ireland had finally ended in 1949 when the Irish Free State become the sovereign Republic of Ireland. This seemed to have finally put an end to the Anglo-Irish question. But one great problem remained – Northern Ireland. Constitutionally it was part of the United Kingdom but its geography obviously made it part of the island of Ireland. This was an anomaly that Irish nationalists found objectionable. They claimed that the 1921 Treaty had deliberately and arbitrarily drawn the boundary between north and south so as to leave northern Ireland with a predominantly Protestant population. In the six counties there were one million Protestants to half a million Catholics. The Protestants had used their majority to dominate the separate parliament set up in 1921. They had then consolidated their political control by securing rights denied to the Catholic minority. An outstanding example of this was the policing system under **the Royal Ulster Constabulary (RUC)**, which the Catholic population came to regard as an armed sectarian police force whose main task was to coerce the Catholic minority and protect the Protestant political establishment.

It was certainly the case that over the decades after partition Protestants came to monopolise the best housing and the best schools, and to have access to the better jobs. The Catholic complaint was that this was a result of the political corruption in Ulster which allowed Protestant councillors and officials to operate a system of favouritism and patronage. It was even said that constituency and ward boundaries were deliberately adjusted so as to maintain permanent Protestant majorities.

One area where local politicians could not control things was admission to higher education, since this was administered directly from Whitehall. By the end of the 1960s nearly a third of the students at Queen's University, Belfast, came from the Catholic minority. It was from among such students that the **Northern Ireland Civil Rights Association** developed.

NICRA's first major public protest occurred in Dungannon in August 1968. In October of the same year a second demonstration, this time in Derry (Londonderry), Northern Ireland's most depressed economic area, ended in violence when the RUC baton charged the marchers to break up what the authorities had declared to be an illegal gathering. This incident is often taken as marking the beginning of '**the troubles**'.

THE ROYAL ULSTER CONSTABULARY (RUC)

Before 1921 the whole of Ireland had a single police force – the Royal Irish Constabulary – which had been largely recruited from the Catholic population. This was replaced in Northern Ireland 1922 with the RUC, an armed force which soon became almost exclusively Protestant. The RUC could also call on a wholly Protestant reserve force, the 'B Specials'.

NORTHERN IRELAND CIVIL RIGHTS ASSOCIATION (NICRA)

was founded in 1967. It condemned the gerrymandering of elections in Ulster and demanded the disbanding of the B Specials and a fair distribution of social and financial resources across the whole population. NICRA took as its model the black civil rights movement in the USA.

Rival demonstrations showed the depth of the Catholic-Protestant sectarian divide. In 1969 disorder grew as protest and counter protest invariably resulted in violence. The Revd Ian Paisley emerged as the leader of unyielding anti-Catholic Unionism which whipped up Protestant hatred. In the summer of 1969, the season of the traditional Protestant marches in Ulster, the first deaths occurred. Responsible politicians on both sides of the border and in London appealed for calm but both communities, Catholic and Protestant, were liable to be attacked by terrorists from the other side. In August James Callaghan, Britain's Foreign Secretary, took the momentous decision to send the British army to Northern Ireland to keep the peace. At first the troops were welcomed by the Catholic community. Residents cheered and clapped as the soldiers encircled the Catholic Bogside area with protective barbed wire.

This happy relationship was not to last. The IRA, embarrassed by its apparent inability earlier to defend the Catholic areas, chose to reorganise itself and take the lead in the struggle. However, not only did it resolve to attack Unionism and head the Catholic Nationalist protest movement, it also targeted, both literally and figuratively, the troops in Northern Ireland as representatives of the hated British imperialist government, which all along had been the cause of Ireland's problems.

For the next 30 years the continued presence of the British Army in Ulster indicated that the province's problems had not been solved. But through the violence and disruption one aspect did become clear. The tide was running against the Unionists and with the Nationalists. Reasonable opinion in every quarter found it hard to justify the continuation of a Protestant political and economic

---

'THE TROUBLES'

A cycle of violence that began in 1969 and was still unresolved in 2000. Its main feature was terrorist conflict between the Republicans and the Unionists, with British troops caught in the middle trying to preserve the peace. It should be stressed that mainstream Nationalists and Unionists always condemned the violence. It was the extremist groups within the two movements which resorted to terrorism.

The Irish Republican Army

The IRA had originated in the nineteenth century as the Irish Republican Brotherhood, dedicated to the creation through violence of an all-Ireland Republic. For political reasons it had joined Sinn Fein which it used as a front. Some of its members had played a prominent role in the Easter Rising and it had been involved in the troubles of 1919–21. Although Eamonn De Valera had belonged to the IRA, during his period of leadership of the Free State and the Republic (1932–73) he had outlawed the movement and attempted to suppress it. It became an increasingly secretive organisation. Despite being banned in the South it clung to the oddly romantic notion that it was the true descendant of the last pre-Treaty Irish Parliament. This made its Army Council the legitimate government of all Ireland. At the end of 1969 the movement split into the Official IRA and the Provisional IRA.

monopoly. Genuine power sharing was the only answer. The movement towards shared power is the basic story that can be detected through the pall of outrages and terror. Of course, it was not a simple story. Progress was never smooth. The path was littered with failed initiatives and disappointed hopes but in the end all but those on the very extremes of the question had accepted that some form of compromise was the only acceptable and workable solution. Optimists could say in 2000 that prospects for a peaceful Northern Ireland were brighter than at any point in the previous 30 years. How things came to reach the position they had by 2000 is best studied as a chronology.

The optimism that came with the formation of the Northern Ireland executive did not survive long into 2000. In the new year, decommissioning remained a major problem with the IRA seemingly unwilling or unable to deliver on arms. The Assembly was suspended in February and David Trimble had to face a challenge from within his own party. Unionist concerns over the Patten Report's suggestions that the character of the RUC should be fundamentally changed added to problems.

KEY STAGES IN THE TROUBLES AND THE MOVES TOWARDS A SETTLEMENT, 1968–2000

1968 (October) NICRA march ended in violence;

1969 (August) British troops sent to Ireland to control the disorder;

1972 (January) 'Bloody Sunday' resulted in 14 demonstrators being killed by British troops during a civil rights march in Derry;
(March) British government abolished Stormont Parliament and imposed direct rule of Northern Ireland from Westminster;

1974 (May) The Sunningdale Agreement created a power sharing Assembly;

1974 (December) Prevention of Terrorism Act applied to Ireland;

1979 (August) Earl Mountbatten assassinated in Northern Ireland by Provisionals;

1981 (May) IRA prisoner, Bobbie Sands, died after 66-day hunger strike;

1984 (October) IRA bomb failed to kill Margaret Thatcher, but killed four others at Brighton hotel during Conservative Party conference;

1985 (November) **Anglo-Irish Agreement**;

1986 (March) Northern Ireland Assembly dissolved;

1987 (November) IRA bomb killed 11 people at Enniskillen;

1988 (March) SAS killed 3 suspected IRA terrorists in Gibraltar;
(October) British government imposed broadcasting ban on IRA;

1991 (February) IRA fired mortars at 10 Downing Street;

1993 (December) **The Downing Street Declaration**;

1994 (August) IRA announced ceasefire;

1995 (October) Loyalists announced ceasefire;
(November) US President Clinton visited Belfast;

1996 (January) US Senator Mitchell laid down six principles of non-violence as basis for all party talks;

1997 (July) IRA announced a new ceasefire;
(August) International decommissioning body set up to monitor handover of weapons;
(September) Peace talks began at Stormont;

THE ANGLO-IRISH AGREEMENT, 1985

Signed at Hillsborough by Margaret Thatcher and the Irish premier, Garrett Fitzgerald. It contained three main provisions:

1. The Republic recognised Northern Ireland as being constitutionally a part of the UK, while the British government acknowledged the strength of nationalist desires for a united Ireland;

2. The British government gave an assurance that it supported full civil rights for all in Northern Ireland;

3. The two governments committed themselves to close co-operation over cross-border security matters.

The response of both Nationalist and Unionists to the Agreement was that too many concessions had been granted to the other side.

THE DOWNING STREET DECLARATION, 1993

Issued by Albert Reynolds, the Irish premier, and John Major, it announced that the people of Northern Ireland would have the final decision on the future of the province.

THE GOOD FRIDAY AGREEMENT, APRIL 1998

created a Northern Ireland Assembly with a new power-sharing government. It was accepted by the Ulster Unionists, the SDLP and Sinn Fein. Of the major parties, only Ian Paisley's Democratic Unionist Party rejected it. The Agreement guaranteed the union with Britain as long as the majority of the people of Northern Ireland wanted it. So, in return for their chance to share in government, the Nationalists and Republicans had, in effect, given up their demand for a united Ireland. For their part the Unionists had, in effect, agreed to the end of their power to control Northern Irish politics and public affairs.

1998 (February) Sinn Fein suspended from talks;
(March) Sinn Fein rejoined reopened talks;
Senator Mitchell set a 9 April deadline for parties to reach agreement;
(April) **The Good Friday Agreement**;
(May) All-Ireland poll on future of Northern Ireland;
(June) Unionist leader, David Trimble, elected to be First Minister of the new executive when it came into being;
(September) Assembly elections results:
Ulster Unionists – 28 seats   SDLP – 24 seats   Sinn Fein – 18 seats;

All-Ireland Poll on Future of Northern Ireland

The first such poll since 1918 resulted in an overwhelming vote for the Agreement. In the Republic there was a 95 per cent yes vote, in the North a 71 per cent yes vote – with half the Protestant electorate voting no.

1999 (April) Sinn Fein announced it could not deliver IRA arms de-commissioning before the new executive met;
(July) Stormont talks collapsed when Unionists refused to participate in nomination of ministers because of Sinn Fein inability to deliver on arms;
(November) Senator Mitchell attempted to resuscitate peace process by proposing that IRA show its good faith by agreeing to commit itself in writing to eventual decommissioning of arms;
Ulster Unionists supported the Mitchell deal;
(December) New Northern Ireland Executive met for the first time;
Irish Republic revoked its territorial claim to Northern Ireland.

ACTIVITY

Having studied section 4, explain the attitudes of the following towards the position and status of Northern Ireland in 1969: the British government, the Irish Republican government, the Irish Nationalists, the Unionists. Trace how those attitudes had changed by the end of the century.

▼ Working on Britain's Role in the Post-War World

The material you have been introduced to in this chapter covers a wide range of incidents and topics. To avoid confusion it is important that you arrange your ideas around the major developments. To help in this, check back frequently to the tables and summaries. If you take the key theme linking all the policies of the period – Britain's adapting to its reduced strength as a world power – you will have a very reliable reference point. Britain's alliance with the USA in the Cold War, its retreat from empire, and its relations with Europe should all be seen in terms of Britain making the practical adjustments that the realities of a changing world and its own relative economic decline necessitated. Northern Ireland is a different case. It might even be argued that it was a domestic matter. However, since it involved relations with southern Ireland, which became a sovereign state in 1949, it falls technically into the area of foreign affairs.

Moreover, the way Britain handled the Northern Ireland issue helps us to see how Britain viewed itself and its responsibilities.

Answering Structured Writing and Essay Questions on Britain's Role in the Post-War World

Types of question	Examples of typical questions
Structured	**1** In what ways did Britain side with the USA on Cold War issues? **2** Trace the steps by which India gained independence from Britain in 1947. **3** Outline the steps by which Britain gave up its colonial territories in the period 1947–80.
Causes	**4** Why did Britain withdraw from Palestine in 1948 but go into Suez in 1956? **5** Why was Britain involved militarily in the Korean War of 1950–53 but not in the Vietnam War of 1963–75? **6** How would you explain Britain's willingness to give up its empire in the period 1947–80?
Historical judgement	**7** Examine the validity of the assertion that Britain's exercise of its Palestinian mandate was 'an unrelieved failure'. **8** 'The UK's entry into the EEC in 1973 marked the loss of the last vestiges of Britain's independence as an international power.' How far do you agree with this view?

Let us consider question 7, the type that asks you to assess success or failure. In this instance you are given a straight proposition, that Britain failed completely in Palestine. Key terms to note: 'mandate', 'unrelieved failure'. Remember, failure and success are best measured against original aims and intentions. You need therefore to go back to 1917 to put matters into context.

Reasons for Britain's holding the mandate
▼ imperial connections in the Middle East
▼ 1914–18 wartime need to win support of Zionists and Arabs had led Britain to promise land to both groups, hence Balfour Declaration
▼ Britain accepted League of Nations mandate

Aims
▼ Britain committed by the mandate to keep the peace in Palestine and treat the peoples of the region with equal justice
▼ This meant employing a quota system to maintain some sort of Arab/Jewish population balance.

How well were the aims fulfilled?

Here the figures on population patterns (check back to page 88) would be very useful since they show the pressure Britain was under.

▼ Did Britain have an impossible task given Arab/Jewish bitter hostility?

▼ Had the Balfour Declaration, with its contradictory promises, created an incurable situation?

▼ Did the international sympathy for the Holocaust survivors make the creation of an Israeli state impossible to resist after 1945?

▼ Was Bevin hopelessly unrealistic in claiming he could solve the Palestine issue? Did he make the situation worse?

▼ Did the situation in Palestine require the use of coercive powers that Britain in the end was unwilling to take?

▼ Was the only way to solve the problem to allow one of the two sides to win? This is in fact what happened eventually, of course.

The term 'unrelieved' may be worth challenging. Are there no positive aspects to Britain's record? Did it not keep some form of peace, imperfect though it was? Would the blood bath have been greater had British forces not been in Palestine? Against that it could be said that Britain created the problem in the first place by giving contradictory promises and then under Bevin gave up the mandate when things became too difficult.

Answering Source-Based Questions on Britain's Role in the Post-War World

Re-read Sources F, G, H and I (pages 241–42). Then answer the following questions.

Comprehension questions:

1. Why, according to Source H, was Churchill unwilling for Britain to join a European union? **(3 marks)**

2. What can you learn from Sources G and I about Harold Macmillan's attitude to Britain's ties with the Commonwealth? **(4 marks)**

Stimulus questions:

3. Use your own knowledge to explain why Attlee and the Labour Party were opposed to Britain's joining the EEC. **(5 marks)**

4. Using your own knowledge, explain why Britain applied to join the EEC in the early 1960s. **(5 marks)**

Cross-referencing question:

5. How far does Attlee in Source F have the same concerns about the EEC as Churchill and Macmillan have in Sources G, H and I? **(8 marks)**

Source evaluation question:

6. How valuable are these sources to the historian who is studying Britain's relations with Europe between 1945 and 1999? **(12 marks)**

'Lead-out' question:

7. Explain how these sources help to you to understand why Britain experienced frequent difficulties in its dealings with Europe between 1945 and 1999. **(15 marks)**

Further Reading

Books in the Access to History series

Chapters 4–8 of *Britain: Foreign and Imperial Affairs 1939–64* by Alan Farmer lucidly cover the Cold War, the Suez affair and the beginnings of de-colonisation.

General

An excellent introduction to Britain's international role after 1945 is *Armed Truce: The Beginnings of the Cold War* by Hugh Thomas (Hamish Hamilton, 1986). Recommended books which offer insights into all the major topics covered in this chapter the whole period are: Arthur Marwick, *A History of the Modern British Isles 1914–99* (Blackwell, 2000), *The People's Peace, British History 1945–90* by Kenneth Morgan (Oxford University Press, 1999), who is one of the leading authorities in this field, *Hope and Glory: Britain 1900–1990* by Peter Clarke (Penguin, 1996), which is a highly entertaining text, *From Blitz to Blair A New History of Britain Since 1939*, edited by Nick Tiratsoo (Phoenix, 1997), which contains a stimulating set of essays by left-wing writers, and *Post War Britain* by Alan Sked and Chris Cook (Penguin, 1992), which takes a right of centre approach. An important and controversial book explaining Britain's decline is *The Audit of War* by Corelli Barnett (Macmillan, 1986). This could be usefully compared with *Britain's Decline: Problems and Perspectives* by Alan Sked (Blackwell, 1987). Among individual biographies which examine Britain's international role are *Attlee* by Robert Pearce (Longman, 1998), *RAB: the Life of R.A. Butler* by Anthony Howard (Cape, 1987), *Edward Heath: A Biography* by J. Campbell (Cape, 1993), *Harold Wilson* by Ben Pimlott (HarperCollins, 1992), *Michael Foot* by M. Jones (Victor Gollanz, 1993), *Harold Macmillan* by Alistair Horne (Macmillan, 1990), and *One of Us* by Hugo Young (Macmillan, 1994), on Margaret Thatcher. A valuable short introduction to the Northern Ireland issue is *Ireland in Conflict 1922–1998* by T.G. Fraser (Lancaster Pamphlets, Routledge, 1999). Fuller books covering the topic are *Origins of the Present Troubles in Northern Ireland* by C. Kennedy-Pipe (Longman, 1997), *The Ulster Question since 1945* by J. Loughlin (Macmillan, 1998), and *Northern Ireland since 1945* by S. Wichert (Longman, 1999). For a special study of the IRA, students should consult *The IRA* by Tim Pat Coogan (HarperCollins, 2000).

SELECTED GLOSSARY

INDEX